PRODIGAL CHRISTIANITY

PRODIGAL CHRISTIANITY

Ten Signposts into the Missional Frontier

David E. Fitch and Geoff Holsclaw

A LEADERSHIP NETWORK PUBLICATION

JOSSEY-BASS
A Wiley Imprint
www.josseybass.com

Published by Jossey-Bass
A Wiley Imprint
One Montgomery Street, Suite 1200, San Francisco, CA 94104-4594—www.josseybass.com

Jossey-Bass books and products are available through most bookstores. To contact Jossey-Bass directly
call our Customer Care Department within the U.S. at 800-956-7739, outside the U.S. at 317-572-
3986, or fax 317-572-4002.

Wiley publishes in a variety of print and electronic formats and by print-on-demand. Some material
included with standard print versions of this book may not be included in e-books or in print-on-
demand. If this book refers to media such as a CD or DVD that is not included in the version you
purchased, you may download this material at http://booksupport.wiley.com. For more information
about Wiley products, visit www.wiley.com.

Scripture quotations marked "KJV" are taken from the Holy Bible, King James Version,
Cambridge, 1769.
Scripture quotations marked "ESV" are from The Holy Bible, English Standard Version® (ESV®),
copyright © 2001 by Crossway, a publishing ministry of Good News Publishers. Used by
permission. All rights reserved.
Scripture quotations marked "NIV" are from THE HOLY BIBLE, NEW INTERNATIONAL
VERSION®, NIV® Copyright © 1973, 1978, 1984, 2011 by Biblica, Inc.™ Used by permission. All
rights reserved worldwide.
Scripture quotations marked "NRSV" are from the New Revised Standard Version Bible, copyright
1989, Division of Christian Education of the National Council of the Churches of Christ in the
United States of America. Used by permission. All rights reserved.
Scripture quotations marked "RSV" are from the Revised Standard Version of the Bible, copyright
1952 [2nd edition, 1971] by the Division of Christian Education of the National Council of the
Churches of Christ in the United States of America. Used by permission. All rights reserved.

*Library of Congress Cataloging-in-Publication Data has been applied for and is on file with the
Library of Congress.*

ISBN 978-1-118-20326-2 (cloth); ISBN 978-1-118-22835-7 (ebk);
ISBN 978-1-118-24073-1 (ebk); ISBN 978-1-118-26545-1 (ebk)

Printed in the United States of America

FIRST EDITION
HB Printing   10 9 8 7 6 5 4 3 2 1

LEADERSHIP NETWORK TITLES

The Blogging Church: Sharing the Story of Your Church Through Blogs, Brian Bailey and Terry Storch

Church Turned Inside Out: A Guide for Designers, Refiners, and Re-Aligners, Linda Bergquist and Allan Karr

Leading from the Second Chair: Serving Your Church, Fulfilling Your Role, and Realizing Your Dreams, Mike Bonem and Roger Patterson

In Pursuit of Great AND Godly Leadership: Tapping the Wisdom of the World for the Kingdom of God, Mike Bonem

Hybrid Church: The Fusion of Intimacy and Impact, Dave Browning

The Way of Jesus: A Journey of Freedom for Pilgrims and Wanderers, Jonathan S. Campbell with Jennifer Campbell

Cracking Your Church's Culture Code: Seven Keys to Unleashing Vision and Inspiration, Samuel R. Chand

Leading the Team-Based Church: How Pastors and Church Staffs Can Grow Together into a Powerful Fellowship of Leaders, George Cladis

Organic Church: Growing Faith Where Life Happens, Neil Cole

Church 3.0: Upgrades for the Future of the Church, Neil Cole

Journeys to Significance: Charting a Leadership Course from the Life of Paul, Neil Cole

Church Transfusion: Changing Your Church Organically—from the Inside Out, Neil Cole and Phil Helfer

Off-Road Disciplines: Spiritual Adventures of Missional Leaders, Earl Creps

Reverse Mentoring: How Young Leaders Can Transform the Church and Why We Should Let Them, Earl Creps

Building a Healthy Multi-Ethnic Church: Mandate, Commitments, and Practices of a Diverse Congregation, Mark DeYmaz

Prodigal Christianity: Ten Signposts into the Missional Frontier, David E. Fitch and Geoffrey Holsclaw

Leading Congregational Change Workbook, James H. Furr, Mike Bonem, and Jim Herrington

The Tangible Kingdom: Creating Incarnational Community, Hugh Halter and Matt Smay

Baby Boomers and Beyond: Tapping the Ministry Talents and Passions of Adults over Fifty, Amy Hanson

Leading Congregational Change: A Practical Guide for the Transformational Journey, Jim Herrington, Mike Bonem, and James H. Furr

The Leader's Journey: Accepting the Call to Personal and Congregational Transformation, Jim Herrington, Robert Creech, and Trisha Taylor

The Permanent Revolution: Apostolic Imagination and Practice for the 21st Century, Alan Hirsch and Tim Catchim

Whole Church: Leading from Fragmentation to Engagement, Mel Lawrenz

Culture Shift: Transforming Your Church from the Inside Out, Robert Lewis and Wayne Cordeiro, with Warren Bird

Church Unique: How Missional Leaders Cast Vision, Capture Culture, and Create Movement, Will Mancini

A New Kind of Christian: A Tale of Two Friends on a Spiritual Journey, Brian D. McLaren

The Story We Find Ourselves In: Further Adventures of a New Kind of Christian, Brian D. McLaren

Missional Communities: The Rise of the Post-Congregational Church, Reggie McNeal

Missional Renaissance: Changing the Scorecard for the Church, Reggie McNeal

Practicing Greatness: 7 Disciplines of Extraordinary Spiritual Leaders, Reggie McNeal

The Present Future: Six Tough Questions for the Church, Reggie McNeal

A Work of Heart: Understanding How God Shapes Spiritual Leaders, Reggie McNeal

The Millennium Matrix: Reclaiming the Past, Reframing the Future of the Church, M. Rex Miller

Your Church in Rhythm: The Forgotten Dimensions of Seasons and Cycles, Bruce B. Miller

Shaped by God's Heart: The Passion and Practices of Missional Churches, Milfred Minatrea

The Missional Leader: Equipping Your Church to Reach a Changing World, Alan J. Roxburgh and Fred Romanuk

Missional Map-Making: Skills for Leading in Times of Transition, Alan J. Roxburgh

Relational Intelligence: How Leaders Can Expand Their Influence Through a New Way of Being Smart, Steve Saccone

The Post-Black and Post-White Church: Becoming the Beloved Community in a Multi-Ethnic World, Efrem Smith

Viral Churches: Helping Church Planters Become Movement Makers, Ed Stetzer and Warren Bird

Just Lead! A No Whining, No Complaining, No Nonsense Practical Guide for Women Leaders in the Church, Sherry Surratt and Jenni Catron

The Externally Focused Quest: Becoming the Best Church for the Community, Eric Swanson and Rick Rusaw

The Ascent of a Leader: How Ordinary Relationships Develop Extraordinary Character and Influence, Bill Thrall, Bruce McNicol, and Ken McElrath

Beyond Megachurch Myths: What We Can Learn from America's Largest Churches, Scott Thumma and Dave Travis

The Other 80 Percent: Turning Your Church's Spectators into Active Participants, Scott Thumma and Warren Bird

Better Together: Making Church Mergers Work, Jim Tomberlin and Warren Bird

The Elephant in the Boardroom: Speaking the Unspoken About Pastoral Transitions, Carolyn Weese and J. Russell Crabtree

CONTENTS

ABOUT THE JOSSEY-BASS LEADERSHIP NETWORK SERIES

Leadership Network's mission is to accelerate the impact of 100X leaders. These high-capacity leaders are like the hundredfold crop that comes from seed planted in good soil as Jesus described in Matthew 13:8.

Leadership Network

- Explores the "what's next?" of what could be
- Creates "aha!" environments for collaborative discovery
- Works with exceptional "positive deviants"
- Invests in the success of others through generous relationships
- Pursues big impact through measurable kingdom results
- Strives to model Jesus through all we do

Believing that meaningful conversations and strategic connections can change the world, we seek to help leaders navigate the future by exploring new ideas and finding application for each unique context. Through collaborative meetings and processes, leaders map future possibilities and challenge one another to action that accelerates fruitfulness and effectiveness. Leadership Network shares the learnings and inspiration with others through our books, concept papers, research reports, e-newsletters, podcasts, videos, and online experiences. This in turn generates a ripple effect of new conversations and further influence.

In 1996, Leadership Network established a partnership with Jossey-Bass, a Wiley Imprint, to develop a series of creative books that would provide thought leadership to innovators in church ministry. *Leadership Network Publications* present *thoroughly researched and innovative concepts* from leading thinkers, practitioners, and pioneering churches.

To learn more about Leadership Network, go to www.leadnet.org.

To Elmer Max Fitch, a little man on a journey, whose life already witnesses to the radical excessive love of God the Father. May we—you, me, and Mommy—live our lives prodigally together for God's mission in the years that lie ahead.—D.F.

To Cynthia Joy, my true friend and inspiration along the way, and to Soren and Tennyson as you prepare for the journey.—G.H.

PREFACE AND ACKNOWLEDGMENTS

There's nothing quite so irritating as the "much-vaunted expert." Perhaps you know what I mean. We go to a conference. A person comes from some distant place, has an academic degree or two, has a book to sign, and now comes to speak to us on an issue we're all dealing with in our churches (or our lives). He or she speaks as someone who has done the research and presents some insights, tells us what we're doing wrong, and offers a solution or two. We are supposed to be encouraged, but in the end we leave with the distinct impression that it's been a while since this person was actually in the situation we're going through. We want to ask, "How is that working for you really?" but worry this might cause some embarrassment.

Geoff Holsclaw and I would like to disavow any presumption that we write this book as experts. It's true we have some degrees, teach in a seminary, and pastor a church. Nonetheless, we write this book not as vaunted experts but as chastened sojourners. We've traveled the journeys we write about in this book. We have planted and led churches, and we write from these experiences. We are chastened sojourners—sojourners who have failed many times in the things about which we write. Nonetheless, you can still ask us, "How is that working for you?"

Our journey started about twelve years ago. My wife, Rae Ann, and I (Dave) moved to the northwest suburbs of Chicago to plant a church. We'd learned much about intentional Christian community in the city and accepted the call to go to the suburbs to plant a church. We were focused on gathering a community for the peoples outside the Christian bubble, the people who would no longer go to large megahalls or the traditional edifices we still call church. I wanted to be part of a relational community where church was a way of life that gives witness to the kingdom before those who know nothing about the kingdom.

That church became Life on the Vine (www.lifeonthevine.org). Soon after it started, Geoff and his wife, Cyd, joined us. We've been leading this community ever since. Several others have joined us along the way, and we've sent two other communities out to be planted in neighborhoods and helped others as well. During these years, we've been asked over and over again to talk about church in mission in a post-Christianized world. There have been literally hundreds of these theological and practical conversations along the way with people from all over North America.

Somewhere in the middle of this journey we encountered the fracturing of these many conversations. Our various conversation partners were dividing between those formerly known as Emergent and those who had emerged within the Neo-Reformed resurgence, most notably gathering around The Gospel Coalition, an Internet-based network of like minded Neo-Reformed leaders. (Please see note 2 in the Introduction for why we have chosen to refer to these friends by the moniker *Neo-Reformed*.) We observed firsthand the clashing of Emergent and Neo-Reformed visions and how they were coalescing around two opposing ways of thinking about church in mission. As things went on, neither option seemed capable of providing direction for us. From our point of view, both sides seemed to lack the ability to engage, that is, bring the transforming work of God in Christ across boundaries to those outside the influence of the Christian church. We needed guidance for on-the-ground missional engagement. Our churches were engaging issues of injustice, sexual confusion, pluralism of religions, and conflict that had now become part of regular life in the newly post-Christianized cultures of North America. What was the gospel in this situation? Where is the kingdom? How is God revealed in these places?

It is out of this journey that this book came into being.

The Process of Writing This Book

These past twelve years, I (Dave) have been assembling stuff—notes, lectures, presentations, blog posts—reflecting on the issues of the church making its way on this journey. Through teaching classes at Northern Seminary, coaching church plants, blogging, and copastoring, I had accumulated pages of reflections. Dialogues with Brian McLaren, Tim Keller, Tony Jones, Ed Stetzer, Alan Hirsch, and Mark Driscoll (whether online, in person, or through writing about them) were provoking discernments for the church in mission. And so somewhere between Brian McLaren's *A New Kind of Christianity*, published in 2010, and John Piper's "farewell Rob Bell" tweet in 2011 (at the publication of Bell's *Love Wins*), two significant publishing events that drew attention to the Neo-Reformed/Emergent divide, I remember talking with an agent about how to pull all of this together. I wanted to offer some of these hard-won on-the-ground discernments to those who, like me, had grown weary of the fracturing and the bipolar options.

One day, I met Geoff at the local McDonald's to talk and get feedback on my ideas for gathering this material together. All I really remember is that Geoff proposed "prodigal Christianity" for the organizing principle of the book. I was already familiar with Karl Barth's (a famous German theologian) notion of the Son going into "the far country" of sinful humanity in order to return humanity back to the Father (a play on the parable about the prodigal son). This radical, excessive, prodigal journey of God in the Son compromises neither his divine nor his human nature. God fully enters our fallen context. This principle, which drove much of Barth's missional description of God, seemed to galvanize much of what I was working on. It organized all the notes and lectures beautifully, offering a way beyond the impasses of either the emerging church or the Neo-Reformed. The more we talked about it in the following weeks, the more I liked it. In fact, we talked about writing it together. It couldn't have made more sense.

And so this book was born. In McDonald's.

Starting with my main themes, Geoff organized them into the outline for the book. We worked several weeks on that. Then, starting with my notes from teaching the missional theology class at Northern Seminary as well as other classes, I drafted the chapters with the stories I felt important. Geoff then revised those rough drafts, adding an occasional story from his perspective (he's twenty years my junior). He also developed much of the biblical theology that undergirds the book. I revised Geoff's revisions, and then Sheryl Fullerton, our wonderful editor at Jossey-Bass, did a further edit. One of our mutual friends from the Vine, Gordon Hackman, helped with a final edit, along with Geoff. All in all, the final result is a book that reads well and accomplishes much more than what I could have accomplished on my own. I'm convinced the writing is seamless, the theology better, and the perspective broader because Geoff and I wrote this book together.

Some Warnings

What has resulted is this book, *Prodigal Christianity*, which proposes a way of being Christian: in missional communities who live in such a way that we invite the kingdom of God into our lives and the neighborhoods around us. It asks anew the questions: What is the gospel? Where is the kingdom? How is God revealed in the Son and the Spirit? It recognizes the advances made in the past fifteen years from the various Emergent and Neo-Reformed groups. But it asks us to go further, to recognize the lacks in these theologies for mission. The book does not seek a compromise middle ground between these two camps; it proposes a way beyond them that learns from both but defies the categories of each. So be forewarned: this book will probably be looked at as liberal by the Neo-Reformed and as fundamentalist by the Emergents, but we hope you can avoid those labels as you read this book.

We could label the way forward that we propose in this book as "evangelical Anabaptist" or "radical evangelical." For those who find these words troublesome, again, be warned. The book is evangelical in the way of the pioneering evangelicals of the twentieth century who believed unashamedly in the gospel that transforms lives and society. In the words of the old hymn, we believe "Jesus saves." Yet it is also radical in the sense of the radical Anabaptist reformers of the sixteenth century in Europe who knew, in a time of massive upheaval, that Christians must leave the comfortable structures of the past and live together radically under Christ's Lordship for the sake of mission. We must trust the Lord of the harvest and give up control of a lot of things evangelicals have sought to control in the past thirty years. In these ways, this book is both markedly evangelical and intensely radical.

Be forewarned as well that we offer no step-by-step process in this book to change our churches or our lives. Rather, we seek to shape imagination for the way God is working in the world. This, we suggest, will naturally lead to new ways of being God's people in the world. But it will not look the same for everyone, and the steps needed in each context will be decidedly different. If you're looking for a solution to the problems of your local church, you need read no further.

This is not to say that *Prodigal Christianity* does not provide some pointers to help us live the gospel anew in our contexts. The point of the book is to fund imagination for Christians to patiently inhabit our contexts, discern God's work, and practice the kingdom in our neighborhoods. The book challenges us to inhabit the world differently than we do now, build relationships differently, and allow God, through Jesus Christ by the Spirit, to bring the kingdom in over the long term until Christ comes again (1 Corinthians 15:25). As a result, I suspect that if the message of this book sticks, we shall put a different emphasis on discipleship and the way we do that discipleship in our churches. We will focus on leading Christians into living under God's reign in our everyday lives together for God's mission in the world.

This book refuses to exclude anyone. So there are no polarizing arguments in this book. Although we critique both our Emergent and Neo-Reformed friends, we affirm each of them for what they have taught us. We invite everyone from all kinds and sizes of churches to join us in this journey, take a look at ourselves, and seek a way of life that can engage the mission fields of our post-Christian West.

Finally, I warn anyone who thinks we write as authors who have figured it out. As "chastened sojourners," we confess we have yet to fully experience much of what is in this book. But we've seen glimpses, and we live expectantly that these glimmers are harbingers. But this journey in many ways has also just begun for us. By writing this book, we do not invite you to imitate us in any way. We invite you to join with us on this journey, let us join up with yours, or both. As evangelical Anabaptists, we submit the entirety of this book to the Lordship of Christ, one another, and you for feedback, pushback, and clarification. Let us work together for a new faithfulness for our time.

Special Thanks to Some Special People

Special thanks go to Northern Seminary and all my students down through the years who have listened, critiqued, written papers, and encouraged me by their radical lives and ministries. Special thanks to Sheryl Fullerton, our editor at Jossey-Bass, who was an exceptional editor and encouraging; Scott Boren, our agent and provocateur; Gordon Hackman, who helped us with editing; Matt Tebbe, Cyd Holsclaw, and Ty Grigg who read parts of the manuscript and gave us feedback; and of course to Life on the Vine, our church, where we learned so much and have so much more to learn about leading people into the kingdom. We also thank Peace of Christ church in Westmont, Illinois, and Church of the Shepherd in Hyde Park, Chicago, two communities sent out by Life on the Vine that have also helped us learn a great deal about the kingdom coming in different contexts.

There are a lot of stories in this book. We have changed the names, genders, and even surrounding circumstances slightly in them in order to protect each person's privacy. Thanks especially to Drew Marshall of the Drew Marshall radio show for permission to use "A Young Seminary Student Wants to Know If He Should Still Go into Ministry Considering He Is a Celibate Pedophile" from his website.

I thank Rae Ann, my wife, for supporting my work and rolling with the ebbs and flows of being married to an eccentric pastor/apostle/ professor. She continues to join in when moves are hard and change is continual. She's put up with many weeks when I have had to work too much on this book. And to my son, Max, who inspires me with the ways he grows to love and know God each day. Thanks for growing and loving even when Daddy has been busy.

Geoff thanks his wife, Cyd, for all her love, support, and patience while he worked on this book even while finishing his doctorate. She never complained about his early morning commutes to school or the late nights writing and studying. Geoff also thanks his sons, Soren and Tennyson, who are a continual source of joy and wonder as they teach him about the Fatherhood of God.

INTRODUCTION: FOLLOWING JESUS INTO THE FAR COUNTRY—THE WINTER OF OUR DISCONTENT

On a humid Chicago summer night in 2007, forty people from our church, Life on the Vine in Chicago's northwest suburbs, gathered for another Friday night town meeting. These meetings could be called by church members any time a controversial issue needed to be addressed by the church community as a whole. The topic for the night? Sexual brokenness and how we were dealing with it as a church community. Issues of sexual abuse and brokenness run deep and are shrouded in much darkness. But tonight we gathered to hear stories of redemption and hope, forgiveness and freedom. Individuals shared their brokenness, shame, and embarrassment. We lamented the isolation and invisibility of victims that invalidates their hurts and silences their voices. And we discussed the overly prudish restrictions around sex and sexuality enforced by churches that do not know how to deal with it in any other way. Two hours later, we were all a bit shocked at how personally we had connected to each other and surprised at how intimately we had shared our lives. Closing with a time of prayer, we walked out under a stunning star-filled sky, hopeful that life truly can spring from darkness.

But things did not go perfectly after that meeting. A few weeks later, we started hearing concerns—not so much about what was expressed that evening but about a larger agenda carried on by one of our friends and coleaders at the Vine. Like all of us, he wanted to overcome the hurts, the abuses, and the confusions so prevalent in our culture surrounding sexuality. For him, this meant advocating a style of friendship that touched a lot of nerves. As a means toward sexual redemption and healing, this brother was encouraging deep friendships between men and women, even between married men and single women, and vice versa. What made matters worse was that he liked to use the word *intimacy* to describe these friendships. We knew what he meant. Others didn't. To him this was a way of exposing illegitimate sexual boundaries and breaking down overly sexualized situations, all as a witness to God's great redemption of our sexual brokenness and deep calling into relational intimacy. But for many in our church, this looked an awful lot like flirting with sin and possibly a path to destruction for fragile marriages. The whole debate caused quite a ruckus in our community.

As the conflict simmered, two typical responses quickly emerged. The first was tolerant conversation: "Let's just talk about it. Let's build relationships of trust where differences can be appreciated." But the opposite response of dogmatic pronouncement came just as swiftly: "Let's see what the Bible has to say and just be clear in guiding everyone in this very important issue!" Two camps promptly appeared. One believed it was merely a matter of opinion and thought the solution was to be found in tolerance. The other worried that our very integrity as believers was on the line and strayed into absolutes. Sometimes the two responses were ironically mingled into a single dogmatic pronouncement, "You have to tolerate!"

What Were We to Do?

Over these past ten years, we have often found ourselves sitting between the horns of this dilemma. On the one hand, we are asked to be tolerant, accepting of all people, and participate in generative conversations. On the other hand, we are called on to be clear about the truth and give direction to people whose spiritual, moral, or emotional lives are in peril (at least that is how they perceive it). We, as pastors leading congregations in the middle of crisis issues (or at least a perceived crisis), have found peril in both stances. Is there another way? A way beyond splitting the difference or finding common ground? Is there a path beyond what has become the progressive and traditional divide, the liberal and conservative chasm?

Like many others, we and our church community have been slogging forward in these strange and difficult times. We have been moving slowly, striving in hope, stumbling over disappointments, seeing signs of the kingdom in our midst.

That Summer of Hope

Our journey started about ten years ago. In response to countless situations like the one we just described, many questioning Christians began gathering in coffee houses and bars to talk about issues of Christians living in a culture that was presenting never-seen-before challenges. We began experiencing the freedom to ask new and different questions, doubt the old ways of doing things, and explore new paths that had once been forbidden. Indeed, we felt permission to express our doubts, realizing this too as a path of faith.

The excitement grew as new authors and speakers began putting into words the problems and constraints we were all feeling as children of the church in North America. As we started going to conferences, we found out that we were not totally crazy or utterly lost. In fact, a multitude of people were talking about similar things and similar inadequacies of the modern church—its failure to meet the contemporary challenges and offer genuine ways of following Christ. The church of the twenty- and thirty-somethings began using words like *emerging, missional, organic,* and *postmodern* to describe a new way of being church, a different way of being a Christian, a "new kind of Christian."[1] The conversations and church experiments that were happening around this time showed much promise and life. It felt like warm summer rays of hope were burning off the chilly fog of an entrenched church life.

But this summer sun proved to be fleeting. Cooler winds blew in, and our confidence began to waver. Ten years later, in the aftermath of it all, many of us are asking, "Where has all this gotten us? Where do we go from here?"

What Are We Really Doing Anyway?

In the early years, I (Geoff) distinctly remember feeling these cooler winds at an emergent theology conference. I loved debating the ideas nurtured at these conferences. And while many thought these conversations were going off the rails, I nonetheless became involved because of the way they challenged existing assumptions and sought new ways of moving forward. I was onboard entirely. Nevertheless, there was something unsettling about the tone of this particular conference.

During one of the morning sessions, I participated in a lively panel discussion. At the close, one of the conference organizers asked me to conclude the time in prayer. Being somewhat unprepared, I jumped into one of my regular morning prayers. It was nothing particularly profound, but several people came up and thanked me afterward.

Later that afternoon, another person was asked to close a session in prayer. I observed tentativeness in her walk up to the front. She obviously had been as surprised as I had been. She also prayed a familiar prayer, the Aaronic blessing from Numbers 6:24–26. As she prayed, she seemed uneasy with the task, and as she continued, it became apparent she was unsure whether this time of public prayer was appropriate in front of such a group as this. I wondered, *Could these people be embarrassed to pray?* No one had said as much. Surely the organizers were asking people to lead in prayer. But as I observed and probed further, amid the conversations, deconstructions, and reimagining that filled this conference, it was evident that people were unsure whether it was still all right to pray.

My mind struggled with this. I wondered, *Why is it that we should be embarrassed by the simple, ancient, universal act of talking with God?* While the gospel was being extolled as the power of God to right all things, to overturn evil and injustice (rather than merely save sinners from hell), at the same time we seemed to be losing the ability to enter confidently into God's living presence. Had the ground rules of the conversation somehow undermined our ability to have communion with the living God?

Of course, this is only one story. But like one among many falling leaves in autumn, it foretold the fading of that summer of hope. We didn't know where things were going, but we knew they did not quite feel right and that perhaps a deeper chill was coming.

Out of the Cold

Many have since felt these chilling winds surrounding the emerging church conversation. Most visibly there has been a large swath of younger evangelicals in their twenties and thirties taking shelter from the cold by moving toward what is now commonly labeled *Neo-Reformed theology*.[2] In one sense, this move to the reformed fold was inevitable. It was only natural to head back over to a better-known reformed-evangelical theology, now given a postmodern makeover and a new concern for mission in North America.

But this option, though much appreciated, has proved unsatisfying to many of us as well. I (Dave) was asked to join a Web-based missional network during these times. This group invited several missional authors and leaders to join a supportive network for those involved in North American mission. Within a few weeks, the issue of same-sex sexual relations came before the group. In a blog post, one of the new members flatly said that "the Bible was unequivocally clear regarding homosexual relations being outside the will of God for every Christian." To be missional, he then assumed, meant we all would assent to this dogmatic commitment. But that didn't prove to be the case. Many of the others dropped out of the group, and shortly after, all discussion ended and that network died.

This blogger, a member of the Neo-Reformed missional movement, illustrated for me what was lacking in this new version of missional engagement. Although I appreciated his serious commitment to theology and agreed with many of his positions, this leader did not understand the people we were seeking to engage. There was little sense of the cultural gap that lay between him and the people who know next to nothing of the redemption in Jesus Christ. He assumed that merely to verbalize a True position (with a capital "T") on same-sex relations was enough to be a witness to the gospel that brings renewal to those hurt or confused within the sexual culture of our day.

The closer we looked and the more we were seeking to live in mission, the more we sensed how both the emerging church and the Neo-Reformed movement were lacking something for engaging the growing numbers of hurting, secularized, wandering peoples outside our church.

The Winter of Our Discontent: Ten Years Later

So now, ten years later, after many overcaffeinated late-night discussions, after numerous conferences and ministry overhauls, total theological rearticulations, and countless relational conflicts and misunderstandings, we sense that the summery hope of those movements has passed. And we feel a bit left out in the cold.

On the one hand, we are less than satisfied with what the "new kind of Christianity" has become. Brian McLaren, Doug Pagitt, Tony Jones, and others have helped us ask important questions and contributed greatly to creating a generous and compassionate Christianity, and to them we remain grateful friends. But their answers have often lacked the substance on which we could live, and what goes by the name of "the emerging church" now appears to have settled into another version of mainline Christianity.

On the other hand, the Neo-Reformed have invigorated theological discussion and offered serious reflection on the mission we all face in North America. We have benefited from these friends as well. But to us, they appear to be defensive. At times, they seem to revert to doctrinal entrenchment and the attractional habits of the churches from which we had come.

Even *missional*, our own term of choice, has become a confusing venture. The idea of being missional is now attached to nearly every kind of ministry in North America. From megachurches branding their latest programs as "missional" to Protestant mainline churches using *missional* to promote a set of social justice programs, and anti-institutional types using *missional* to spell the end of the church, the term has become virtually meaningless. Has *missional* just become another brand without any real meaning? And so now our last protection against the stormy blast is lost. We have no way to identify ourselves. Now it certainly *is* getting cold out here.

What Do We Do Now?

Has this decade been a waste? Is a new direction still possible? If both options (emerging or reforming) have proved unable to provide sustainable ways of Christian living amid the cultural challenges we face in North America, is there a way forward?

As we will show throughout this book, emergent and Neo-Reformed run on the same "operating system." Although each has promised us a "third way" beyond the conservative-liberal theological wars, they nonetheless keep us trapped within a bygone cultural consensus of Christian dominance that no longer exists. One side assumes people will listen to us as we speak about justice in "the way of Jesus." The other side assumes people will listen to us because we speak of orthodoxy and the Bible. The truth is that these ways make sense only to those who are already convinced.

In contrast, we sense the need to escape these kinds of cultural Christianity. We seek something beyond these third-way strategies that keep us locked into old habits, circling back to old positions. To us, the road signs for the so-called third-way options should warn, "No Outlet." If we are looking for a third way, it is because we have already lost our way.

Is there a path leading to a Christianity capable of bearing witness where little or no Christian consensus exists? Where is the Christianity that journeys into the difficult places, the places where the Christian language is not yet spoken, where the witness to God's Kingdom in Christ has not yet reached the edges of humanity, the places where brute force often has the last word? Where is the renewal of what the church has always been but sometimes forgets to be: a people sent in mission? Where are these signposts that can direct us into the missional frontier?

Prodigal Christianity

These questions have stirred the two of us as pastors and professors to write this book as an encouragement and a challenge to all who find themselves in this same winter of discontent. We believe a compelling way forward lies ahead for Christians in the new post-Christendom cultures of North America. In fact, we believe this way forward is intrinsic to the very reality of Jesus the Son and his coming into our world.

In the familiar parable, the prodigal son (Luke 15:11–32), Jesus tells of a son going off "to the far county" and losing his inheritance through excessive and wasteful living. But at the end of hope and basically living as a slave, the son remembers his father and figures he would be better off as a servant in his father's house than a slave in a foreign country. So the son journeys home. His father sees him from afar and runs to meet him. The outpouring of the love of the father on the prodigal son is a stunning picture of God loving us. We all know it well. It speaks to our relationship as sons and daughters of God our Father who has poured out his love on us through Jesus Christ.

The son is not the only prodigal character in the story. As New York pastor Tim Keller reminds us in his well-known book *Prodigal God*, it is really the father who is the prodigal, celebrating the return of his son extravagantly, excessively, and beyond all expectations. The father is the reckless one—reckless in grace. When the son expects nothing, the father gives everything. When the son expects to be a servant, the father reinstates him as a favored child. The older brother famously complains that his father is being wasteful and excessive in this celebration of the younger son. Through this parable, we learn that just as the father is recklessly lavish in regard to his son, so also God the Father "is nothing if not prodigal to us."[3] God is reckless, extravagant, even wasteful in his grace toward us.

One more twist to this parable is important. It comes to us from the famed twentieth-century German theologian Karl Barth. Barth suggests that to really understand this parable, we must read the journey of the prodigal son alongside the journey of another son: the Son of God, Jesus Christ.[4] This Son did not consider it his right to stay with the Father, but humbled himself and became a slave (Philippians 2:5–8). Indeed, Jesus, the Son of God, like the prodigal son of the parable, traveled across all boundaries into "the far country" of sin and death (Luke 15:13). But this son, in stark contrast to the prodigal son of the parable, is not rebellious but obedient. He is the obedient son in all things, and in that obedience, he returns to the father, bringing with him all his redeemed brothers and sisters.[5] For Barth, the point of the parable is that God radically sends God's own son into the far country to bring back all who are lost.

Barth thinks this interpretation completes the other interpretations of the parable. He puts forward this interpretation over against German theologians of his day who saw no atonement in this parable and therefore argued Jesus's work on earth is purely about the father's love. No, says Barth; the journey of the son reveals the true nature of the parable, expressing the radical missionary nature of God, that the Father has sent the Son into the far country to redeem the world. God is a prodigal God, not just in graciously receiving us back when we sin but by recklessly leaving behind everything and, in the person of Jesus, journeying into the far country. God recklessly pursues the world by entering into the very depths of the far country. This is the way God works. This is the way God is.

This book charts our way into the far country. It unfolds a Christian way of living that is determined by this prodigal nature of our God in Jesus Christ by the Spirit. That this journey changes everything is not an overstatement. This way of living is radical and generous and yet particularly defined as the way of God. This journey will break down the boundaries around the postmodern, post-Christian, sexually broken, relationally scarred, estranged, wandering, and marginalized peoples of our day. It will be a journey that takes us to the frontiers of God's mission. To be Christian is to learn to become prodigal.

Such a prodigal Christianity will be generous. It may be so generous and welcoming that it will seem scandalous. Yet it compromises nothing of the transformative nature of the gospel. A prodigal Christianity will not rely on pronouncements given from a seat of authority. But we will enter humbly and vulnerably, bringing God's hospitality to the places of mission. A prodigal Christianity will not rely on the basic foundations of Christendom because it always journeys far beyond these places into the missional far country, where there is no prior witness. Yet prodigal Christianity will not merely accommodate the new cultures it meets because it comes bearing a story, our story, the good news (gospel) of the prodigal God. This prodigal Christianity is always defined by the missional journey of the prodigal God with whom we live and breathe. It is a faith and a life that understands God is always going before us in Christ. And so we freely enter this journey, working in continuity with all God has done in Christ to reconcile the whole world to God. We go knowing God has already gone before us into the far country. This is the journey this book invites us into. For this journey we need some signposts.

Signposts

As a boy, growing up in Hamilton, Ontario, I (Dave) took hikes in the early spring in an area called the Red Hill Valley. It was just six blocks from my house, but it was another world. The valley, hewn out of the Niagara escarpment by the water flowing through the Red Hill Creek into Lake Ontario, was rugged at times (especially for a ten year old) as the trails wound up and down various elevations within the gorge. And if the weather suddenly turned warm, the air off the colder Lake Ontario could produce a lot of low-lying fog. And so I remember starting off on those trails (the famous Bruce Trail System) of the Red Hill Valley on a foggy Saturday morning imagining all that that lay before me. It was a mysterious unexplored land with famous wildlife like the Coopers hawk and flying squirrels. There were jagged cliffs high up the gorge. And if the other hikers and I reached the end of the trail, there was the marvelous Mt. Albion falls that to a young boy's eyes were every bit as majestic as Niagara Falls itself. The Red Hill Valley was an extraordinarily beautiful place yet with many potential pitfalls.[6]

The pathway was marked by signposts. Each signpost was simply a splotch of color (usually on a tree) and an arrow. There was nothing else. At best it gave a clue as to a direction to go but little else. You could not really know what lay ahead. And if the day was foggy, you could not even be confident of the actual direction you were going: east, west, north, or south. You could navigate only one signpost at a time, moving from one to the next as the trails carried you deeper into the valley. Yet if you followed the blue splotches along with the arrows long enough, you eventually arrived at your glorious destination, Mt. Albion falls.

The signposts, essential for reaching the destination, were inherently vague. They didn't tell everything, just enough to guide you on the next steps of the journey. Truthfully I seriously wonder whether we would have even gone into the very depths of Red Hill Valley gorge if each signpost had displayed in digital photographic accuracy all that lay ahead. It would have been a bit too scary. The signposts were just enough to get a young boy to the marvelous destination that awaited him.

In my childhood, the Red Hill Valley was a marvelous, mysterious, and beautiful place that could not be described by a sign or even in a book's description. All we could do was follow the signposts and discover it.

In the same way, the far country, the territory that God has called us to as believers, is incapable of being fully known in advance. We reach it from a journey leading us through the marvelous, awe-inspiring, and beautiful places where God is at work far beyond the comforts of our own backyards. We will walk it together in this book following certain signposts: splotches that point us in the right direction but still require us to discern what this will mean for our own contexts, places, and neighborhoods. We have no idea what this will look like for all the different places where we live, inhabit, and minister. The best we can offer are signposts. As we follow them in small, discerning steps, God will lead us into mission.

This is what we are offering in this book: a way forward into God's mission, the missional far country to which God is calling his people in these new and difficult times. We offer ten signposts for this journey.

The first four signposts direct us into the life of the Triune God, the sending God, who sends the Son, the Spirit, and then the disciples into the world to fulfill the mission of redemption. These signposts deal with the basic questions of culture, God, Jesus, and witness. Signpost 1 directs us into the cultures of post-Christendom. Signpost 2 points us into a relationship with the missionary God. Signpost 3 directs us toward the way God comes to us in Jesus, the incarnation. Signpost 4 directs us into the way of God's truth in the world, communities of witness.

After these four signposts come three more that direct us into the daily means by which we, the church, travel this journey. Signpost 5 directs us into the story that we live, the Bible. Signpost 6 points us into the way of our salvation, God's way of setting the whole world right again, the gospel. Signpost 7 shows the way God's reign breaks in and transforms everything through local communities of the kingdom.

The final three signposts then point us into some of the most difficult terrain we face in North America today. Signpost 8 leads us into God's mission among the sexually broken. Signpost 9 leads us into God's mission among the systemic social injustices of our day. And signpost 10 leads us into God's mission among the pluralist versions of truth in our world.

Each signpost gives us a vision for joining the mission of God through Christ in his Spirit. Together these ten signposts direct us into the rich journey of life with the God of mission, the prodigal way of following God into the far country.

Please do not think of these signposts as ten easy steps to a new church. The way ahead must be carefully discerned. We cannot rely on the instincts of the past because we're moving beyond the tired dichotomies of Christendom. Each one of us must follow these signposts in our own contexts.

This book is not a program, an ideology, or a destination. It is a way of being God's people on a journey in and among the hurting and lost peoples of North America, a journey that always leads us deeper into the love and redemption of the radical-reckless-loving-prodigal God. The way forward awaits. Let us journey on.

PRODIGAL CHRISTIANITY

POST-CHRISTENDOM

INTO THE FAR COUNTRY: THE JOURNEY
INTO POST-CHRISTENDOM

"WOW!" THE BARISTA EXCLAIMED, moving herself farther behind the counter. "A real pastor?" Her reaction was something between amazement and fear as if she'd just seen an extinct bird that she thought might contaminate her with some alien disease. But there I (Geoff) was, working in my small church office—a local coffee shop in the neighborhood—and I was experiencing what had now become commonplace: the disjunction between what people think about the church and my trying to live the gospel in everyday life. Sue, the barista, got over her shock, and we went on to have many good talks in the future, but she very much represented the new situation my church and I find ourselves in.

If you've been a Christian in North America and spent any time outside church buildings, you know what we're talking about. We sense our culture pressing in—in movies, in local schools, at the mall, or as we drive to the church gathering on Sundays. We see signs of it in the looks on people's faces as they travel on the train to work, scurry to get their children to a Little League game, or head to a restaurant with friends. People are living as if God doesn't exist or, at least, as if God doesn't matter. Society used to have a general place for God. Now, sightings are rare, and if they materialize, they are soon forgotten.

When we're at the doctor's office, in conversations around the watercooler, or standing in the checkout line at the grocery store, we hear language that shows how the culture has changed. We hear words of praise for Oprah's "faith" or someone seeking "to be true to yourself." People are still seeking a form of spirituality, but it is often an inward-focused spirituality centered on actualizing the true self, and not usually something learned "in church."

It's obvious that the world has changed from the days of previous generations. We are all busy, running after our own "gods," and seeking "what works." And when someone talks about Jesus, it is no longer clear whether that person is talking about the same person traditionally accepted as God. We are living in a post-Christian culture in North America.

"Are You One of Those Christians?"

Seven years ago, my wife and I (Dave) moved to a new neighborhood. Soon we found ourselves sitting around a fire pit, meeting our neighbors at a block party. When they discovered I was a pastor, they wanted to know about our church, and then the questions began. "Are you an evangelical like George Bush is an evangelical?" An arctic-like chill settled over the conversation, the disdain palpable. For them, Christians had become branded as narrow, exclusivist, and judgmental. It was apparent that if we were to talk about Jesus with people like this, we would have to start all over. The conversations would be as much about deconstructing what they did believe about me and my faith as it would be about giving witness to who Jesus was for our lives and the salvation he was bringing into the whole world.

These are the places we Christians are living in. These are the times of a new post-Christendom West. Imagine, then, seeking to plant a church—a fresh living expression of the gospel—in this post-Christian landscape.

Ten years ago, together with my wife, Rae Ann, I set out to plant Life on the Vine Christian Community in the northwest suburbs of Chicago. We had ten people join us in the effort. Shortly after, Geoff and his wife, Cyd, came along. We joined together to figure out how to be a church amid these challenges. We had no idea of the difficulties we faced.

In a few years, we had thirty people and decided we needed to reach out to the community. We tried everything. We tried doing a daily vacation Bible school in order to attract busy neighbors who, you would think, would be happy to send their children to a recreational venue in the neighborhood. As it turned out, only Christians came. We tried providing a date night, offering baby-sitting services for families in the neighborhood who couldn't afford it. Again, only Christians came. Someone proposed we do a fair on the grounds we had been given to start this church. The costs were prohibitive. The chances of competing with the local school district or megachurch in offering these kinds of services were just about nil. Back then, these ideas were what was called outreach.

What we learned quickly was that non-Christian people in our neighborhoods would not come to an event or service held at or associated with a Christian church. Even non-Christians with friends who are Christians will resist. The question, then, was why would we even try these events. In a culture that distrusts Christianity, a society that no longer sees the church as positive, why do we seek to attract people to come to us? Why not instead use this time and energy to be in our neighborhoods, at our local park district gymnasiums and fairs, donating our time, getting involved, knowing the people, and bringing the gospel there? We were living in a culture that no longer wanted to do the things churches do, yet we were doing them anyway.

One Sunday I learned that some people from our church were protesting the local high school board's decision to make all the school's bathrooms unisex. Two weeks later, Geoff was asked to join his neighbors in the same protest. The only problem was that Geoff's neighbors were protesting against the very people in our church who were arguing for traditional gender-based bathrooms. We saw firsthand how the church had lost its former place of authority in the community and was instead viewed with suspicion. In this case, it was Geoff, speaking as a neighbor within the community, not as a pastor, who was listened to.

Meaning Anything

Today it seems anything can mean anything, or nothing. People now expect much less out of our ideas as Christians and much more out of us as people; much less from the truth of our ideas and much more from the truth of our lives; much less from what we claim to know and much more from the life we've experienced. People are now simultaneously more suspicious and critical of grand ideas but more open to individual lives; more cynical of overarching explanations but more receptive to honest questions. Most people are open to a plurality of sources and traditions and are noncommittal about the truth of any one source.

Just look around your neighborhood. There is a family down the street from me (Geoff) where the wife was raised Jewish but recently declared her atheism (and is now trying to convert me!) and the husband is an agnostic from an ex-Lutheran family. Raised without overt spiritual direction but openness to all, one of his daughters is now flirting with Buddhism as a way of life, and another daughter, living in Africa and serving the poor, has joined the local Catholic parish (although she tells me they are much too conservative). And they all think of me as the nice guy who runs the equivalent of a nonprofit self-help center.

When trying to navigate this new cultural landscape, it often feels as if all the street signs have been pulled down, the lights aren't working, and the road has been blocked or torn up in some places. We can't get around with any ease and frequently get lost. Some of us, like Dave, remember growing up as children when navigating these cultural landscapes was relatively straightforward. Now it feels like wandering among the rubble. Others of us, like Geoff, never felt this certainty; the maps and paradigms handed to us seem outdated, destined to frustrate and discourage.

Aren't We All Christians Still?

What is to be done in the sign-stripped, mapless, and road-blocked world? There are two common responses from Christians regarding this (what some have called) postmodern mind-set (soft-relativist, strong pluralist, antiauthoritarian but pro-downtrodden). Some want to fight the cultural changes that are drifting away from universal truth, credible authorities, and a common story for understanding life. For them, engaging in mission requires showing that relativism is wrong, pluralism is mistaken, and objective truth is out there. Before any one can even share the truth of Christ, apologists must defend the idea of truth. Before anyone can even proclaim the gospel, evangelists must establish the validity of the scriptures. The assumption is that people must begin thinking a certain way before they can think about the gospel. These people often self-consciously stand against postmodernity and its negative effects on the truth of the gospel.

A similar approach is to ignore the cultural changes and stick with what works. If hellfire and brimstone was good enough for Jonathan Edwards and the First Great Awakening, then it is still good enough for us. All are still "Sinners in the Hands of an Angry God," and to preach anything less is to compromise the gospel. It is assumed that people already live in fear and guilt, and the job of the church is to relieve people of this terrible burden.

In everyday life, this often means trying to persuade people of their guilt so that the gospel can then be offered as the means to relieve them of it. It's a nice maneuver when it works. But fewer and fewer people are susceptible to this kind of guilt. We no longer live in a culture where people already know about a Holy God, the Judge. People do not live with the idea that the whole world is careening headlong toward some final judgment. They are more concerned about their social security than they are about eternal security. Arguing people back to the truth or back to guilt is merely a retreat to a lost modern mind-set and forgotten Christian culture where we can still assume that everyone is basically a Christian.

Aren't We All Postmoderns Now?

Another reaction to these cultural changes is to fully embrace the postmodern mind-set. This mind-set, made so popular by Brian McLaren, Tony Jones, and the emerging church, refuses to argue people back to the truth. Instead of retreating into a bygone cultural bunker, they revise faith for a new generation. Instead of engaging in conflict against the contemporary situation, they push us to enter a conversation with these new thought patterns.

Not retreating but revising: Isn't this what Christians have always done? The apostle Paul became all things to all people so that all might be saved (1 Corinthians 9:22). And like the men of Issachar, we are called to understand the times so that we might know what to do (1 Chronicles 12:32). We know the gospel is not one-size-fits-all. Otherwise we wouldn't need four gospels with four different perspectives written to four diverse audiences. Revising instead of retreating makes Christianity relevant to the new postmodern generations.

But being relevant is not the only motivation behind the emerging church. It is not just that Christianity has lost touch with the contemporary mindset. Nor is the problem just that Christianity has believed the wrong things, losing touch with the modern world by becoming too narrow, rational, and dogmatic. Rather, Christianity has believed in the wrong *way*.[1] Those of the emerging church feel that embracing Greek philosophy caused us to focus too much on ideas and right beliefs. As a result, Christianity lost its Hebraic inheritance of relational truth and the right way of belief.[2] This recovery of a relational mind-set moves from a gospel of guilt to a gospel of compassion and mercy. Rather than a vengeful God seeking justice on all sinners, now the gospel calls all to seek justice for the poor and the oppressed. Instead of mounting arguments for absolute truth, caring for all is the absolute commandment.

We applaud both standing up for the truth and broadening the scope of the gospel. These are both essential aspects of the journey into the missional far country. But the moves to retrench and defend or revise and relate require something more. The categories of modern versus postmodern are helpful, but we require something more earthy, on the ground, and in the middle of the struggle. We need a way to engage the cultural dynamics of day-to-day life while compromising nothing of what God has done in Christ for the world or his very presence in the world. We need to journey deep into people's everyday lives, trials, hurts, and desires. To do this, we need a signpost that can direct us to where people outside the church are living, that is, the new cultural worlds of post-Christendom.

The First Signpost: Post-Christendom

Recently one of our church's missional communities invited its neighborhood over for an Octoberfest celebration. One of the members of this community had been learning how to home-brew beer, and he used the occasion to share several of his best recipes with the gathering. Sixty people came and spent the evening getting to know one another in his backyard. One neighbor named Pete came after being invited by a member of the missional community. He knew no one else except his neighbor. He started to ask a lot of questions like, "How do you all know each other?" "Why did you all choose to live so close to one another?" "Why do you all drink in moderation?" One of the missional community members answered him awkwardly by saying, "We're here to plant a church." Pete could hardly get his mind around that answer. He said "A church? [long pause] Well, I'll drink your beer, but I won't drink your Kool-Aid!"

This incident illustrates the new situation many of us find ourselves in as Christians in North America. The place of the church is fading and, even worse, is under suspicion. The reality of God is fading in the social consciousness. Yet many Christians, pastors and churches, ignore this reality. Oddly, we go on living and organizing ourselves as if nothing has changed since the 1950s. Talk of modernity and postmodernity, although helpful, misses the core issues we're facing. We need another diagnosis. For us, the issue lies squarely in the fact that the contemporary world is moving toward post-Christendom.[3] But what is post-Christendom?

Speaking in terms of Western history, *Christendom* refers to the Middle Ages of Western Europe when all of society (church, state, schools, work, art) was united under the umbrella of Christianity. All of life—work, commerce, education, politics, family, and money—was ordered toward the church and around the core beliefs in Christianity. The Reformation did little to change this. It only put more options on the religious menu. We could now be Lutheran, Reformed, even radical Anabaptist, as well as Catholic. When the New World was discovered, Catholic Europe established Catholicism in Latin America, and Protestant Europe established Protestantism in the United States and Canada. This was all Christendom in one way or another, and it lasted for a long time in North America.

Fifty years ago, it was not uncommon for our parents (or grandparents) to watch *Andy of Mayberry* and see Andy in the pew on Sunday and Barney singing in the choir. In those days, stores were closed on Sunday. Popular evangelist Billy Graham could go to a city and hold what was basically an evangelical Sunday morning service in the local municipal stadium, and thousands would come. A majority of people would go to church on Sunday, and those who didn't go would feel slightly guilty. Many Protestant churches held a Sunday evening service to do evangelism, expecting their regular members to bring non-Christians to hear a targeted gospel message. Regular church people would attend a midweek service, as well as serve with the Boys and Girls Clubs. Life revolved around church. Even public television had to watch its p's and q's regarding religion and sexuality. Government gave its nod, and the public schools basically cooperated with the Christian agenda. These were the days of Christendom in North America.

But in many places (but not all!) today, these times are gone. The culture has shifted, and Christendom has all but disappeared in large parts of North America. We are now changing from one set of cultural patterns to another. We suggest this shift into post-Christendom can best understood by three "posts-": postattractional, postpositional, and postuniversal. These three describe the cultural conditions that have come after post-Christendom. They describe what has changed and help us see how old ways of being church may simply not relate to the new cultures after Christendom in North America.

Postattractional

There used to be a time when people gravitated toward the church building on Sunday and, especially, in times of personal or social spiritual need. It was easy to attract people to the "church." But today the poles have reversed: the church is more likely to repel people. We now live in a postattractional time.

People in this post-Christendom world no longer think about going to church when they wake up on Sunday mornings. When they find themselves in a crisis, they don't turn to the church. In fact, the church often finds itself under suspicion as an institution. "The church only wants my money!" is a common sentiment. Today we find that churches have to justify our existence. It is not true everywhere, but if you find these dynamics in your neighborhood, you know you're living in a postattractional, post-Christendom place.

Postpositional

The second post- describes how the church no longer carries respect or influence in post-Christendom. The church used to have an inherent position of authority in the community. The pastor (educated, trained, and ordained) would be consulted on educational and civic matters. People would trust him (and almost all of them were men) as the source of help and direction with regard to spiritual matters. When I (Dave) was a grade school child in the 1960s, my teacher would ask if my father, a local pastor, would like to see a copy of the musical *Jesus Christ Superstar* because we were studying it in school. Today, asking clergy to comment on class curriculum would be virtually unheard of, even resisted. In many places, the authority of the church and the pastor are viewed with apathy, distrust, and even hostility. In fact, not just the church but all other previously authoritative institutions have fallen under suspicion.

Now, churches, pastors, and ordinary Christians must earn authority, and it has to be earned relationally. The character of our Christian communities must be exposed to the light of relationships and developed slowly over time before a picture of the kingdom can emerge in our neighborhoods. People are more drawn in by the life of a local gathering than by a set of moral dictates coming from an established power. If you find yourself in a neighborhood where the church is suspect and clergypersons who wear collars are seen as strange, you're living in a post-Christendom neighborhood.

Postuniversal

Language and worldview are no longer universal to everybody we meet (of course, these things were never really universal to all people). Post-Christendom culture is postuniversal in these regards.

As a result, outside of our church, we can no longer assume we are speaking the same language when we talk about Jesus, God, and sin in our neighborhoods. Indeed, it is difficult to even speak of a singular, universal culture to which all belong. Instead of saying we are in a postuniversal culture, we should say we are in cultures (plural) that are postuniversal. North America now, more than ever before, represents peoples from diverse religious, ethnic, and economic heritages. There is no single common culture or conceptual language from which to discuss God, faith, and redemption. If you find yourself in a neighborhood where people don't know what you are talking about when you say, "Jesus is Lord," or they say, "Who are you? Tim Tebow or something?" then you know you are living in a post-Christendom neighborhood.

Post-Christendom and Intellectual Shifts

These three "posts-" describe the dynamics we're all dealing with in post-Christendom. These dynamics are interwoven with various intellectual shifts (broadly understood as postmodernism) that are becoming commonplace among people who graduated from college since the 1990s.[4] They are noticeable when we sit down in coffee houses or hang out in a health club or attend a local town meeting. It's the world that is happening all around us.

For instance, sitting in a café in Santa Fe, New Mexico, one morning about six years ago, I (Dave) noticed a poster on the wall. Titled "How to Build Global Community," it was a call to a new understanding, a plea for justice, a way toward peace. Around the global images of culture on the poster were listed over thirty catchphrases that communicated its message. A look at these revealed the depths of the new cultural situation we find ourselves in.

For instance, the poster declared, "Visit people, places, and cultures—not tourist attractions." Here's a slogan that cuts to the core of our new cultural suspicions: the people of the new post-Christendom cultures distrust what seem to be programmed experiences manufactured for consumption. They see through the staging of political events. We swear allegiance to a group only when it is personal and real. Or, as the poster says, "Listen to the people tell their stories." There is a hunger for real life and a cynicism toward corporate determination. This poster in a little café tells us we're living in a postattractional milieu.

A second look at this poster reveals the slogan, "Question consumption!" It shouts out, "Notice the workings of power and privilege in your culture," and, "Know where your bank banks!" All of these slogans reveal suspicion toward external and imposed authority. Those born in the cultures of post-Christendom believe that all systems of knowledge have power interests. Michel Foucault, one of the more famous postmodern philosophers, provides the tagline for this. He asserts that "all power is knowledge." In so doing, he is reversing the popular mantra of industrial America: "Get a good education!" or, in the words of Francis Bacon, "knowledge is power!" Foucault warns us to be aware of power agendas in all forms of societal education.

We are often taught that knowledge creates the power to change the world. Each Saturday morning, the *G.I. Joe* cartoon taught me (Geoff) that "knowing is half the battle." To know things was the power to change things. In this way *G.I. Joe* was more than a cartoon; it was teaching valuable life lessons. What I didn't know at that time was that the *G.I. Joe* morning cartoon was Hasbro's way of producing consumer demand by expanding its market through television. Hasbro was exerting a subtle power on my way of knowing and my desires through its cartoon even while it claimed to give children the helpful knowledge and confidence to take control of their lives.

Similarly, think of ads for medications. They offer themselves as merely informational—"If you struggle with ... ask your doctor about ..." Just the facts. But so much more is going on. They are forming in us anxiety about cholesterol, blood pressure, or depression and then offering a solution in the form of a particular drug. These ads offer knowledge, but they also exercise power in forming our desires (partly in the form of what they don't tell us—that there might be other ways of dealing with these problems than just popping a couple pills).

This happens everywhere. Opening a checking account or getting your first credit card introduces one to the power of debt and interest and opens one to a new way of thinking about money. Listening to certain news outlets shapes our thinking about politics. Buying produce from chain stores forms our understanding of agriculture. Under the guise of giving us helpful knowledge, just as Hasbro did (and still does), each activity exerts a subtle form of power. We become enslaved to or at least formed by the power interests at work in these systems. The poster in Santa Fe shows how postpositional this context has become.

That poster offers yet another lesson in its compelling phrases: "Think of no one as *them*," and, "Imagine other cultures through their poetry and their novels." These catchphrases express a plea not to impose one's own cultural prejudices on other peoples. Instead it urges us get to know their language and understand what makes them tick. The postmodernist philosopher Jacques Derrida is famous for claiming, "There is nothing outside the text."[5] By this, he means we are all captured within a culture and a language. We all live in and from a (con)text. By "language," we don't just mean languages like English, Spanish, Swahili, and Chinese. Rather, it includes the cultural patterns of meaning that shape and organize our lives. These might be the language and thought patterns of Latino immigrants working in California, the experience of racism in the South (for blacks and whites), or northeastern political passion. None of these is neutral. All of them form, shape, and even control us. We enter these experiences formed by language before we can truly understand them. There is power at work here. There are stories. There are no more metanarratives that explain everything for everybody as postmodern philosopher Jean Lyotard tells us.[6] We are living in a postuniversal world where we can no longer assume we are speaking the same (conceptual or cultural) language. It's not that easy!

I (Geoff) remember preaching early on at Life on the Vine. Being from California, I used what I considered a harmless slang phrase that refers to getting angry. I later found out that people thought I was swearing (oh, and to make it worse, I was referring to God with these questionable words). So while we were all speaking English, my West Coast language was inadvertently offensive to the language of midwestern ears.

Similarly, we all live in overlapping networks of languages, cultures, and histories generating different hopes, passions, fears, and expectations. And just like moving from the West Coast to the Midwest, we must learn to inhabit these languages before we can proclaim Jesus within them. This is all a testimony to the postuniversal nature of our North American society in which this poster serves as a centerpiece.

More than just some catchphrases, then, this poster is a signpost pointing us away from our secure places. It directs us far into another country. It leads our church lives, everyday lives, and individual lives (we assume these are all part of one life) into the postattractional, postpositional, postuniversal cultures that lie at our doorstep. Our neighbors are too distracted to notice another well-produced program on a screen or a piece of entertainment in a theater. They quickly move from one "truth" to another. They live too fast and are too cynical. Only an encounter with something real, humble, and embodied, where they encounter a set of eyes, a conversation, and an authentic life, will cause them to take notice. These are the souls of the new post-Christendom cultures of the West. This is where they live. This is where we must go.

Not Prodigal Enough

In Santa Cruz, California, on my college campus, I (Geoff) was talking with an ecofeminist student about her desire to save endangered species. I admit I was trying to evangelize her! But we kept turning toward issues of the environment instead. No matter. I was well trained in the art of debunking evolution as a philosophy, exposing how this worldview actually gives no basis to care for the environment because it didn't have a place for a Creator who gives intrinsic worth to creation (and so on and so forth). I was a Bible-believing, philosophy-reading student ready to destroy all intellectual strongholds standing against the gospel. The only problem was that she wasn't interested in questions of origins (Where did the earth come from?), or ethics (How do we know what is good?), or my very compelling answers. She wasn't asking those questions. Rather than entering into her world, I was just repeating the questions and answers I had learned from my established church culture. I was proclaiming the mainstays of traditional faith in an apologetic mode.

Mark Driscoll's book, *Vintage Jesus: Timeless Answers to Timely Questions*, does some of these same things. It answers questions such as, "Is Jesus the only God?" "How did people know Jesus was coming?" or "Where is Jesus today?"[7] There is nothing wrong with asking or answering these questions, of course. The problem is that these are proposed as timely questions meant to minister the gospel to a seeking world. Yet these questions assume people have a background from which to ask about Jesus. They are therefore Christendom questions. They reflect a Christendom confidence that everybody already knows who Jesus is and that he is important. It does not teach us how to engage those who know nothing about Jesus and suspect people who do. This approach isn't nearly prodigal enough.

Of course, knowing the dangers of the fundamentalism of my youth, I could have taken a different approach when talking with this student environmentalist. I could have wrapped the faith with an evolutionary cover, making it accessible and relevant to the passions of this young woman. I could have embraced, affirmed, and accepted this alternative worldview, inventing a new Christianity compatible with her hopes and aspirations. Isn't this what it means to be reckless in faith, entering the missional far country? Isn't this the best example of an excessive faith, ready to change and adapt for every situation, not holding anything back?

But this too leaves something to be desired. In our welcoming and affirming of all cultural nuances and alternate worldviews, we also want to be able to discern God: the God we know in and through Jesus Christ. Christ has said, "Behold I am making all things new" (Revelation 21:5 ESV). Again and again we are told in the Bible that he is at work "reconciling the world to himself" (2 Corinthians 5:19 ESV). We must not lose attentiveness to God's activity in the midst of our conversations. When we are in our neighborhoods, talking and helping, we must not find ourselves surrendering what we believe is good and right, losing the ability to discern the dark underbelly of things. If we do, then we will eventually find ourselves unable to enter into our surrounding neighborhoods prodigally, as God comes in Christ. God comes in Christ as one of us, affirming and accepting and loving. But God also comes overcoming evil and injustice by healing and restoring the broken. He comes as God bringing his saving reign into the world. In the same way, both of these aspects together are the sign of a prodigal Christianity following a prodigal God.

The Opportunities of Post-Christendom

Accepting the postattractional, postpositional, and postuniversal realities of mission in North America gives us an opportunity to learn again the prodigal nature of God, for the Triune God crosses all boundaries into our world of poverty and affliction in the Son rather than merely attracting us by magnificent displays of power and glory. He climbs down from a position of prestige and authority and becomes like us in our weary and despised state. He gives up a universal perspective and inhabits the flesh of a Jew in the Roman Empire. A prodigal Christianity understands each "post-" as opportunities for faithfulness rather than problems to be solved. Neither retreat nor revision will do. Instead we are sent into the depths of our neighborhoods to discover the prodigal God at work—the God revealed among the meek, in ordinary neighborhoods, within the languages and struggles of everyday life.

Each of the three "posts-" is seen in the Son, the one sent by God into the far country. We notice first that the Son becoming human didn't run an attractional campaign to gather large groups of people to himself. Jesus didn't have a single location or a simple message that drew crowds, and he was actively tearing people away from the stability offered by physical structures and social ties. To those desiring to follow him in some sort of easy and stable manner, Jesus responds, "Foxes have holes and birds of the air have nests, but the Son of Man has no place to lay his head" (Mark 8:20 NIV). When the disciples and the crowds wanted to consolidate early ministry successes at Capernaum, when they wanted to dig in and expand their ministry platform, Jesus had nothing to do with it. He simply responded, "I must preach the good news of the kingdom of God to the other towns also." Why? "Because that is why I was *sent*" (Luke 4:42–43 NIV). Living into the postattractional reality of post-Christendom is to follow in the prodigal way of the Sent One.

Likewise, God sent the Son into the middle of the largest empire in human history. Caesar, as its ruler, claimed to be a god and expected to be worshipped as such. In contrast to this, God sent his Son, "who, being in very nature God, did not consider equality with God something to be grasped." He did not consider it necessary to flaunt his divine nature before the crowds, "but made himself nothing, taking the very nature of a servant, being made in human likeness." Not only this, but the Sent One was "found in appearance as a man, he humbled himself and became obedient to death—even death on a cross!" (Philippians 2:6–8 NIV).[8] The one who was already equal with God (the position Caesar aspired to) not only puts aside this status but took the place of the lowliest of low and died the death of a slave, for only slaves and other non-Romans could be crucified. This humility, this obedience even unto death, is the prodigal place through which the presence of the Sent One is made known.

Jesus had no assumptions about power and prestige. He did not seek after places of influence and significance and did not rest on the seat of authority. In utter recklessness, the Sent One abandons the security of position, the pretense of power, the concern for control. In the eyes of Roman authority, this move from godhood to slavery was nonsense. For Roman authority, only a completely wasteful god would squander the opportunity to rule and dominate. Yet it should not surprise us that this is the postpositional posture of the prodigal God. And this posture of humility is the mark of those following God into the missional far country.

Finally, we should notice that the Sent One shows us what being post-universal looks like. The Sent One is not an abstraction living above the daily grind, a lofty thought beyond everyday concerns, a universal perspective outside our common blind spots. Rather, "The Word became flesh and blood and moved into the neighborhood" (John 1:14 Message). The world-creating Word, the life-giving Word, the Word before the beginning and after the end, this Word took on flesh and blood, a common human body (a Jewish body to be precise), and moved in down the street (if you lived in Nazareth). The Word became local, not universal; concrete, not abstract. The Word left the virtual world, became analogue, and dwelled among us. The Word does not come to us as data to a hand-held device, but as a hand holding a hand.

Don't we mostly think of God as abstract, universal, outside space and time, beyond our experience, and above our comprehension? That God would become flesh in Jesus of Nazareth was a great scandal to the Greek philosophical mind. They thought God must be without a body, outside time, beyond emotion—like the Roman Caesar, scandalized by a God who would give up a position of authority; a God who would give up universality and take up particularity scandalized the Greek philosopher. This is the "scandal of particularity." It is only a prodigal God who would come in this way.

In the same manner, we must follow the prodigal way of the Son. We must enter each local context, each neighborhood, each place of work, and each social space. This is the journey of the Sent One who came and dwelled among us, who did not make us come to him, who came vul-nerably and humbly, not out of a position of power, who came walking among us in flesh and blood in a way of life. He came communicating a message in his very life, using parables from local (agri)culture and speaking the language of his day (Aramaic). To live into the postuniversal landscape of our post-Christendom situation, we must do no less.

These days, when our compasses are spinning and all the street lights are out, when our familiar routes are blocked and our maps are torn, this first signpost of post-Christendom directs us toward a prodigal Christianity that does not stand still in order to attract, does not sit in the seat of authority, and does not walk in the ways of the universal, but instead delights in the paths of the prodigal God.

MISSIO DEI

WITH THE PRODIGAL GOD: THE JOURNEY
INTO GOD'S MISSION

IT'S A NORMAL MORNING at the local McDonald's. I (Dave) am sitting in my favorite booth, working away, while people of the community from every race, class, and job status pass through. While I sit there, getting my work organized for the day, many come, sit around, have something to eat, drink coffee, and talk for anywhere from two minutes to two hours.

Among this very normal suburban crowd, I know a man who left the Roman Catholic priesthood in his thirties and now looks to Buddha to teach him the ways to God. I have a secular Jewish friend who resists talking about God or his personal life, but he gives me medical advice. I meet regularly with a friend here who has slept in his car for three years. He has been confused about voices he says are from God. He's convinced evil people are trying to confuse him and undermine him getting anywhere in his life. It is painfully clear that "god" has been twisted into the many dysfunctions he carries with him. I have many ex-Catholic friends who distrust Christianity of any kind because they are convinced the church is out for their money. I know a man who is sold on science and evolution and blames the church for boxing God into a seven-day creation scheme. And then, of course, there is a smattering of practicing Christians who don't seem to know what to do with this mosaic of beliefs. This McDonald's has become a reflection of society today: life in the new post-Christendom worlds of North America.

This is the world we live in. There is no consensus as to what the word *god* means. When a friend stops in at McDonald's and tells me his wife is leaving him, his sister is dying from kidney disease, or his daughter was admitted to the hospital on suicide watch, I have no idea how he will react if I suggest that we pray together. He might respond saying, "Right. I need to get in touch with my inner spirit?" or, "I pray best with my Sutra," or even, "Sorry, but I can't believe in a God who allows such evil in the world."

This lack of consensus in our society about "god" is evident everywhere. Several years ago, for instance, Oprah ridiculed her Baptist pastor by telling her audience how he would preach at the top of his lungs, "God is a jealous God!" In response, Oprah said, "God is not like that." Being jealous, she said, was the equivalent of being insecure and "God needed to get over that." God is the good spirit at work in the world. In contrast to her pastor, God for Oprah is the inner light of our souls that we all need to get in touch with. She has been called America's high priestess. With a TV audience of over 40 million Oprah had the largest church in North America and revealed how many people think today about "god."

Meanwhile, for at least ten years, self-proclaimed atheists have been snubbing the idea of God and selling thousands of books on the *New York Times* bestseller list. "God is not great, He poisons everything!" said Christopher Hitchens. God is a piece of ideology that stands in the way of human progress according to Sam Harris. God represses intellectual growth. God means we must embrace seven-day creationism versus the advances of science. God is the tool of the church to guilt people into a medieval moralism. God is responsible for violence in the world, including the Christian Crusades and Islamic terrorism. It is stunning how prevalent this view of God is among the average North American.[1]

Princeton researcher Kenda Creasy Dean tells us that for most churchgoing American teenagers, God is a personal moral therapist available on call when they need to solve a problem and make life happy. This may be an upgrade from the god of Hitchens, but it hardly relieves our confusion about God.[2]

In the strange new worlds of post-Christendom in North America and Europe, who God is, what he has done, and what he is doing in the world is an open-ended and disorienting discussion. Our churches appear dumbfounded and astonished at their inability to communicate about God. It seems we are comfortable reciting only what the Bible says about God and telling the world to get with it. As we discussed in chapter 1, these days it feels as if all the street signs have been pulled down, the lights are blinking the wrong colors, and the familiar roads have been rerouted. In the midst of the post-Christianized cultures, we need some direction in order to see and know God. Signpost 2 points us in the direction of the God of mission whose very character is revealed in the *missio Dei*, the mission of God. But before we get to this signpost, let's examine the current status of this discussion about God.

The All-Powerful Yet Distant God

Like many uprooted immigrants who set out for a new land, we are looking up at the distant stars for a direction. Like good sailors, we are searching for something constant, steady, and unchanging to orient ourselves. We want a north star to guide us. And this hope for a fixed point to navigate by aptly summarizes what drives us amid the current confusions and misconceptions about God. A neighbor once asked me (Geoff), "When you think about God, do you get a picture of an old man behind a desk running the universe?" Isn't this the typical conception of God: the old man behind the cosmic desk? In theological terms, God is all-powerful, all-knowing, holy, high above all things, and firmly in control. Or perhaps instead of sitting behind a celestial desk as the galactic executive keeping all the stars spinning and the rate of gravity constant, we sometimes see God sitting behind a colossal court bench, a stoic judge banging the cosmic gavel and meting out judgments over humanity. Sometimes the judgments are favorable, which are called forgiveness. Other times they are convictions, followed by swift sentencing.

But to those wandering around McDonald's on any given morning, these pictures of God are distant and alienating. There is little doubt that these images make sense of parts of the Bible. But isolated from the rest of Scripture, they present God as daunting and untouchable. And so more and more North Americans simply shrug their shoulders and say, "I'd rather go it alone, thank you." It doesn't help that every time a world disaster hits, we get pronouncements from prominent Christian leaders that highlight God's judgment ("Hurricane Katrina is God's judgment on New Orleans!") in a way that seems detached and dispassionate.

Thankfully, the televangelists do not speak for all of us. But most of our churches, when teaching about God, begin with God's most austere attributes. It's a habit that goes as far back as the Puritan preachers like Jonathan Edwards who proclaimed first God's holiness and our sin, and only then, after we've being properly crushed with shame and guilt, did they proclaim the wonders of God's grace and love. Today, hundreds of years later, we are still starting with God's transcendent attributes illustrated from the Old Testament. God is holy, unchanging, and almighty. God is all knowing, just, sovereign, and everywhere at all times. We come to God's personal attributes—such as love, mercy, forgiveness, and grace—only after God's impersonal traits have been dutifully expounded. As a result Christians have often subconsciously subscribed to a static and distant view of God.

These ways of approaching God are well accepted within the church and make a lot of sense within the confines of Christendom because here, in Christendom, we know the whole story behind these attributes. But in a society that has lost its memory of God and his story in scripture, these attributes come off as dispassionate and aloof. God comes off as "behaving badly," as David Lamb puts it in his great book.[3]

The problem becomes obvious: this approach to God leaves out the full breadth of God's story. Somehow we abstracted these attributes from the whole story of God and lost the sense of how God is active and at work in the world, welcoming all women and men into an abundant life. Stunningly, we have lost the imagination for the way God has sent the Son and the Spirit into the world to bring God's kingdom. We have lost the prodigal God who comes to us into our own lives, neighborhoods, and places of work.

Sovereign or Just Plain Cruel?

After the tragic tsunami disaster of Japan in 2011, one of the nation's great pastors, John Piper of Minneapolis, led his congregation in a wonderful prayer: "Father in heaven, you are the absolute Sovereign over the shaking of the earth, the rising of the sea, and the raging of the waves. We tremble at your power and bow before your unsearchable judgments and inscrutable ways." Piper beautifully leads the congregation into the presence of the transcendent God whom Christ taught us to pray to as "our Father." We can sense the comfort received in the midst of such an awful moment through this prayer. The pastor then leads further by praying, "O God, we humble ourselves under your holy majesty and repent. In a moment—in the twinkling of an eye—we too could be swept away. We are not more deserving of firm ground than our fellowmen in Japan. We too are flesh . . . Grant us, your sinful creatures, to return to you, that you may have compassion." Placing us in relationship before the sovereign God, the pastor leads us into the great comfort we have in Christ: "For surely you will abundantly pardon. Everyone who calls on the name of the Lord Jesus, your beloved Son, will be saved." The pastor pleads that "every heart-breaking loss—millions upon millions of losses—be healed by the wounded hands of the risen Christ. You are not unacquainted with your creatures' pain." The pastor then closes with words from an old hymn: "O let them not judge you with feeble sense, but trust you for your grace. And so behind this providence, soon find a smiling face."[4] Over against the moral-therapeutic gods of our day, this pastor draws us into a place of worship before the almighty God, a God in we whom we can trust even if we don't always understand what is happening.

If you heard this prayer, however, without the background knowledge by which it makes sense, you might be left with a sense of emptiness, disquiet, and distance. God is sovereign, but he is also just plain cruel. You might be left with the feeling you get when a doctor informs you of a serious health issue while using a mechanical tone of voice. You hear him, but inside you're yelling to yourself, *Hello! You're talking about my life or death here, Doc!* Many are yelling the same thing to this pastor. Truth be told, God is not dispassionate but is passionately acting for the rightness of the world. Yet when forced to start with the justice and anger of God, before anything else, the fullness of God's life is lost to the average person. These post-Christians leave shaking their head confused. They are saying to themselves, *Maybe that makes sense to you, but I'd rather go it alone.*

And God Does Us a Big Favor

And yet most of us North American Christians still start from this vision of God the Just, God on High, God the Holy One who confronts our sinfulness and reveals our condemnation in the face of God's righteous wrath. But (as this line of thought goes) God also mercifully sends the Son to die for our sins, paying the price for our unrighteousness. "Phew! What a relief," we sigh. "Now we are pardoned, set free from our guilt." Sometimes this is explained as God loving us so much that God comes down to do for us what we could not do ourselves. God pays the price of sin by sacrificing the life of God's own Son so that we might live. This has been the common version of the gospel in Western Christianity for centuries (parts of which should not be hastily dismissed).

And yet, to the millions of people in post-Christendom, this message is heard differently. To the uninitiated, this message sounds like a petty dictator from on high demanding satisfaction for every transgression, no matter how small. Or perhaps worse, this looks like a narcissistic God who creates a world that falls into sin so that he can then come to the rescue and feel good about himself—much like a villain who creates a disaster and then shows up like a hero to save the day. It seems in many cases that God is coming to do us a big favor we never asked for.

As we mentioned briefly in signpost 1, over the past one thousand years in the Christian West, the dominant moral issue has been personal moral guilt. Western society cultivated the guilt of falling short of God's standards—the fear of falling outside God's redemption. There's nothing false about this. In fact, the result was often a well-ordered Christian life where the most urgent issue was the management of one's personal burden of guilt.[5] Today, however, the ubiquity of guilt no longer holds in many parts of North American culture. That part of the gospel that made so much sense to people growing up in a Christian home or living in a Christian society has lost its context. Certainly forgiveness and repentance will always be central to living with God. But it may no longer be the starting point it once was.

Funeral Pyre

Two years ago, a dear friend of our gang at McDonald's died at an elderly age. Many of us decided to go over to the church for the funeral. Most, if not all, of my (Dave's) comrades did not practice any form of Christian faith. Nonetheless, they decided to honor Mel.

The funeral started wonderfully with stories testifying to Mel's amazing life and ministry. And then the pastor got up. For the next hour and a half, he told everyone in the hall that if you had not "accepted Christ's provision for your sins," you would never see Mel again! Text by text, he relentlessly went over how God was a just God and how eternal damnation was our fate apart from trusting in Christ and his provision for sin. Although it was Mel who had passed away, this pastor was making it clear that everyone else was in danger of being thrown on the funeral pyre.

Despite his best efforts, this pastor could not generate the guilt and fear necessary for his gospel message to make sense. Instead I watched in horror as my friends became extremely irritated. Snide remarks started to come out. And with each one, the pastor would respond by extending his sermon another five minutes! My friends left more alienated from God's work in Christ, and I don't believe it was entirely their fault.

I was certain that God was working in my friends and around them. They just needed a vision of God's working in and around their lives. The testimony of God's work in and through Mel's life was probably the place to start. My friends needed to see that in Mel, God was already reaching out to touch them personally, offering healing to the broken and victory amid death. But all this was short-circuited by a message of guilt and fear. Though much of what the preacher said was true, his words and presence did not reach far enough into the prodigality of the Triune God at work in the lives attending that funeral.

So Now God Is Everywhere, Right?

A giant pendulum swinging back and forth is absolutely mesmerizing, even hypnotic, and it's very predictable. So for those of us uncomfortable with the distant God of our past church life, it is inevitable that we would swing over and notice that the God of the Bible is at work in the whole world. From God constantly working outside Israel through events and rulers like King Cyrus (who sent Israelites back home from exile) to God working outside the church through people like Cornelius (in Acts 10), God is now and has always been at work in the world by the movement of the Spirit.

For those of us disenchanted with the distant God, we welcome this side of God who is active in our world. As Lesslie Newbigin said many years ago, "One of the most popular slogans in the missiology of the past decades is 'God is at work in the world.'"[6] God is close enough to touch, taste, and feel at every moment in life. Celtic Christians pictured God as a wild goose: uncatchable, unpredictable, freely roaming the world.[7] The wild goose as a figure for the Spirit of God blasts through the boundaries of exclusion and injustice, and it is our work and our joy to chase the wild goose around but never capture it, following wherever it leads but never guiding it. This understanding gives us new inspiration. It fuels our passion because it is God's love and compassion that drive us into partnership with all God is doing to free the enslaved and empower the hurting. The good news, in this view, is that God is bigger than the church and its activities, and we are invited to join in.

But can you feel the pendulum swinging? Swinging from the distant God to the everywhere God?

Ten years ago, both of us led one of the first Emergent cohorts in the country. The emerging church, and its primary organization, Emergent Village, was gathering much attention. Its authors, pastors, and leaders were at the forefront of making us aware of God's mission in the world. They were challenging us to get out of the building and join in with what God is doing in the world. We jumped in on the conversation by starting a local cohort in Chicago called "Up/rooted" (the idea being that when we are rooted in the mission of God, we are also always uprooted by that mission). After several years, we handed over the leadership as others emerged and as our time commitments shifted. We went to many meetings but couldn't make them all.

A few years later, we read with interest some reports from the Up/rooted website of a meeting neither of us could attend. The conversation for that night centered on the subject of whether its meetings should end with the Lord's Prayer. Years before, the two of us had started Up/rooted meetings with a few liturgies that would gather us together around what we believed about God and the world. The two most common were reciting the Apostle's Creed and praying the Lord's Prayer. We felt these acts united us around the historic Christian faith no matter what denomination or group we were with. But now it seemed this tradition was a concern at Up/rooted. Two atheists had apparently come to the meeting along with an Emergent Jewish person, and they had deemed these practices to be exclusive.[8] Some of the opinions expressed on Up/rooted's blog maintained that the liturgy itself was too excluding. It "inevitably draws a line. Why do people recite words together?" Instead we should be asking, "How can we better serve each other and love God? How can we be human together?" But after these liturgies had been eliminated, others in the group reported feeling hollow, like loose ends dangling out of nowhere. They felt groundless because the Lord's Prayer was replaced with silence.

What had happened in that group over the first five years of its existence? Our sense was that the Up/rooted group had moved from being a group of Christians committed to discerning what it meant to follow God in the world to an inclusive discussion of where God was working in everyone and in everything. The center of the group had shifted. The difference between saying, "God is at work in the world," and saying, "God is at work everywhere," had been blurred. The questions that became increasingly more important for us as we journeyed through these Emergent discussions was what it means to say "God" and how one might know where God is working.

If God Is Everywhere, Then God Is Nowhere

Certainly Christians must make spaces to be with non-Christians and have open conversations. There should be open listening and discussion all around, along with engagement and discernment of where God is at work in each encounter. But it is a mistake to give up our particular story as Christians—our core identities given to us in the history of the Triune God from Creation; to the birth of and history of Israel; to the life, death, and resurrection of God's Son in Jesus Christ. To do so loses the radical sense that God has distinctively arrived in mission in the Son and the Spirit in order to overcome sin, evil, and death.

Rather than a distant guiding star, the idea that "God is at work in the whole world" can function like an enveloping cloud, close enough to touch, covering everything, so that no matter where we look, no matter where we go, God is already there. There is a certain progress toward the God engaged in mission, but claiming to see God everywhere can obstruct our ability to distinguish the illuminating work of God from shadowy semblances. Like Newbigin, we think that saying that God is at work in the world "is in a sense indisputable," but we must also remember that "proclaiming the reign of God over all events and things must involve some kind of interpretation of what is happening in the world."[9] And this interpretation of God's work is more complicated than merely proclaiming that God is at work. The ability to interpret and discern where God is at work comes from knowing the distinct history of Father, Son, and Holy Spirit working through time in the world in mission. Indeed, to say God is at work in the world is to say that God has begun a new work in Jesus Christ made manifest in the world by the Spirit. Neither a distant star nor an enveloping cloud is sufficient to navigate these post-Christendom cultures.

Brian McLaren wrote a book in 2007 entitled *Everything Must Change*.[10] We love the book. It's full of hope and calls us to live more faithfully into the mission of God. And yet we felt in this book the same incompleteness we felt about the Up/rooted meeting. Should the title of this book be *Everything Must Change!* (a command) or should it be *Everything Has Already Changed* (a description), calling us into the fundamental work God has already begun in Jesus Christ? The challenge that everything must change certainly calls us out of the worn walls of typical Christian living. But within the enveloping cloud of the everywhere God, it feels as if everything is up to each one of us. God's ubiquitous mission shifts, almost accidentally, into our mission to change the world, something we must do. We swing radically from a distant God who isn't doing much in the world to the mission of God that we must do for God.

So we applaud our Emergent friends who worked to proclaim the fullness of God's mission in the world and invite everyone into it. But we need more: we must go beyond the pendulum swinging between the distant God and the everywhere God. We must realize this pendulum shares the same pivot point, attached to the ceiling of Christendom, all of which hinders a deep understanding of the second signpost, *missio Dei*. Rather than retreating (distant star) or revising (enveloping cloud), we must move forward with the God who is on the move in the world in very concrete and distinct ways. Until we can get this we will be unable to follow this second signpost.

Signpost Two: The Journey into God's Mission for the World

We may not think of God as the one who has invaded the world in the Son. Nor do we live as if God has remained active in the world through the Spirit. But we must get back to this place. And to get back, we need to start at the beginning—the beginning of the good news of Jesus, the beginning of the gospel of Jesus Christ, the Son of God.

> In those days, Jesus came from Nazareth of Galilee and was baptized by John in the Jordan. And when he came up out of the water, immediately he saw the heavens being torn open and the Spirit descending on him like a dove. And a voice came from heaven: "You are my beloved Son; with you I am well pleased." The Spirit immediately drove him out into the wilderness. And he was in the wilderness forty days being tempted by Satan. And he was with the wild animals, and the angels were ministering to him. Now after John was arrested, Jesus came into Galilee, proclaiming the gospel of God, and saying, "The time is fulfilled, and the kingdom of God is at hand; repent and believe in the gospel" (Mark 1:1, 9–15 ESV).

Mark's gospel begins with Jesus announcing the kingdom of God, the arrival of the reign of God: "The time is now! The place is here!" But not only does Jesus announce the kingdom; he is also acknowledged as the Son of God and anointed by the Spirit of God in his baptism.[11] Rising out of the water, Jesus sees the "heavens being torn open," a dramatic event—an apocalyptic event—a fulfillment of Isaiah's prayer: "Oh that you would rend the heavens and come down" (Isaiah 64:1 ESV). Tumbling down from this tear in the heavens come the startling words of divine affection and acknowledgment: "You are my beloved Son; with you I am well pleased." The parallels to Psalm 2 are astonishing—not merely as a proof text for the phrase but because this psalm is a coronation psalm used traditionally to celebrate the anointing of Israel's king over all the nations. Here, in Jesus's baptism, he is being anointed king, embodying the hopes of Israel that one day God would come and make all things right. The kingdom is breaking in.

And yet we also learn at his baptism that Jesus lives his sonship in close relationship with God the Father ("you are my beloved Son"). Nothing is more characteristic of Jesus's understanding of God than this notion: that God is his father, his *Abba* in Aramaic (the language Jesus spoke). This understanding of God is so characteristic of Jesus that he begins the Lord's Prayer with, "Our Father" (Matthew 6:9). When explaining salvation to the Gentiles, the apostle Paul says that they too, like Jesus, have received the spirit of adoption and can cry out to God as "Abba! Father!" (Galatians 4:6; Romans 8:15).[12]

This spirit of adoption reminds us that the Spirit descended on Jesus, the Son of the Father, anointing him to do the work of the kingdom. This is the work of bringing justice to the nations, good tidings to the afflicted, sight to the blind, and freedom to the captives, and to proclaim the arrival of God's favor (Luke 4:18, quoting Isaiah 61:1–2). It is by this Spirit that Jesus proclaims that the kingdom of God is at hand. It is by this Spirit that Jesus draws all daughters and sons to the Father, that they might cry *Abba*. It is by this Spirit that a new creation springs forth from the rubble of human striving and suffering.

Indeed, just as the Spirit of God hovered over the waters of the deep from which creation emerged out of chaos and darkness, so now the Spirit hovers over the one emerging from the waters of the Jordan, the one who will confront chaos and darkness. With the tearing of the heavens, with the voice of God, with the descent of the Spirit, we see a new creation beginning. The Father, Son, and Spirit—God the three in one, God the Trinity—are acting in Jesus's baptism to begin new work, tearing open a new possibility for a wandering and estranged world. It is as if "God has ripped the heavens irrevocably apart at Jesus' baptism, never to be shut again. Through this gracious gash in the universe, he has poured forth the Spirit into the earthly realm."[13] This is an astonishing moment: from this single episode, the Father, Son, and Spirit should never be confused with a distant and dispassionate God.

We see the Trinity (one God as three persons) powerfully at work in Jesus's baptism. The Triune God is not a static, singular metaphysical being, set apart from creation, distant and removed. Nor is the Triune God the "father judge" sending the "sacrificial son" on a mission to earth (to die!), and then returning to the godhead. Rather, God is the sending God, the dynamic God, the lavish and excessively risky God, who comes crashing in, breaks through the heavens, and enters our world, becoming one of us. The Trinity, this archaic doctrine from early Christianity once written off as too hard to understand, too philosophical, too intellectual to make any difference to the way we live, is now front and center in little communities of mission all over North America. Revealed in Jesus's baptism is the Father, Son, and Holy Spirit, the prodigal God powerfully at work, breaking in to our world, announcing the kingdom, and, because of this, everything is changing.[14]

Missio Dei *for the World*

For Mark, Jesus's baptism is the beginning. For the gospels of Matthew and Luke, Jesus's birth is the beginning. While for Matthew, this beginning stretches back to Abraham (Matthew 1:1), for Luke, it stretches back to Adam, the first son of God (Luke 3:38). But the gospel of John reaches back before all births, before all beginnings, and echoing the words of creation in Genesis declares, "In the beginning was the Word, and the Word was with God, and the Word was God. He was with God in the beginning" (John 1:1–2 NIV). Jesus is the beginner of all beginnings because he is the one through whom all things (all beginnings) are made (John 1:3). John is making explicit what Mark had kept implicit in his narrative. Is it any wonder, then, that when Mark describes the baptism of Jesus, it sounds so similar to the creation of the world? Jesus is the new beginning because he was there creating the first beginning.

The point here, however, is not only that the Triune God is invading the world, tearing open the heavens in an all-or-nothing rescue mission. Rather, the main point is that this arrival, this coming down of God, is the defining characteristic of God: God is always going, coming, sending in mission. John tells us that the Father sends the Son. Just after the famous John 3:16 (NIV) passage, "For God so loved the world, that he gave his one and only Son, that whoever believes in him shall not perish but have eternal life," we get to verse 17 (NIV): "For God did not *send* his Son into the world to condemn the world, but to save the world through him." Not only does the Father send the Son into the world to save it, the Son also sends the Spirit into the world, resting on the disciples (John 16:7–8).[15] The disciples are also caught up and drawn into this divine sending when Jesus proclaims, "Peace be with you. As the Father has sent me, even so I am sending you" (John 20:21 ESV). *Sending* and *being sent* is fundamental to who God is and what God does (they are one and the same).

Recently in churches across North America, this sending and being sent, this movement of the Triune God invading the world for salvation, has moved from the margins to the center of our understanding of God. Many now speak of it as the *missio Dei*, or the mission of God. It is always in God's character to send and be sent. It is essential to the nature of God to engage in mission, to go and draw near. This Triune God is never distant and aloof, drawing near only in the past but today removed and unmoved. God is always drawing near, entering in, walking beside the world in all its distress and uncertainty, in all its poverty and depravity. The prodigal God is on a mission.

Joining the Journey

I (Dave) remember the first time someone challenged me to pray for my neighborhood, the people I worked with at my financial services office, the people I would meet every day. I thought I was supposed to pray for them by name, for their salvation, or for an opportunity to speak with them about their need for God.

This challenge felt mechanical. I had in mind that this meant to pray for my friends to somehow see their need for God's forgiveness and that I would have an opportunity to give them the answer: the gospel of being forgiven from sin. The friend challenging me said, "No, God is already working there, in each person's life. Just pray that you will have eyes to see what God is doing so you can participate with a word, or a prayer, with laughter, or a tear." If the Triune God is already in mission, then I need to see the worlds in which I regularly walk as the arenas of the Spirit—places imbued with the presence of God. This was a fundamental shift. It changed the way I walked into every space of my life. *Missio Dei* means that God is already at work in our lives and the lives of all around us.

I started to change the way I inhabited places: work, the coffee shop, the train on the way to work, a neighborhood conversation, a school board committee meeting, the food pantry, and of course my own family life. I started to pay attention to things I normally would miss. I began to listen for God. I tried not to make God into an evangelism project that I had to do a few hours a week. I simply paid attention to my existing routine and daily tasks. I looked for what God was doing in all the relationships and interactions of my life.

One of my tasks that starts each of my days is reading and grading. I am a professor and need about two hours each day to keep up with my work. So about four years ago, after my time with God in the early morning, I started to go to the local McDonald's. I went there the same time every day, drinking coffee, doing my work, and trying to be present for God and other people (without compromising getting my work done). I began to pray before I got there that God would open my eyes. Much to my shock, I started to see a whole world I had been missing where God was already at work. Whereas before, I might have been focused only on my work and gone from place to place, paying attention to no one, now I was trying to listen, inhabit, and take note of what God was doing. Over the years, God has done wonderful things. I was beginning to understand God through the lens of *missio Dei*.

A typical episode goes like this. John, whom I have gotten to know over two or three years, is hurting financially. He comes in to the coffee shop one morning with an impacted tooth in a swollen and infected mouth. In between my work, we sit and talk for a while about what's going on. This takes about ten minutes. I easily discern (because we've known each other for two years) that he's in trouble: he's in great pain with no recourse to get help. I give him a number of a dentist I know and suggest he make an appointment. I give him my cell phone number so that he can have the dentist call me and I will inform the dentist that I (or my church) will pay for the dental work. I ask him if we can submit to God's kingdom and allow him to bless these relationships and heal his mouth.

A day later, the dentist calls, I agree to cover the bill (through our mission fund at church), and John gets his mouth fixed. I see John in a couple of days, and we thank God. I tell John that I did nothing: "This is the way God works through Jesus Christ and His people." And the thing is, I never got a bill. The dentist did it pro bono.

This simple episode took about fifteen minutes of my time. Yet I feel as I had done almost nothing—just cooperated with God. But in that fifteen minutes. God worked. A little slice of the kingdom broke in. In that local McDonald's, these kinds of things happen regularly.

Many will say to me, "Dave, you're a pastor. This is why this works for you." But frankly, I have found that being a pastor is a more of a hindrance than anything else. I've had to overcome stereotypes. Ironically, most of my friends at McDonald's would probably tell you, "Dave sticks to himself a lot. He works a lot in his cubicle over there. He's really asocial." As a result, I must adamantly insist that I cannot attribute any of the good things that have happened at McDonald's to me. I am committed to getting my work done! Nonetheless, God has helped me counsel and pray with people in the midst of divorce, share grief with a widow, pray with a man whose son is in the hospital in depression, proclaim the gospel at a funeral for a friend's sister, talk theology with an agnostic: and I could go on. I am thoroughly convinced God has been amazingly at work, and I have merely been available. I simply began to know God differently, as the God of mission, and pay attention.

God is at work in all the places we already inhabit. He is bigger than the arena of our own immediate church programs and ideas about evangelism. He is a prodigal God recklessly working in people and situations of all types. If we truly believe God is at work in the world, we must take the time to pay attention, listen, and discern what God is doing in the lives of those around us.

Following God into the World

The second signpost, *missio Dei*, therefore points us squarely into the middle of this world where God is, discerning where God is working, knowing that what God has done in the past continues into the present—not as something that we must do but as something God is always already doing. But this work is also a sending with a beginning, a beginning that does not instantly expand to cover everything, but starts small, with one particular person in one distinct place, Jesus of Nazareth, the Son of God. And from this sending, an extension goes forth.

When the people want Jesus to remain in Capernaum after the crowds start to explode around him, he responds that the ministry of the kingdom of God is meant for all the other towns as well, "for I was sent for this purpose" (Luke 4:43 ESV). But not only did Jesus understand that he was sent; he also sends his disciples, telling them, "Whoever receives you receives me, and whoever receives me receives him who sent me" (Matthew 10:40 ESV). He says in the upper room, definitively, "As the Father has sent me, even so I am sending you" (John 20:21 ESV). So now we have a string of three: the disciples are sent; and whoever receives them, in some sense also receives Jesus; and not only that, also receives the Father who sent Jesus. All who claim to be Christ's disciples are extensions of this sending. All Christians are by nature sent into this mission. We, all of his disciples, have been caught up in the radical prodigal mission of the Triune God.

We cannot navigate this journey into the far country according to a distant star or within a darkening cloud. There is something very concrete going on in this sending. But we need something more as we move forward. The *missio Dei* can take us only so far. It is for this reason that the second signpost leads directly to the third, incarnation, where the mission of God is given concrete flesh and blood in the life of Jesus, the definitive place of God's mission.

SIGNPOST THREE

INCARNATION

ON THE GROUND: THE JOURNEY
INTO EVERYDAY LIFE

"WILL THE REAL JESUS please stand up!" This sounds like a line from a game show, but in fact this was the course title of my (Geoff's) undergraduate cultural anthropology class at University of California, Santa Cruz. The purpose of the class was to explore the processes by which important cultural figures are formed and transformed within the cultural consciousness.

In this class, we explored Jesus as a cultural figure. In addition to the four gospels, we read Nikos Kazantzakis's *The Last Temptation of Christ* and Norman Mailer's *The Gospel According to the Son: A Novel*, and we watched the films *Jesus of Montreal* and Monty Python's *Life of Brian*.[1] The basic premise of the class was that there is no "real" Jesus, just a bunch of different stories that people started telling about him. And because everything is just a story about Jesus, there is no authoritative version. For the professor, this meant that for those seeking to understand Jesus, *The Life of Brian* was just as valid as the gospel of Mark. For all we know, Jesus was just the accidental leader of an unintended religious movement. Members of the class ended up concluding that Jesus was just a Jewish rabbi, or just a miracle worker, or just a social revolutionary, or just a religious mystic, all depending on what authors resonated most with each student. The one thing that was *NOT* taken for granted in this class was that Jesus was God.

It is the same today for many in our society, the neighborhoods we live in, and the places we work. Jesus is a great sage, or a wise man, or a profound moral leader, or a revolutionary, but most people don't know how to say he is God. Certainly there are still people out there who get offended at the intolerant idea that Jesus was unique, supreme, exalted, God in human flesh. More often than not, they just assume you don't mean what you say when you say, "Jesus is God." "Oh sure, of course," they reply. "What you really mean is Jesus is a great leader who embodies a way to God [or a wise sage that taught us about God, or . . .]" And then, stunningly, there are even more people for whom the question, "Who is Jesus?" is not even relevant to them. Jesus has become so marginalized in parts of our culture that we discuss him only in terms of a cultural curiosity in a course on the sociology of religion. We study him much the same way we study Socrates in a philosophy course or Julius Caesar in a history course.

When our church, Life on the Vine, was new, we sent out ten thousand postcards to people in our neighborhoods. We artfully displayed a collage of various depictions of Jesus (classical paintings, icons, and European, African, and Asian portrayals) with the question in bold print running across it: "Who is Jesus?" On the back, we invited the neighborhood to have a discussion with us about the question. We were playing off the cultural curiosity around Easter and hoped that we could welcome a constructive conversation around the question.

The card was not well received. Local "Bible-believing" Christians accused us of straying into relativism with so many different depictions of Jesus. They worried we were losing the truth of Jesus. Meanwhile many others accused us of being intolerant. Were not other religious leaders just as worthy of discussion? We got nasty phone calls asking, "Why are you focusing only on Jesus?" No one, and I mean NO ONE, came to any of our gatherings from this postcard.

Where does this leave us Christians living in a world like this? If we follow the first signpost (as we must) into the diversity of post-Christendom and also follow the second signpost into the mission of God (who is neither distantly aloof nor vaguely everywhere), where does Jesus fit? And what does he have to do with God's mission to restore the world?

Is Too! Is Not!

One response to this new cultural situation is to simply proclaim the divinity of Jesus Christ louder and with more confidence. "Jesus is God!" goes the cry. "We must stand up for this belief! We must defend Christ's divinity in the face of secular unbelief and disinterest!" Then we often turn to science, history, and philosophy to try to prove the divine life of

Jesus, claiming that it is irrefutable to any intellectually honest person. But unfortunately this quickly devolves into a spat where we yell back and forth with unbelievers—"He is too!" we say; "He is not!" they respond. We are more separated from the nonbelievers than we were before.

Another response has been to see Jesus as the ultimate example of a human life filled by God. His life is the highest model of one living in the love of God, or the greatest example of one entering the kingdom of God. We see Jesus as the compelling representation of someone who leads others to God, who might even be the way to God, and who reveals the truth of God. Often this perspective does not hold the divinity of Jesus in high regard but rather desires to emulate his humanity as a way to follow after life with God.

Both of these responses put forth something that is eminently true about Jesus. But is either response sufficient to match the prodigal act of God sending the Son into the far country? As we probe these options in the coming chapters, it becomes clear to us that we must go beyond these approaches. In Jesus, we are being invited into God's very own life through the Son who has journeyed into the very center of our lived existence. The third signpost, incarnation, unrelentingly points us in the direction of join-ing the Son's journey into the far country of our everyday lives.

Once upon a Time?

But let us start with what we are *not* talking about. There is a tendency to make the incarnation into a divine act in history that happened a long time ago. God comes to earth like Superman landing in a capsule from outer space. Jesus, the Son, invades the world, accomplishes what he needs to do for our salvation, and then just as quickly leaves and returns to the Father. Like a Navy SEALs special forces operation, he (as God) parachutes in, rescues the prisoners, and then is immediately airlifted out, leaving some instructions for those left behind on how to live and where to rendezvous when he returns.[2] In this view, it seems Jesus came to do only two things: prove his divinity and then die for our salvation. With this past event in mind, we are now supposed to worship the revelation of God in Christ (divinity) and trust him for our salvation. In short, it is (1) because of a past event, (2) we are forgiven of sins so that (3) we can enjoy eternal life in the future. But where does that leave us now? What does Christ's work have to do with our everyday lives? How does Christ's work in the past and the hope we have for a future life with him affect our life in the present?[3]

When we are engaging those outside the church, this view of the incarnation often leads us into defending the divinity of Christ and the truth of our future salvation. In response to all the doubters about Jesus, we spend a lot of intellectual energy trying to make the case that Jesus is God and has saved us from hell. As a result, there are countless books, professors, pastors, and conferences defending the divinity, the supremacy, and the sufficiency of Christ. In this process, however, we too easily make Jesus into a concept, a proposition to be upheld, or a truth to be defended. We thus detach ourselves even further from him than before. We become distanced from the person of Jesus and a dynamic living relationship with him.

To be clear, we affirm the divinity of Christ as absolutely central to our faith and life in God's mission. Yet we must be careful about being defensive here. Certainly his reality in the world as Savior and Lord must be testified to, given witness to, pointed to (which we will get to in signpost 4). But a defensive posture about Christ's divinity reveals we ourselves have not gone into the far country with Jesus, for if the reality of God in Christ has truly entered our lives, then he needs no defending. We need only bear witness to the reality of his working in our lives. *For us, then, the past-event version of incarnation is not prodigal enough.*

The Way of the Father's Kingdom

Many have seen the dangers of making Jesus all about his life on earth as God. Many have seen the problem of making God's salvation in Jesus all about the future. And many have pointed out that overemphasizing Christ's unique divinity and his unrepeatable act of salvation on the cross has the strange effect of making Jesus irrelevant amid the daily challenges of poverty, sickness, and pain that plague our lives and our world. Jesus is so unlike us that his life does not connect with ours, and we are left merely praising his divinity and salvation and nothing more. As Brian McLaren reminds us, this exclusive view on the divinity and salvation of Jesus seems to say he is not the one who saves from poverty, captivity, blindness, or oppression "even though Jesus uses these very words to describe his mission" (Luke 4:18–21).[4]

It was inevitable, then, that many pastors, writers, and leaders of the past decade began returning to the gospels in order to look at the life of Jesus for clues that pointed beyond the past event of his divinity and salvation. Many began to see that Jesus was the revealer of God "not only in his teaching . . . but in his very way of being."[5] Jesus, in his everyday way of living, came to be seen as the model of discipleship, of what it is like to live in the Spirit, of the sacrificial love that is the very center of God's work in the world. Jesus is the ultimate example of a life lived in the Father's kingdom, and he shows us how to engage the culture for God's transformation. In the life of Jesus, his interactions with the poor and oppressed, his condemnation of the rich and powerful, his sacrificial humility and redemptive love all show us how we as humans can truly live life in the kingdom of God. The secret message of Jesus is not that he is the divine savior but that all of us can actually live like Jesus by doing the same things he did.[6] Jesus is not just a divine event lost in the past but a living human possibility. His life can live through our lives if we follow the model he left behind.

For this view, the significance of Jesus's life is not so much that he was divine but that he was human, and he revealed what a truly human life could look like freed from sin. Jesus was free to serve the least of these because he was not seeking status. Jesus was free to teach the law of love because he was not bound to the law of sin and death. Jesus was free to challenge the establishment because he did not seek his own self-preservation but would lay down his life for his friends. In the life of Jesus, we truly see that God has entered into our world as a human and has shown us the way to truly live within the coming kingdom of God.

This understanding of the incarnation works wonderfully to put our focus on discipleship. It puts the emphasis on following Jesus. It enables us to see that God has offered us a way to enter into life with God and God's kingdom. Jesus models this way. It draws us into full and earnest discipleship because to follow Jesus "is to be like him, to take seriously what he took seriously."[7] People like Brian McLaren, Mark Scandrette, and Marcus Borg have opened up in their popular writings this kind of fullness of the incarnation in ways rarely accessible to Christians in North America.[8]

Is There More?

But this view of God's incarnation still leaves us asking for more. We love the way it takes us into the world through the imitation of Jesus. We love the way we are taught to walk into the kingdom the same way Jesus walked. But even this journey fails to recognize how radical God comes into our lives through the humanity of Jesus. It fails to take hold of the way in which Jesus himself has promised to be present in his authority and reign wherever we go and engage in the kingdom. As we will see below, the incarnation is not merely a model for us, but something that extends through us. God has won a victory in the sending of the Son. His power, rule, and victory are a reality breaking in right now. Jesus is not merely a model of God's kingdom; rather Jesus is God's kingdom coming. Thinking of Jesus only as the way into the kingdom misses the point of the prodigal Son's journey to the far country: that in Jesus, God has entered our world in human flesh to be with us and bring his kingdom to completion in the world. It is radical and excessive, but also humble and vulnerable. Ascribing anything less to Jesus risks domesticating the incarnation, or denying it all together.[9]

In signpost 2, we explored the everywhere God and how God's mission seemed to be found in everything. Saying "God is everywhere" can subtly change God's mission into our mission of doing stuff. The same thing happens here. If Jesus is only a model, then it seems everything is still up to us. The announcement is lost that in Jesus, God has changed everything and now is changing everything. The truth that God is loose in the world is reduced to the idea that God has modeled for us a way to live. Devoid of God's cosmic victory over sin, death, and evil in Christ, the "way of Jesus" easily drifts into becoming another religious mentality, a moralistic social gospel that leads us not into his kingdom but into burnout.

Over the years, our little church has journeyed into helping at soup kitchens, homeless shelters, domestic abuse treatment facilities, and jails. We have helped an urban church struggling with inner-city violence by raising funds and standing with them in solidarity. It was exhilarating at times. But it is also exhausting. One of our communities once spent a year faithfully working in a local food pantry, only to see it disintegrate in conflict. Meanwhile, another food pantry just blocks away was flourishing. When the people tried to restart the former food pantry, it became apparent that this was about ego gratification, not extending ministry. We needed to discern how the kingdom was being extended here or not. There were times when subtle change as well as stunning transformation happened in people's lives and their communities, but at other times, there seemed to be a lot of effort for dubious ends. We've learned we have to discern the way God extends the presence of Jesus into the world through us. We were just beginning to discover how his kingdom breaks in when we follow him into the far country.

Signpost Three: The Journey of God into Everyday Life

So it seems that Jesus is all too divine to be any good (for our everyday lives) and also all too human to do anything (against the reality of evil). Neither option seems adequate to capture God's radical movement into the world. The prodigal act of mission in the incarnation is more than either past divine event or present human model. It is also God's continuing presence with us. The incarnation of God extends into history, our lives, the here and now. It extends into the present, from the past, and into the future. When we talked about moving past the distant God and the everywhere God, we turned to the baptism of Jesus as the initial unfolding of the Triune, God's mission in the world. Let us pick up the story there.

The Incarnation

In Mark's telling of the story, Jesus, after his baptism, begins his ministry by declaring, "The time is fulfilled, and the kingdom of God is at hand; repent and believe in the gospel" (1:15 ESV). The rest of Mark's gospel tells us what it means to say God's kingdom is at hand and how we are to respond.

In essence, Jesus's life, death, and resurrection are the proclaiming and making present of the kingdom of God. This is witnessed in the first act of Jesus's ministry. He enters the synagogue, and all are astonished because he teaches with such authority, unlike their typical leaders (1:22). Then everyone is equally amazed when he confronts an evil spirit in the synagogue and then later heals Peter's sick mother. Mark sums up a typical day in the life of Jesus with these simple words: "He healed many who were sick with various diseases, and cast out many demons" (Mark 1:34 ESV). Jesus teaches—people are amazed. Jesus confronts evil—oppression flees. Jesus stretches out his hand—health and wholeness returns. This is the proclaiming and making present of God's kingdom.[10] This is what it looks like when God is at loose in the world, no longer contained in heaven—now teaching, confronting, healing, restoring, and making all things new. Jesus, the Son of the Father, filled with the Spirit, is the proclamation and presence of the kingdom in power, overcoming the evils of bodily sickness, social exclusion, and spiritual oppression. This is what is happening in the incarnation.

At least that is what we read in the first half of Mark. Then Jesus starts talking "crazy." He starts talking about rejection and betrayal, about death. It's as if you are rich and famous, having a good old time on top of the world, and then one of your friends starts telling you that it's all going to fall apart and you are going to be left with nothing. You probably would want to take your friend aside and tell him to chill out so you can enjoy the fame and power. And this is exactly what Peter tried to do with Jesus.

Jesus had begun to teach the disciples that he "must suffer many things and be rejected by the elders and the chief priests and the scribes and be killed, and after three days rise again" (Mark 8:31 ESV). Jesus presents his future as suffering, rejection, and death. Peter didn't sign up for this: he expects a royal palace and a prominent place in it, so he takes Jesus aside and "rebukes" him for this craziness (the Greek word for *rebuke* is the same used when Jesus is casting out demons; it seems Peter was trying to exorcise Jesus). Jesus responds by telling everyone present, "If anyone would come after me, let him deny himself and take up his cross and follow me" (8:34 ESV). Jesus tells them in no uncertain terms that the way of God's kingdom is the way of humility, the humility of a child (9:37), the way where the first will be last and the last first (10:31), where the highest place of honor is the place of the servant (10:43). For Jesus, the way of the kingdom is the way of the cross.

The exaltation of the first half of Mark's gospel leads to humiliation in the second half. The revelation of God powerfully at work early on leads to the realization of where the ultimate power truly lies: in humility and service. From the display of divinity to the difficulty of humanity, Jesus unites everything of what it means to be truly God and what it means to be truly human, a unity that leads directly toward the cross: "For even the Son of Man came not to be served but to serve, and to give his life as a ransom for many" (10:45 ESV). This revelation of humility, make no mistake about it, is at the core of what is happening in the incarnation.

Mark unfolds this mystery of the incarnation further with a very important word, used only twice throughout his gospel. The first time, we have already seen, is in the baptism of Jesus, where the heavens are "torn" or "ripped" open (Mark 1:10). This was an apocalyptic moment when God is no longer contained in heaven, but in Jesus, through the Spirit, the kingdom of God comes crashing into earth. The second, and only other time this word for *tear* or *rip* is used is at the moment of Jesus's death, when the curtain in the temple was "torn" in two (15:38). Some believe that the tearing of the temple curtain means that now all people can come in and worship God, that there is no longer a barrier that divides humanity from God. In the death of Jesus, humanity is delivered from its separation from God. And this is certainly true. But there is also a second dynamic at work in the tearing of the curtain. With the tearing of the curtain, God is getting out. Divine presence is no longer safely up in heaven. Neither is it securely in the temple. Instead, in Jesus's death, God is set loose in the world for mission, fully as God and man.[11] God's very presence is bursting out into the world in and through the death of the Son. This too is an essential aspect of what is happening in the incarnation.

We remember how the Roman centurion responds to Jesus at his death on the cross. He looks up at Jesus and proclaims, "Truly this man was the Son of God!" (Mark 15:39 ESV). Scholars tell us this is the high point of Mark's gospel—the climax toward which the entire gospel is directed. This particular man, this human individual suffering the same tragic end of all human persons, in solidarity with all humanity, dies. But this human person is also truly God.[12] And so this singular, climactic moment reveals that this person on the cross is God present and at work in the world. God comes not to destroy or even impose his will on us. God comes instead to be present with us and work in and through suffering with and for the world. This is how God comes and works for the redemption of the world. This also is what is happening in the incarnation.

And so in the incarnation, we have God entering human life to show us who God is and how God works. His baptism as the Son of God leads to his death on a cross as the Son of God.[13] His humility is intertwined with his exaltation. As the ancient hymn says, Jesus,

> who, though he was in the form of God,
>
> did not count equality with God a thing to be grasped,
>
> but made himself nothing, taking the form of a servant,
>
> being born in the likeness of men.
>
> And being found in human form, he humbled himself
>
> by becoming obedient to the point of death, even death on a cross.
>
> Therefore God has highly exalted him
>
> and bestowed on him the name that is above every name,
>
> so that at the name of Jesus every knee should bow,
>
> in heaven and on earth and under the earth,
>
> and every tongue confess that Jesus Christ is Lord,
>
> to the glory of God the Father. (Philippians 2:6–11 ESV)[14]

This is the incarnation. This is the way we must learn if we are to follow Jesus. It is not a matter of splitting the difference between Jesus's humanity and his divinity, of seeing him as one part divine savior and one part human role model, and then giving each one its due. There is a bigger issue at stake here: the true prodigality of the coming of the Son.

Extending the Incarnation

In Christ, the Almighty Creator has come to be with us. And yet somehow this central reality of God's work in Christ has been lost in much of the North American church. But if we look closer at the Scriptures, we can see it everywhere.

The gospel of Matthew opens and closes with the idea that God is with us. The words of the prophet Isaiah resound in Matthew, chapter 1: "Behold, the virgin shall conceive and bear a son, and they shall call his name Immanuel," and Matthew adds the translation of *Immanuel*: "which means, God *with* us" (Matthew 1:23 ESV). Jesus's life is the fulfillment of God's promise to be with us. Then, at the very end of Matthew, in the last verse, Jesus declares, "Behold, I am with you always, to the end of the age" (28:20 ESV). At the beginning, Jesus is called Immanuel, God with us. At the end, he claims that he will indeed always be with us. The mission of God is not a solitary intrusion into the history of our past and now a model for our present lives. No. The prodigal God comes to be with us—in our humanity, in our everyday lives—until the end of the age. The incarnation of God extends to the present and beyond.

Jesus's words in John 20:20–23 spell this out in a different way. Here, in the upper room, Jesus sends the church (his disciples) into the world and gives his Spirit as part of that sending. Famously he says, "Peace be with you. As the Father has sent me, even so I am sending you." Then he breathes on them and says, "Receive the Holy Spirit. If you forgive the sins of any, they are forgiven them; if you withhold forgiveness from any, it is withheld" (20:21–23 ESV). Here we see the unique power and authority of Jesus the King bestowed on his disciples as a ministry of the Spirit. As the Son sends the Spirit on his disciples, Jesus is extending his authoritative presence through all who bear the signs of his kingdom: peace, the forgiveness of sins, the unbinding of the powers (Luke 10; Matthew 18). This is the authority of the resurrected and exalted King (Luke 10:17–19). His rule comes wherever his disciples gather together and submit to him and to what he is doing. They cannot control the Spirit or his power (Mark 9:14–29), but by submitting to them, they become the instruments of extending his reign.

We don't mean this in some abstract or vague manner. It's more than saying God is with us as the everywhere God (who might just as well be nowhere). Rather, God is with us as an extension of the incarnation, as the extension of the life and ministry of Jesus. Indeed, Jesus handed over his entire ministry to his disciples. He called twelve disciples and sent them out to proclaim the gospel, cast out demons, and heal the sick (Mark 6:12–13). These are the same things Jesus was doing: preaching the gospel, freeing from oppression, and healing from sickness. This is the kingdom coming in power. In sending his disciples, his authority is being extended (Mark 3:14–15).

But the disciples also participated in this coming kingdom in humility (a lesson they were slow in learning). Speaking of his coming crucifixion in Jerusalem, Jesus said the disciples would also drink from the same cup (of suffering) that he drinks (Mark 10:39). This is the way they will learn to be servants to all. This is the way they will learn to walk in the middle of God's work. This way (to repeat for emphasis) of the cross is inextricably intertwined with God's coming in power.

This "sending" by Jesus of his disciples is more than "just repeat what I did" or "follow my model." There is a kingdom dynamic set loose in these disciples. Jesus promises that his very presence will be with us in all of these activities. And so whenever we practice forgiveness and reconciliation in submission to "his name," the very authority of the King binds and looses in heaven what is bound or loosed on earth. Whenever "two or three are gathered in my name, there am I among them," Jesus says (Matthew 18:20 ESV). He says that whenever we welcome a child in his name—and by "a child," he meant anyone on the margins of society—then we also welcome the presence of Jesus himself (Mark 9:37). Or whenever we care for the "least of these"—the hungry, thirsty, naked, or imprisoned—we find Jesus with us there (Matthew 25:31–46). When Jesus sends out the disciples to proclaim the gospel, he says that when they preach, people will actually be hearing Jesus (Luke 10:16). You shall have "authority" over demons and "the enemy" (Luke 10:19). In all of these instances, Jesus's kingdom is the context, and it is his authority as King being made manifest. Followers of Jesus are making the kingdom of God present as a continuation of his life, as an extension of the incarnation. The mission of God reaches a climax in the incarnation of Jesus, but this mission does not end there. It is extended in the disciples because Jesus promises to be Immanuel: *God with us*.

Body

We should not be surprised to find that the apostle Paul describes Christians who gather under Christ's reign as his "body." The church, Paul says, is Christ's body; although we are many individuals, we "are one body in Christ, and individually members one of another" (Romans 12:5 ESV). In our baptism—and whenever we talk of baptism, we must think of the Triune God working in the baptism of Jesus—we are "baptized into one body" by the Spirit (1 Corinthians 12:13 ESV). Jesus himself called on the disciples to participate in a common meal, where he said, "This is my body, which is given for you. Do this in remembrance of me," and taking the cup, he says, "This cup that is poured out for you is the new covenant in my blood" (Luke 22:19–20 ESV). The apostle Paul explains what is going on in this meal by asking rhetorically, "The cup of blessing that we bless, is it not a participation in the blood of Christ? The bread that we break, is it not a participation in the body of Christ? Because there is one bread, we who are many are one body, for we all partake of the one bread" (1 Corinthians 10:16–17 ESV).

Here we see the mystery that all who partake in the communion table are participating in Christ's incarnation. The New Testament is claiming that the community of disciples is Christ's body—he in us and us in him. God in Christ has not come once upon a time and then left us. He continues to be with us in a deep and abiding manner by the Spirit. And whenever we engage in the ministry of Jesus, we are not merely modeling the way of the kingdom of God. We are actually extending the incarnation, the way of the Son, into the far country.[15]

Wrong Way

When I (Dave) was visiting a missional church in New Jersey many years ago, I met its dynamic but weary pastor. He had been working for years to spur people toward mission in the neighborhoods. But his young, diverse congregation could never really mobilize. They saw mission as something they were supposed to do, not something God was doing already in and around them and all they had to do was submit and participate. They could not escape thinking of themselves as the agents of God's mission as if they had to do it. They did not see themselves as people who were extending the reality of God's kingdom as it was breaking in around them. They did not understand God was with them, extending the life and ministry of Jesus in them. They struggled with the notion of a common life together that participates in God's mission. With no way for this church to take shape in the neighborhoods, it died from exhaustion and disillusionment. The pastor left to return home six months after my visit, exhausted and depressed.

We have seen this happen across the country with small missional congregations. Apart from God going with us, the only alternative is for us to act individually as his personal agents of mission. Unfortunately, this repeats the same problem of making Jesus's life into a model, but now it is often called "being incarnational."

Is the Church Incarnational?

In the past ten years (really twenty), much ink has been spilled describing the church as incarnational. As opposed to the attractional model of the modern church in America, where a church puts on worship services and expects people to come, the incarnational model challenges us to be a people who inhabit neighborhoods, go where the people are, live among them and listen to them, know their hurts and their hopes. From this incarnational perspective, we are called to minister and proclaim the gospel while following the Spirit in specific circumstances. According to this approach, the incarnation of God becomes a model for entering into local cultures, a model for mission.

This approach draws on the best of both models of the incarnation addressed above: the divine and the human. In what has become the common incarnational approach to ministry, we recognize the divine uniqueness and supremacy of what God has done in Jesus Christ. Yet we also see the fully human in the way God entered into life, condescending to walk vulnerably and humbly as one of us. In the words of Alan Hirsch and Michael Frost, "When we talk of incarnational mission, we hope to, in some real way, directly draw inspiration and motivation from the unique act whereby God entered into our world into the human condition in the person of Jesus Christ."[16] Hirsch elaborates:

> God came into the world in an act of profound identification not only with humanity as a whole, but with a particular group of people. That He was in the neighborhood for 30 years and no-one noticed says a lot about God and how He engages the human situation. The Incarnation thus shows us that God speaks from within a particular culture, in ways that people can grasp, understand, and respond. The Incarnation gives us the primary biblical model of engagement—this is how God does it and we who follow his Way should take a similar path. Incarnational mission requires that we contextualize the Gospel in ways that honor the particular cultural and existential situations of various peoples without compromising on the mission itself. If missional means going out (being sent) into the world, then incarnational means going deep down into a culture.[17]

Hirsch clearly elaborates the incarnation as a model, as a way to follow Jesus into his mission. And yet Hirsch does not flinch on the divinity of Christ, the radical disruption of grace, or discontinuity that comes from God's engagement with the world. For Hirsch, this means that proclaiming the good news of God's salvation is at the heart of incarnation.[18] This is not just a personal experience of the Spirit or a public work of transformation in society. This incarnational model leads us into the marvelous ways of transformation in context that come through individuals becoming, as he says, "little Jesuses" walking across all boundaries to be present incarnationally in "every nook and cranny of society."[19]

Nevertheless, despite how close we are to Frost and Hirsch's understanding of incarnation and mission, we still must ask, Is this enough? Prodigal enough? Notice how their way of speaking ("little Jesuses") about the incarnation emphasizes the individual. We have no doubt that Hirsch and Frost believe discipling is "a communal activity"[20] and justice enters the world as a result. But what about the communal activity itself as the very place where Jesus is made known, where his authority as Lord breaks in? Frost and Hirsch tend to leave little room for the practices of the church in mission. Church, for them, comes after mission.[21] But we believe there is something profoundly social happening in the incarnation that is more than individual. Christ's inbreaking authority becomes present in people in their life together as they submit to his reign. As we meet around the Table or reconcile our disagreement together, a new order of creation is bursting forth and breaking in, a new way of being together is beginning, a foretaste of the kingdom itself. Jesus himself as Lord is present among us. This is church. This is mission. God's coming in the Son sets forth a chain of events—through a people—that looks like a nuclear reaction but can best be called a people revolution that is changing the world.

The Journey with Christ into and for the World

One of the most famous missionary texts in all the Bible is Matthew 28:18–20, otherwise known as the Great Commission:

> Now the eleven disciples went to Galilee, to the mountain to which Jesus had directed them. And when they saw him they worshiped him, but some doubted. And Jesus came and said to them, "All authority in heaven and on earth has been given to me. Go therefore and make disciples of all nations, baptizing them in the name of the Father and of the Son and of the Holy Spirit." (ESV)

Jesus, on the verge of ascending to the right hand of the Father, gives his disciples his last instructions. He concludes the commission by saying, "Behold, I am with you always, to the end of the age." He, in no uncertain terms, is and always will be "Immanuel, God with us" (Matthew 1:23). On that mountain, then, we see that the incarnation of Christ is more than the divine Son worshiped, although the disciples worshipped him ("when they saw him they worshipped him"), and more than the example or model to be followed, although Jesus does tell the disciples to bring others into the way of Jesus ("make disciples . . . teaching them to obey everything I commanded you"). Here we see that the disciples, and the church after them, are sent into the world under his rule and reign ("all authority has been given unto me") bringing Christ's very presence as Lord with them wherever they go. Christ's presence is extended into the world by his disciples participating in his in-breaking authority as part of the Triune Mission.

The mission of God (*missio Dei*) has moved forward with the Son in a new way. It is now the Son to whom "all power and authority" has been given. His reign now encompasses beyond Israel, beyond Judea, into the whole world "in heaven and on earth." He shall reign "until he has put all enemies under his feet" (1 Corinthians 15:25 NIV). This is God at work for "the reconciling of the world in Christ" (2 Corinthians 5:19 NIV). This is the *missio Dei*.

In this new reign, we are sent ("Go!") into the far country. We go not into a church building but into the whole world to bring his very presence and authority. In essence, we extend the incarnation (his "withness") and bring his kingdom (what already exists and is at work in the world) into visibility before the rest of the world. The world is thereby able to see glimpses of the kingdom. We become witnesses.

A while back in the life of our church, a couple named Richard and Amanda ran into some financial trouble. Richard had lost his job, and not for the first time. They had fallen behind in the rent, and Richard had gotten into a vigorous, almost violent dispute with his landlord. There were also complaints of domestic abuse. Richard was a violent man, an ex-felon. It was not uncommon for him to lose his temper, haul off, and hit someone. For months, we were in a discipling group together, learning the ways of Jesus. Yet we were seeing very little progress with Richard. What were we missing? Was there something more to be lived into here? Why was there no power or authority to move forward?

Matthew 18:15–20 tells us about the practice of reconciliation. Here, Jesus tells his disciples what to do whenever they have disagreements. The one who has been wronged is to go to the person who has wronged him or her. This person is to go, as it were, and "put it out there," to talk about the sin out in the open. If they cannot agree and resolve their relationship in peace, they are then to bring in another person.

Jesus calls us to come together in these times and be brothers and sisters committed in love, submitting all things one to another before the King. If there is still no peace, then they are to bring it before the church, whether that means the elders, or a church council, or perhaps the entire community for discernment (and remember that the goal is not punishment but reconciliation and discernment—that is, a way forward). Jesus says that when we do this (the process of reconciliation) and submit it to his Lordship ("in my name"), he will be there (Matthew 18:20). Indeed, the very reign of God breaks in at that moment so that "whatever you bind on earth shall be bound in heaven, and whatever you loose on earth shall be loosed in heaven" (Matthew 18:18 ESV). God's rule breaks in and shatters the chains that bind and brings forth new life in the kingdom.

After weeks of no resolution, with Richard and Amanda on the verge of losing their apartment, we invited all the parties to get together and talk through the issues. We invited the landlord to bring a friend who had witnessed any wrongdoing. We invited Richard and his wife to bring witnesses. We invited those from our community who had been walking with Richard through this. We gathered around a table and invited everyone to submit this matter to the Lordship of Jesus Christ (even the nonbelievers like the landlord) and then we simply started to ask questions.

In the course of the evening, the presence of the Holy Spirit began to break down manifestations of pride in Richard's life. Areas of his sin were being revealed to him, so much so that he couldn't stand it. Richard literally raced out of the building and climbed up a tree to hide. The landlord was so amazed at what was happening that he committed to giving Richard free rent for two months. This began an intense several weeks for Richard in dealing with the anger that had constantly led to losing his job and failing to pay his bills.

Was this just a simple process of earthly reconciliation mediated by a neutral third party, or was the reign of Christ breaking in? Was the landlord just overcome by generosity, or had the life of Jesus started to rearrange the relationships between renter and landlord, boss and worker? We believe the latter. In this simple process, we were extending the very presence of Jesus. One simple meeting, one simple practice, ordered by Christ himself, as part of everyday life, extended the reign of Christ in our midst.

We can see this same principle evidenced in many practices Jesus gives to his church to carry on in the world (which we explore in detail in signpost 7). In Luke 10, when we inhabit a neighborhood, eating and enjoying fellowship at a table, bringing peace and proclaiming the gospel, Jesus says that "the one who hears you hears me, and the one who rejects you rejects me, and the one who rejects me rejects him who sent me" (Luke 10:16 ESV). In a real way, then, even though we know the kingdom is already at work, the presence of Jesus is extended visibly through the proclaiming of the gospel by the sent ones. Likewise, when we clothe the naked, visit the sick, or feed the hungry, when we are present alongside and with the poor, it is Jesus who is there present in this ministry ("as you did it to one of the least of these my brothers, you did it to me"; Matthew 25:36–37 ESV). Here we see Christ's presence, within God's greater kingdom, being made visible in the church's ministry to the poor. The same dynamic can be seen when we minister to children in a genuine welcoming relationship (Matthew 18:4) or when we share the hospitality of the kingdom that comes forth from the Lord's table (Luke 22:29). We cannot help but think that the little church in New Jersey might still be going strong if it had united around these practices of his kingdom in the neighborhood.

Each one of these practices carries us out into the world, into the missional far country. We practice reconciliation within the church in order to extend this same reconciliation into the world. We eat at the Lord's table together and extend this hospitality in the meals we share with and in the world. We serve the poor in our life together as disciples so as to recognize and serve the poor in the neighborhood. We proclaim the good news in the gathering in order to proclaim it into every area of life we inhabit in the world. Each time we do, Christ's presence and the kingdom of God are made visible in the world. These practices are not internal to the church as a nice and cozy country club, but are the very ways of entering the world as the body of Christ.

These are just a few examples of how the presence of the prodigal God invades the world through the Son by the Spirit, making visible the new creation of love and forgiveness. Each time we enter into the world in these ways, we go on a journey deep into the far country. But we do not go alone. The presence (and reign) of Jesus goes with us, giving us courage and strength to walk in the new creation he is bringing. This prodigal Son is not merely a divine deliverer, not only a human model, but a Son who was sent by the Father and in obedience (as opposed to the disobedience of the son in the parable) is bringing the whole world into reconciliation with himself. As we go with the Son, his reign breaks forth and becomes visible by the Spirit. And when this happens, all we can do is stand in awe as witnesses to what he has just done. Becoming his witnesses is the fourth signpost of a prodigal Christianity, to which we now turn.

WITNESS

IN THE WORLD: THE JOURNEY INTO THE WORLD

IN 2005 NIKE ROLLED OUT its Witness media campaign, centering on National Basketball Association (NBA) superstar LeBron James. From early adolescence he had been assiduously recruited by NBA scouts and was drafted right out of high school in 2003. After being named Rookie of the Year and NBA All Star in his first year in the NBA, he took his team, the Cleveland Cavaliers, to the 2005 playoffs. The Nike campaign called on all who would listen to "witness" the greatness that was unfolding before us.

James was rising to basketball immortality. Early on he was nicknamed "King James" and "The Chosen One," presumably because he was the one who would lead the hapless Cavalier franchise to its first championship or perhaps be the one to help countless fans forget Michael Jordan. In 2007, Nike ramped up the Witness campaign during James's first NBA Finals appearance, where they hoped that James would finally be crowned the champion everyone knew he would be. A ten-story poster hung in downtown Cleveland so all could see his greatness (a marvel in itself).

Alas, the San Antonio Spurs swept the Cavaliers in four games, and the Cavs never reached those heights again. LeBron continued to play brilliantly on the basketball court, but he never came any closer to winning a championship, so he took his talents to South Beach, Florida, to play for the Miami Heat. For Cavalier fans, the "King" had not delivered, and now the "Chosen One" had gone.

Nike's repeated announcement in print, television, or radio was, "We Are All Witnesses." But this had proved hollow. Witnesses to what?

Cleveland and the rest of America felt duped. Had it not been all hype, stirring up a religious fervor just to sell athletic shoes?

Nike helps us see a little bit of what the word *witness* means. *Witness* is more than a role played within the U.S. court system. It is more than a casual observer. *Witness* communicates that we are participants in something big happening in the world. This something must be bigger and greater than us, or else why would such an event require a witness? It will change how we understand the world (at the least the world of basketball). But in the end, James failed to deliver on the promise. And with the changing of his jersey, all the witnesses that Nike had gathered disappeared in disillusionment.

In a world that is broken and bankrupt, diseased and dying, killing and corrupting, it is all too easy to think that God's kingdom has not come. God has failed to deliver. When we turn on the news or look down the street, we are tempted to agree with the many people in our world who doubt the reality that Jesus is Lord. As outlined in signpost 3, Jesus came proclaiming and making present the kingdom of God. But where is the evidence of this new in-breaking of God's kingdom? And where is the witness? This kingdom sometimes seems like another failed media campaign, a message that is simply not true. In a world such as this, the idea of truth seems to be broken, if not mortally wounded. And yet we have been sent as prodigal Christians into these wounded and broken places to somehow proclaim the kingdom. God is calling us into the missional far country. How in this world does the truth of the Son invade this far country? How is his kingdom made known?

Why Another Church?

When Life on the Vine Christian Community began as a little church plant in the northwest suburbs of Chicago over ten years ago, we were roughly ten to fifteen people gathering amid a large suburban population—somewhere around 800,000 people within five miles of us. Yet there were few churches. As best I (Dave) could tell, 75 percent of the existing Christians went to three extremely large, busy megachurches that offered spectacular Sunday services for thousands of people. The people who attended them were mostly folks who were familiar with the Christian message. They had some sort of church background in their past and were seeking a place to sustain their faith within the hectic pace of modern life.

As Life on the Vine began to meet as a church gathering, the question was whether there was any reason to begin another church. Was there a need for another witness to the gospel? Why not just herd everyone into one of these three other venues more efficiently to receive what they needed from God?

I remember meeting with someone who, while looking around this strange social world of the suburbs, asked me this very question: "Why another church?" She mentioned the very large megachurches and said, "Why do we need more churches when we have these large successful ones? Who can beat them at doing such a good job at church?"

But for us, a different picture was coming into focus. In our area, 70 percent of the people had no witness of the gospel of Jesus Christ. Sure, there were huge, open venues that people could flock into if they wanted a well-produced gospel presentation. But the average post-Christendom adult looked at these churches suspiciously. They viewed them as impersonal and slick, feeling more like corporations trying to sell something than sacred spaces. They were saying in their deepest hearts, even if never out loud, *I do not trust this as a place to find God.* In many ways, these churches had become so seeker sensitive that those actually seeking something sacred felt more like customers than spiritual pilgrims. Unless these post-Christians somehow got up out of bed on Sunday, overcame their distrust, walked into a large auditorium, and sat and watched one of these services, they stood little chance of encountering a witness to the gospel. The chances of this happening were small, and decreasing by the day. In essence, for those living in the land of post-Christendom, there was no accessible expression of the gospel by which they could encounter the love, forgiveness, hope, and renewal that God was working in and around them.

According to the statistics (as with all statistics, they are debatable), the percentage of Christians hadn't changed in thirty years in the northwest Chicago suburbs. Outside of those remembering their "Christendom upbringing," few were being engaged by the gospel. For us, the northwest suburbs were the lost territory defined as the far country. This was where God was calling us. But how were we to go there?

How Do We Enter the Far Country?

As we have seen in the previous signposts, navigating our post-Christian culture means we must rely on God, who is on mission, who is neither distant and aloof nor ambiguously everywhere. To do this means we enter into these places, inhabit them, and extend the presence of God in Jesus, who proclaims and makes present the kingdom of God. But what exactly are we supposed to be doing? When challenged by issues of justice, salvation, sexual wholeness, and pluralism in our schools, work, and neighborhoods, how do we enter these places with the reality of the gospel of Christ and engage others with it? How do we manifest the presence of Christ, the good news of the gospel?

In the churches we grew up in, there were two responses to these questions, each representing a way of understanding "truth." On the one hand, if the church faced a new cultural challenge in its life together (say, of same-sex relations or whether Buddhists can be Christians), the senior pastor, usually a magnanimous leader, would research the issue, do a sermon on it, and tell the congregation exactly what to do based on the truth of the Bible as he (most often this person was male) saw it. Everyone who agreed with him would stay, and the rest would leave. Those who stayed now had the truth to dispense to those people outside our church who didn't have it yet.

On the other hand, faced with a similar cultural challenge, another church would respond by gathering a bunch of people together in order to have a discussion about the issue. They would discuss same-sex relations, justice, or the environment. They would be sure to "tolerate" all opinions. None of the disagreements were ever resolved corporately, and they never really did anything different afterward. In this kind of church, each Christian was left to pursue the witness of Christ as best as he or she saw fit individually. This is how people in this church would engage the culture around them.

Both approaches leave us asking for more. But before moving to the signpost of witness, let's look a little more closely at these two options.

Standing for the Truth

Sometimes it seems that everyone has an answer for everything. Or rather, everyone has a different answer for everything. When we face personal financial stress and busted budgets, the economic world will train us to think about the daily cycles of making and spending money as if it were the center of the universe. When we face physical illness and go to the doctor, the medical world dictates our options, becoming the "lord" of the body. When our children do not achieve properly at school, the social worker is there to guide us, becoming the master of our family life. Every day we are tempted to think these authorities and their answers are more real than God's kingdom.

In all these ways and more, we are trained daily to become witnesses to other authorities and another reality. These overlapping worlds of post-Christendom (economic, scientific, medical, therapeutic) impinge on us, telling us what to believe and who we are. As a result, the first temptation for many Christians when facing a strange and difficult cultural situation is to assert ourselves. Like a cornered animal, we want to lash out and protect our territory. Many infer that because we are living in a "relativist" society, we Christians must be ones to stand up for the "truth."

Philosopher and theologian Douglass Grootius argues that the current "truth decay" (the title of one of his books) in our society is a threat to Christianity itself.[1] Neo-Reformed author and pastor Kevin DeYoung warns that "God does not get glory by our being uncertain and ambiguous about who he is, what he has done, and why [he] is supremely valuable. God gets glory when we lovingly and truthfully declare theological, propositional truths about his internal excellencies, his saving work, and the weight of his glory."[2]

But sometimes "standing for the truth" (armed and defensive) can take an ugly turn. The "proclamation" of the gospel to our neighbors and friends can become more about "proving the truth" and getting them to believe what we do. If they do not believe, we can become threatened and threatening, often withdrawing relationally (telling ourselves that they are merely persisting in their rebellion). Sadly, it becomes more about us and our beliefs (the truth) and less about entering into the other person's life and allowing God to work.

This approach to encountering others often puts the question of truth before the act of witness. Strangely, we demand to know what people believe about truth before we offer any witness to the truth. We think that if people do not believe in "absolute" or "propositional" truth, then it will be impossible for them to believe the truth of the gospel. But such a "stand for the truth" can reduce people to disembodied minds (as if the most important part about them were their brains) and reduce the gospel to the transfer of information.[3]

Geoff's wife, Cyd, was working in a financial services firm made up of employees from one of the largest churches in the area. They all decided to get involved in an evangelistic effort sponsored by the church. The church was going all out putting on a movie-dinner night with full-surround sound and gourmet food. They were inviting hundreds to hear the gospel. They were all so convinced of the "truth" behind this event that they could hardly contain their excitement. They invited everyone in the office who was not part of their church to come. Unfortunately, they were turned down by a few holdouts who not only felt no interest in the event but felt a strange unease in it all.

The church people soon shunned those who had rejected the invitation. It was as if they subtly said, "You rejected our invitation. You had your chance, so now there is no reason to have a relationship with you."

These holdouts felt isolated and excluded as the rest of the office went off to the dinner-movie night. Yet Cyd continued on in normal relationships with her coworkers, listening to them as they explained how they felt. Surprisingly, one afternoon, they told her how she was the one in the office who really lived as a Christian and helped them understand what it meant to be one.

The movie-dinner night way of "standing for the truth" can strip us of the ability to be witnesses. We acknowledge the need for grounding in the truth, but when we are too quick to make bold pronouncements, we compromise our ability to witness because we have not truly entered into the cultural world to be with people: to listen to, seek God with, and learn from those with to whom we are witnessing.

Boldly Proclaiming the Gospel?

One summer Friday evening, I (Dave) was sitting in the town square park near where we live visiting with some good friends—parents of one of my son's best friends. Jackson was a secular Middle Eastern immigrant who had rejected the Muslim faith of his growing-up years in Iraq. His wife, Patty, was a lapsed Catholic who viewed Christians as judgmental, especially when it came to gay people. As we were sitting there, I noticed a group of seven or eight people in their twenties praying in a corner of the park. As they broke up, one of them headed toward a couple sitting on a bench across the park from us. I decided to observe.

The young man, in his late twenties or early thirties, went boldly up to the man on the bench, handed him a tract with a picture of a $1 million bill on it, and said, "Excuse me. Can I interrupt your evening to ask you the million-dollar question? If you were to die today, would you know the eternal destiny of your soul? It's an important question, wouldn't you agree?"

The man skillfully deflected the question, but the young evangelist, with skill and passion, kept coming at the man, asking about his fears of death and hope for an afterlife. The man was a lapsed Catholic himself and said the question didn't really make sense to him. Nonetheless, the young evangelist persisted: "Would you allow me to lead you in a prayer right now by which you would know where you're going when you die?" The man patiently said he thought it would be disingenuous but appreciated his concern. I watched as the young man pushed for the prayer three more times until he gave up. It was about a twenty-minute conversation in all.

The telling aspect of the story occurred as I was returning to my wife and friends. Jackson came up to us and said, "Look, we've got to leave! Now! You see those people over there. They are going to harangue us to no end." Pointing to the evangelists, he noted that they had been there last week and were relentless and rude and wouldn't leave him alone. Despite my best efforts to get Jackson to give them a chance, he and his family left. As I looked over my shoulder, I saw the entire park emptying out. It was a stunning scene.

The evangelists were from one of the largest churches in our suburbs. The first of the church's four values is to "proclaim the authority of God's Word without apology." Another one of its four pillars is "sharing the good news of Jesus with boldness." It appears that these two commitments had created the illusion that entering a park without knowing someone, without listening, and without understanding the context at all is enough to boldly proclaim the gospel.

While I commend these believers' zeal, I must admit the question lingered with me as to whether these folks were actually witnessing to the gospel. Bold? Yes. But did this boldness exhibit the character of the Sent One? Unapologetic? Perhaps. But their confidence came off as disregard for those with whom they conversed. Had they not assumed too much, that they knew who these people were and their problems? Hadn't they really just intruded with little care into the lives of these people? Had they really entered with their lives as Jesus had with his life, or had they merely proclaimed a gospel of information (about a judgmental and distant God who is not really "with" us anymore)? Indeed, it seemed to me that this approach to evangelism had become a disincarnate witness, denying the nature of the prodigal God who always fully enters into our lives, who is already at work around us if we would only pay attention.

This all-too-common approach is not prodigal enough to be faithful to the sending of the Son. It does not enter humbly and vulnerably into a context to witness, giving testimony to what God is doing right here, right now in our midst. As we navigate our post-Christendom world, this approach is too much like an individual person shouting orders from a street corner. And these days, people are all too ready to ignore it.

Let's Talk About It and Talk About It and Talk About It . . .

Many of us have felt that something is lacking with the "standing for the truth" paradigm—this unilateral tendency to speak at people while attempting to convince them of the gospel. Doing evangelism in this manner is like entering into hand-to-hand combat or a battle of wits. But it is not, on its own, witness. When we do this, we engage a person presuming already to know what the person's problem is. The trick is to help the other person see the problem. We just need to help others ask the right questions so we can supply the right answers. Unintentionally, this has often been our stance of witness. These are the habits of a Christendom that assumed the same problem and answer for everyone.

About ten years ago, the emerging church movement rose up and began criticizing these strategies. They had come from places that did this kind of evangelism. The emerging church stressed a more humble, chastened view of truth and engagement with others. The tactic most often deployed was that of conversation. The emerging church and its most prominent organization, Emergent Village, suggested that churches start conversations in safe places that are open to all. These conversations would be spaces for questioning, seeking, and doubting. There would be only listening and acceptance, with no judgments made. Only acceptance. These conversations would uncover the stifling power structures among us. Conversation was the process by which we could make room for marginalized voices. For many, this was the way of the kingdom. *Conversation* was the word of the decade (we once counted thirty uses of *conversation* in one Emergent presentation alone). Groups sprouted up around the country to promote these conversations.

Something was happening in these conversations that was unequivocally different from what we had known before. There was humility here, a vulnerability and a chastening. A different posture was being taken, something that was often called "epistemic humility." There was an awareness of our own in-grown biases. Some feared this would lead to relativism or, even worse, utter meaninglessness. But the Emergents rightly longed for what Lesslie Newbigin called "proper confidence."[4] It was assumed that we were all entering an ongoing communal interpretation of Scripture and belief.[5]

We applaud what Emergent was doing. We approve the elevation of conversation as a place the church must inhabit in the world. Over against a defensive engagement with culture, we need places to listen and discuss. Over against the aggressive pronouncements of the truth, we need places to sort things out where doubts are welcomed. The emerging church was making space for questioning, deconstructing, for listening to unheard voices. In a sense, we were learning that conversation is a key way of entering the world for the kingdom of God. It felt like the way of the kingdom in the world.

At their best, conversations enter the world of others, listening to them and humbly inviting them into discussion. Conversations are hospitable, vulnerable, and open. In all these ways, they are incarnational. Nonetheless, as we experienced them in the emerging church, they were still lacking something. Although conversation embodies the posture of incarnation, it does not go far enough in our opinion. It is not prodigal enough. Let us explain why.

Lost in Conversation

A couple of years ago, a conflict broke out in our church over the issue of cross-gender friendship. One of our leaders, a married man, was accused of "dating" single women. He would ask single women out for a cup of coffee. He would mention on Facebook that he was "going on a day bicycle trip" with a single woman. He talked openly of "intimate" friendships with women who were not his wife. For many, this was all very confusing, even suspicious. But for others, this was bringing in the kingdom by breaking down the overly sexualized relationships between men and women that keep us from understanding true intimacy in friendships between and across genders. He was making way for a desperately needed discussion on friendship and the lack of it in our culture. For many involved, his work with cross-gender friendship was healing and wholesome, and he was witnessing to the redeemed reality of God's kingdom.

Nonetheless, our community was asking important questions. Faced with cultural (and theological) issues about the proper intimacy expressed between men and women, some in our community responded by questioning him about these issues. As pastors, we instructed those with complaints to go directly to this man and deal with the issues in person. But it seemed that agreement could not be reached on the interpersonal level. Indeed, the issue spread from those initial complaints to the wider congregation. People began asking more questions: Where did the church stand on this issue? What example was this setting for our young men who may not have the requisite maturity for such intimacy? Was this promoting sin?

We continued to have conversations, and our understanding grew. And yet as much as we needed conversation, we needed more. We could not merely have an endless conversation while some claimed that one of our leaders was promoting "emotional adultery" through the dating of single women by married men (though we were sure he was not). But how could we both affirm that his ministry was breaking down the walls between men and women, while still honoring our brothers and sisters who did not see the issue the same way? We needed clarification, not just conversation; discernment, not just discussion. We needed some way to lead our congregation forward, not just split it.

Ongoing conversations on issues facing the church are fine for open forums, but for people living these issues in life together, conversations must touch the ground in concrete actions and decisions if the kingdom of God is to break in. We must discern what God is doing in the here and now and respond. We must move into the very center of Christ's in-breaking kingdom. When we do, Jesus promises to be there. He promises that "whatever you bind on earth shall be bound in heaven, and whatever you loose on earth shall be loosed" (Matthew 18:17 ESV). The very authority of God's kingdom breaks in and carries us into new life in him. Apart from this, we are not being incarnational because nothing is taking on flesh and blood in real life.

Most of the Emergent conversations we took part in during the early years never actually touched the ground. When we met, we could talk about how to address the mistreatment of Muslims in a neighborhood in Dearborn, Michigan, but our group itself had no stake in the issue. It was abstract. We would talk about issues surrounding gay, lesbian, bisexual, or transgender relationships, but at the end of the evening, we would each go home to our own families and churches, and that discussion would go nowhere. Nothing would happen for God's justice in the world. We'd talk for hours about care of the earth as God's creation and then go home to our own little worlds. The discussions would never hit the ground. They would dissolve into the individual activity of each person who would work for justice for about four hours a week and then leave. And although people would sometimes get inspired and each place of service would benefit in some way, there would be little improvement for justice on the ground in the real world.

It really matters, though, how we stand alongside Muslims who are being judged and mistreated based on the acts of some terrorists. It matters how we deal with the complex sexual issues of our culture. It matters how we care for God's creation. These are not mere ideas requiring therapeutic discussions or a few more volunteers. These are people and situations where God is working to reconcile the world (2 Corinthians 5:19). And so it is essential to become witnesses to what God is doing. We must be the instruments through whom (not by whom) God's reign becomes visible. We cannot afford a perpetual discussion about where to go without ever really going, suspended in neutral toleration. In post-Christendom, an overemphasis on conversation now looks like a bunch of people standing around talking, and talking, and talking, and nothing ever comes of it.

This is why we've become convinced over the past several years that more than a "gospel" pronouncement or a "kingdom" conversation, the church is called to be a "witness." The problem is not only what to say about Jesus or what to do as individuals in order to be like Jesus. It is also how we live in Jesus so that his kingdom becomes present and visible in and through us in the neighborhoods. More than a pronouncement *of* the truth or a conversation *about* the truth, the church is called to embody a witness *to* the truth.

Signpost Four: Witnesses to the Kingdom

So let's go back to our initial question. Within a broken and bankrupt world, how can we claim that God's kingdom has come? Is it really true that Jesus is Lord? Or is this merely a failed media campaign that is fading and eventually will be forgotten?

At the beginning of the book of Acts, the disciples voice these same questions. After his death and resurrection, Jesus spends forty more days teaching them about the kingdom of God (1:3). They wanted more details and ask, "Lord, are you at this time going to restore the kingdom to Israel?" (1:6 NIV). They had experienced his life and ministry, his reconciliation and restoration, his healing and hope, and now they wanted to know if the kingdom of God was really coming after all: "Is this everything or is there more?"

Jesus answers, "It is not for you to know the times or dates the Father has set by his own authority. But you will receive power when the Holy Spirit comes on you; and you will be my *witnesses* in Jerusalem, and in all Judea and Samaria, and to the ends of the earth" (1:7–8 NIV). Some see in this text a rebuke, as if Jesus were saying, "When the kingdom is coming is none of your business." Others see Jesus as still working to get the disciples out of their narrow nationalistic mind-set ("restore the kingdom to *Israel*"). But according to theologian Michael Goheen, Jesus is doing neither. Instead, he is "shifting his disciples expectations from *when* to *how*." In no uncertain terms, Jesus is telling them that the outpouring of the Holy Spirit, which will enable their role as witnesses into Jerusalem and the world, is "precisely how the kingdom is to be restored to Israel for the sake of the nations."[6] The kingdom shall come through the power and authority of the King extended through the disciples by the Spirit within them. This indeed is what he means when he calls them "witnesses."[7]

The great missional theologian Darrell Guder suggests that when we think of mission, we must think of witness. He says, "Mission is *witness*," because the

> concept of witness, as we find it used in a variety of ways in the New Testament, describes the essence of the Christian experience from Easter onward. The New Testament cluster of terms based on the root for "witness" (*martyr-*) . . . defines comprehensively the missional calling of the church.[8]

New Testament scholar E. G. Selwyn notes that the term for *witness* (*marturian*) is used six times more frequently in the New Testament than the term for preaching (*kerygma*) when discussing the gospel.[9] In other words, New Testament writers more easily thought of the gospel being carried into the world through the process of witness rather than by any singular act of pronouncing or proclaiming.

It is important to say, nonetheless, that witness does not diminish the importance of verbally proclaiming the good news in people's lives on a daily basis. Quite the contrary! Witness provides the context from which such proclamation might make sense. Darrell Guder tells us that *witness* serves as an overarching term in the New Testament, drawing together proclamation (*kerygma*), community/fellowship (*koinonia*), and service (*diakonia*).[10] The term *witness* refers to an entire way of life that points to and embodies the reality of kingdom in the world.

The Witness of God (and Its Truth)

As we saw in the previous signpost, we'd be wrong to think that witness is something we do out of our own effort. It is something God does through us. We've learned this is a hard experience for North Americans to make sense of. Witness is God continually acting in, through, and around us.

This is why the Spirit is given. Jesus promised that when the Spirit comes to all disciples, it will bear witness about Jesus (John 15:26), just as the Father bears witness to the Son (John 5:37) and the Son bears witness to the Father (John 14:7). Witness is the work of God's Triune mission in the world, in which the Spirit takes the principal role after the resurrection. As the Holy Spirit inhabits us, we go forth into the world, extending the reality and truth of the kingdom of God. Our entire lives bear testimony to the in-breaking of God's kingdom in Christ. In this way, it is truly the Spirit that bears witness to Jesus when we live as witnesses.

The Spirit's power, however, does not guarantee triumph. Indeed, when Jesus promises the Spirit in John 15, he is reminding his disciples, on the night before his own death, that they too will be persecuted, falsely accused and put on trial, and killed as witnesses, as martyrs. After all, the word for *witness* in Greek, *martyrion*, later refers to those who died for bearing witness, from which we get the English word *martyr*.

Martyrdom is the complete giving of one's own life for the claims of the gospel. It is the ultimate place where the act of witness and the life of flesh and blood meet. In these situations of persecution, trial, and potential martyrdom, Jesus promises (sends) the Spirit to come to our defense and lead us in truth. The Spirit, who is called the "Spirit of truth" three times in John (14:17, 15:26, 16:13), will lead us in all truth during these times of distress, giving us the strength not only to be witnesses but martyrs if necessary. *Witness* does not mean there will be no suffering. Yet even in the worst of suffering and persecution, God's kingdom is breaking in, making visible the truth of the kingdom in Jesus Christ (and so the church has often exploded in power over the rebellious political forces on the world in the midst of its people dying as martyrs).

The Spirit's presence ensures that witness is not something we have to do, defend, or somehow make happen. It is something we live together in Christ for God's mission in the world. In the process, our lives give credibility to what we say. "Witnesses are not expected, like lawyers, to persuade by the rhetorical power of their speeches, but simply to testify to the truth for which they are qualified to give evidence," and because of this "it is in the very nature of Christian truth that it cannot be enforced," but only held forth.[11]

Witness therefore can never be coercive. By definition, it walks the way of the cross and resurrection, submitting to God's power to make all things right. It can only be offered as a gift. But some might ask, "If we pull back from defending the truth, aren't we giving up on the truth?" No. But we do refuse to impose the truth on others. For to impose the truth denies the very life, death, and resurrection of Jesus, who neither compelled nor imposed himself on others but lived as an open witness to the alternative reality God was birthing in him.[12] This is the way of God's love. And we must do likewise.

It is therefore inherent in the Son's journey into the far country that the world comes to know the truth of God's kingdom not by us defending the truth, but by our witnessing to it; not by having well-policed conversations about the kingdom, but living lives that testify to the truth.

Witnessing from One Reality to Another

One night as our missional order gathered around our dining room table, I (Dave) posed the question: "In what ways do you experience being with the poor in your everyday life?" Missional orders at Life on the Vine are groups of people who gather to share fellowship around a meal, develop sustaining relationships, talk about what God is doing in our neighborhoods, and respond together in prayer, thanksgiving, and commitments to be faithful. It is a place where the Spirit can shape witness.

This group had been gathering only a few months, and from the looks on people's faces, the question was horrifying. You could feel their angst around this question. They were feeling guilty. Their eyes were heavy with visions of being with homeless people, taking on the full responsibility of ministering to them: inviting them in, giving them food or shelter or both. This would be exhausting. This would surely cost enormous time, energy, and financial resources. Worse than this fear was the shame in feeling it. We did not know how to get beyond the fear and threat.

I told my story of how I had overcome the fear of being with hurting people. God had been leading me to regularly spend time in common places where I would often cross paths with hurting people. I would do my normal work there, but as opportunity would arise, I would make commitments to spend time with people as God led. It was simply being available: a conversation partner, listening and observing, and when certain needs came up, to ask questions as given permission, to be open to learning from this person as God worked. As I made a commitment to one homeless person, there was truth (but not pronouncements!) to be discerned almost every week.

We were probing together what God is doing in his life, in my life, in our lives. We would often turn to scripture to understand how God was working, for example, when a struggle with an estranged family would come up or a job opportunity. When other men from our church gathering would meet with me there, he'd ask about them. He would see reconciliation take shape between us as Christians. By and large, we got to know the inner details of each other's lives. In one year's time, being with one homeless man had cost me $238. When some bigger needs came up, the church had funds, and therefore it didn't cost me anything. Several times when he needed funds, he worked at my home or at the church building. God was providing. God's kingdom was breaking in.

This was no heroic effort or gigantic program. This was just the sharing of everyday life in the kingdom with this one man in my neighborhood.

As we heard a few more stories, the feelings changed. We realized that our task, when it came to the poor among us, was quite simply to do nothing. Absolutely nothing. We simply had to be present, available, in relationship to the poor, to listen to God's Spirit, and then respond when God spoke in and through these relationships. We were to let the kingdom of God flourish in and among us and thereby be witnesses.

This, we discovered, is what witnesses do. This is what Christians do. We are present with people, dirty laundry and all, and share everyday life so that others can catch a glimpse of a different reality. We do not need to make anyone or anything a project. Instead we are witness to the hope, hospitality, and healing that God is bringing into the world. Our lives, our friendships, our entire way of life together point to something beyond ourselves: what God is doing to redeem the whole world in Jesus Christ. This is what it means to be a witness.

The Journey into Witness

Prodigal Christianity is a life of witness characterized by two things. First, it is characterized by a testimony that points away from oneself to the works of Christ in our midst. As with John the Baptist in the gospels, our lives point to Jesus: "He must increase, but I must decrease"(John 3:30 RSV). With the apostle John, we recount "what we have heard, what we have seen with our eyes, what we have looked at and touched with our hands" (1 John 1:1 RSV). The act of witness testifies to what is going on that others might not be able to see. But witness participates in God's work; it cannot generate it. There is no burden here to do or prove something. Witness is about everyday attentiveness and faithfulness to God's kingdom that helps others learn to see it for themselves.

Second, witness is characterized by a shared life that embodies God's work among us. We are "a chosen people" so that in our lives, we might "declare the praises of him who called [us] out of darkness into his marvelous light," so that they might see our "good deeds and glorify God" (1 Peter 2:9,12 NIV). "By this," Jesus said, "everyone will know that you are my disciples, if you have love for one another" (John 13:35 NIV).[13] Witness therefore takes shape as we live God's new creation, with reconciliation and justice as signs of the kingdom as it lies ahead for the whole world. Through our transformed lives, the world sees something it did not know was possible: it sees the kingdom breaking in.

Any true witness is therefore social

It is more than just words we say; it is something we live. And this cannot happen purely as individuals. Witness happens socially as reconciliation, righteousness, and new creation take place horizontally (in lived relationships) and vertically (with God). We cannot reduce witness to mere proclamation or conversation.

Just as God came to us as one of us, filled by the Spirit, ushering in a new way of life, so we too must enter in to our neighborhoods and live the gospel as a way of life so that others can join in with us. Just as God came into humanity for all to see, touch, and hear so as to reveal God's coming kingdom, so we too must enter our neighborhoods with God's presence in order that the kingdom might become just as visible for everyone to see. To stay abstract or aloof is not the way of the prodigal God. Just as Christ became concrete, embodied flesh, we must embody our witness through our lives together in our neighborhoods.

And so we have learned that God's salvation in Christ extends into the very material circumstances of our everyday lives as people gather in his name to pray in the kingdom for their city, town, or neighborhood. Signs and wonders will appear. His reign over sin, death, and evil will take hold in the circumstances of our everyday lives. It will be something to behold.

The Journey So Far

In the first signpost, post-Christendom, we noted three shifts calling us to three new directions. We were called away from the stance that merely seeks to attract people to us; instead, we were challenged to go to them. We were called away from the postures of power that assume a position of authority; instead we were challenged to enter into deep relationships of vulnerability and integrity. And we were called away from assuming a universal perspective; instead we were challenged to live into particular places and situations. In each case, this is the way of witness.

With the second signpost, *missio Dei*, we were reminded that God is the sending God—sending us as witnesses to this mission. The God who sends us is never distant and aloof, dipping into the situation for a moment and leaving. Rather, God is the prodigal God who has dared to enter recklessly into our everyday lives. Our witness in and through Jesus Christ is the persistent and attentive participation in what God is doing in and around us. It is responding to God in obedience and faith, always pointing away from ourselves to God's work among us. This too is the way of witness.

With the third signpost, incarnation, we saw that just as Jesus came proclaiming and making present the kingdom of God, so Jesus goes with us in our sending. He extends his kingdom into the far country through us when we continue the practices of forgiveness and reconciliation, welcoming the stranger, proclaiming the gospel, the hospitality of the Lord's Table, praying "thy kingdom come," and visiting the sick. In these ways and more, before a watching world, God's kingdom breaks in (much more is coming on this in signpost 7 on the church). The kingdom bleeds from every area of our lives into all parts of the world. This too is witness: the Holy Spirit as empowered extension of the Incarnation.

Discerning the Kingdom: The Last Piece

Living as witnesses assumes that God is already at work and that what we need to do is discern this work by entering into each situation together, inviting one another into the presence of Christ. Signposts 2 and 3 make possible our following signpost 4 into post-Christendom (signpost 1). Because we assume God is at work, we can wait patiently, listen, pray, inhabit Scripture, and discern the Spirit in each situation. But we will not know what to say or do prior to discerning what God is doing. Only through discernment can we participate in God's kingdom work, thereby becoming the vehicle for the divine in-breaking of Christ to do his work in and among us. This is the prodigal nature of all witness.

Acts 10–15 give us an example of this type of kingdom discernment. In Acts 10, Cornelius receives an angelic vision telling him to send for Peter. The next day, Peter receives a vision of his own that enables him to receive the Gentile visitors. But Peter does not immediately understand the meaning of his vision and is still pondering it when the men from Cornelius arrive (v. 17). The Spirit tells him to go down and meet the men and go with them (v. 19). Cornelius and Peter are both tending to the Spirit and discerning it, and because of this, the Spirit begins to take them on a journey that will change the entire church. At Cornelius's house, the first words out of Peter's mouth confirm that he feels out of his element but is nonetheless committed to discerning God's work there (v. 28). Peter then begins a "presentation" of the gospel (although not as we usually think of it; this is the subject of signpost 6), and while he is still speaking, the Spirit comes onto all who are listening. They immediately begin to speak in tongues, astonishing all who are present (vv. 44–46).

This passage seems to back up the idea that all we need to do is present the gospel, that is, tell the story of Jesus so that lives will be changed. But this is not the end of the story. A bit later, after the Gentiles had been part of the church for a while, some began to teach that although it was good and fine that God welcomed the Gentiles, all male Gentiles still needed to be circumcised (i.e., they still needed to follow the Jewish laws). In Acts 15, in what is often called the Jerusalem Council, the church gathered to discern together God's work among the Gentiles. They eventually discerned that the Gentiles did not need to be circumcised, a new understanding that developed over time and in community. It came to them through prayer, listening to each other, and totally submitting to the Spirit's work among them.

After much discussion, Peter rose and began witnessing to the group about what happened to Cornelius, reminding everyone that "God, who knows the heart, *bore witness* to them, by giving them the Holy Spirit just as he did to us" (15:8 ESV; emphasis added). After this, James turned to the witness of the scriptures about how God would allow the Gentiles to call God by God's own name (15:15), concluding that it was as Gentiles, not as Jewish converts, that God was welcoming them. In light of these witnesses (the witness of Peter, the Holy Spirit, and scripture) the council writes a letter to the whole church and announces its communal discernment with the words: "It seemed good to the Holy Spirit and to us" (15:28 ESV). The unity of Gentiles and Jews, the great work of God unifying all people in Christ, was being displayed before everyone. This was witness at its finest.

Like those days with Peter and Cornelius, witness today entails regularly discerning the kingdom among us and what God is saying and has said in Scripture. It will entail a community of people where God is working. This is the prodigal journey we must travel.

So having entered the way of witness, let us travel deep into the ways the prodigal God speaks within the story we have been given (scripture). Let us walk recklessly into the middle of God's making right what is broken in the world (gospel), and move boldly into the center of the kind of people God has called us to be (community). As with the church in Acts 15, this also is where we must go. These are the three signposts that come next. Only by following this path can we go beyond the way of the singular pronouncement by the senior pastor or the meandering conversations of interested people and make our way into the missional frontier.

SCRIPTURE

LIVING OUR STORY: JOURNEYING BY THE BOOK
THAT IS MORE THAN A BOOK

WHEN I (DAVE) WAS GOING to high school in the 1970s, we were not allowed to have a Bible club on the grounds of the public school. But the school did offer The Bible as Literature as a course in the English department. There we studied the Bible as an influential piece of literature in Western society. What I experienced then, as a teenager, is even more prevalent today in large parts of North America. The Bible is at best a text for cultural study. It sits on the library shelf next to other religious and spiritual classics, carrying little, if any, authority of its own in our culture today. When we follow the Son into post-Christendom, we also discover a post-Bible society.

But not only is the Bible now nothing more than a cultural artifact; it is actively disdained when offered as an authority in the public realm. Whether we are talking about politics at the neighborhood school board or at the local coffee shop, we get smirks, hints of suspicion, or even hateful stares if we suggest the Bible has something to say to a pressing policy issue. If we reference the Bible while talking about sexuality, we are seen as repressive fundamentalists. And it would be out of the question to refer to the Bible when talking about economic policy. The famed atheist Christopher Hitchens, in his *New York Times* bestselling book, *God Is Not Great*, calls the Old Testament one gruesome long "nightmare" of irrationalities, pettiness, and, even worse, divinely sanctioned genocide. He finds the New Testament even worse.[1] Bart Erhman, in his own bestseller, *Misquoting Jesus*, mocks the inspiration of the Bible because

God has not bothered to preserve the original writings, allowing instead multiple copies of corrupted manuscripts.[2] These are common sentiments among the masses today. The Bible is seen as archaic, lacking scientific integrity, and open to abuse.

Add to this the fact that our culture is innately suspicious toward interpretation. The automatic rejoinder to any authoritative statement is the proverbial, "Well, that's your interpretation." All interpretation is conditioned by your cultural viewpoint, and the Bible is no exception. Our society is accustomed to seeing the Bible misused. Does anyone really need to be reminded that the Bible was used to justify slavery in pre–Civil War United States? Did Pat Robertson really just use the Bible to declare God's judgment in another natural disaster? Is it any wonder the Bible has lost its position as the guiding moral compass of North America?

And to top it all off, authority in general has gotten a bad name. For years, I led a Christian community in Chicago, where any kind of challenge or judgment of a person's way of life was viewed as an abuse or dismissed. Whether it was a personal challenge or a charge from the pulpit, the normal response would be, "Sorry, but I don't need your judgment." We live in a culture of client-centered therapy (the patient is always right) and self-help encouragement (the truth is within you) where authority is what you decide it is.

And so we walk in a world where the Bible's authority is forsaken and forgotten, a curious relic more than an animating force. But there's a different path into the heart of scripture's authority and the way it operates in and through Jesus Christ among his people by the Spirit. It is the prodigal journey that shakes loose our common concerns about the Bible and allows it to regain its function as a conduit of God's kingdom. This journey reconfigures all authority according to the reign of Jesus. There is a trajectory here, a signpost, we must follow. But how we follow it makes all the difference.

(Sacred) Authority Through (Secular) Science

Disoriented by the confusion surrounding the Bible in society, battered by reactions against judgmentalism and authoritarianism, we react by defending it. We build arguments that support the reliability and authority of the Bible as God's Word (this tendency is by now familiar, linked to the desire to defend the divinity of Jesus, or to defend some conception of truth). This approach rightly sees the need for some sort of authority in our lives. It connects to the desire to be confident in the Bible, trusting its authority in uncertain times.

Many pastors and leaders have sought to defend the Bible according to the most accepted of all standards of authority in Western society: modern science. Early in school, we are taught that the scientific method leads us to the most trustworthy results. Regardless of one's beliefs about God or the particular findings of science (age of the universe, evolution, determinism), few people question the progress of modern science and its many advances. What can be scientifically proven is considered true. What cannot be verified is false or, at best, merely a matter of opinion.

We are therefore tempted to deploy the scientific method to prove the authority of scripture. Are the biblical sources historically accurate? Do biblical stories match archaeological evidence? Do biblical claims correspond to scientific facts? Does the meaning of the text link up with the reality to which it refers? Because these are the types of questions our scientific mind-set asks, we feel the need to answer them as well. In the desire to feel justified before science, we attempt to make scripture measure up to the standards of truth that seem so obvious to the modern Western mind.

This scientific mind-set trickles down from proving the authority of scripture to the process of reading scripture. The way down this road begins by emphasizing that "all Scripture is God breathed and is useful for teaching, rebuking, correcting, and training in righteousness" (2 Timothy 3:16 NIV). Because God inspired the words, the sentences, the paragraphs, and the books of the Bible and all of them refer to historical and current realities, they must all be scientifically accurate. From uniting the inspiration of scripture to the scientific method comes the concern for "inerrancy" and a focus on "propositions." In the words of Al Mohler, the president of Southern Baptist Seminary, because "the Bible is 'free from all falsehood or mistake' . . . inerrancy is an essential safeguard for the Bible's authority as the very Word of God in written form . . . to affirm anything short of inerrancy is to allow that the Bible does contain falsehoods or mistakes."[3] For Mohler, although "Christians understand truth to be more than propositional . . . [it can never be] less than propositional."[4] This is the baseline commitment for Mohler. The Bible is fundamentally understood as a book full of factual truth statements, otherwise known as propositions.

Can We Love Propositions?

The famed Baptist preacher from Minneapolis, John Piper, made the startling observation in his 2011 book, *Contending for Our All*, that some of the early church fathers believed that false propositions about Christ could send you to hell. Heresy, in other words, is lethal to your soul. Piper then went on to say something that sounds rather odd: "Loving Christ includes loving true propositions about Christ."[5] We know what Piper is getting at here: seeking Christ entails seeking truth. But there is a danger here. Scripture, when viewed in this way, can seem like a static collection of divinely perfect scientific propositions. As a result, knowledge of God can equally seem distant and aloof, imparting true information to our minds only through a written text.[6]

We therefore must avoid reading habits that make us look at the Bible as an austere textbook. The Bible is not a static account of historical things in the past. It is not a user's manual written so we could know how to drive our lives (or have Jesus drive it, as it were). Instead scripture is a dramatic unfolding of the story of God's redemptive work in and for the world. Such a Bible leads us into the prodigal love and the journey of God into the depths of the far country. A view of scripture overly focused on its scientific rationality is not prodigal enough to engage our concrete lives and the people we live around. It inadvertently makes scripture into a disincarnated text addressed only to our minds, making disincarnated disciples who are more concerned with proper ideas than they are with missional lives.

Is Inerrancy Too Liberal?

Nonetheless, it is good to uphold scripture as historical, true, and trustworthy. Coming into a deeper relationship with God depends on knowing that God is actually doing something in history and that scripture guides us reliably into this knowledge. Yet we have to be careful that we do not make the Bible into merely a collection of provable statements that have little intrinsic connection to our lives as we seek God's mission here on earth.

In my (Dave) ordination interview I was asked if I believed in the inerrancy of scripture. I answered, "Yes, I affirm it, but it is too liberal for me." Confused looks crossed the faces of my ordination council. So I went on:

> Inerrancy begs the question "inerrant according to who?" and too often the "who" consists of scholars, scientists, and archeologists. They are the ones we allow to determine whether there are errors or not in the Bible when we consent to this strategy. They are the ones we are reacting to when we defend the Bible using "inerrancy." And so too often we end up defending scripture over against such critics on their terms,

the science and historiography of the universities. We inadvertently end
up basing the authority of scripture on an authority outside of (extrin-
sic to) scripture, outside of the work of God. We inadvertently put a
human authority over the Bible. We diminish the Bible. This strategy
therefore ends up putting us in the position of forever looking over
our shoulders to see if science has another problem with the Bible. So I
believe the Bible is without error, but I need more than that!"

My ordination council seemed somewhat satisfied with this answer.
But what I really wanted to say was that the Bible is not a textbook—a
set of mechanically delivered yet scientifically true propositions about
God. It is the living extension of the gospel itself in Jesus Christ.

After Inerrancy

These days, inerrancy is out because interpretation is in. I (Geoff) had this
epiphany while talking with my dad. We were sitting in the front yard,
under the walnut tree, talking about everything I was learning in college.
My dad began talking about the doctrine of inerrancy and how important it was for upholding Christian faith. He was talking about how, if
scripture is not inerrant, we could lose all knowledge of God, the truth of
the gospel, and our confidence in salvation. If scripture isn't historically
and scientifically true in all things, then we are left adrift in cultural relativism. At least, that was the general drift of the conversation.

This didn't sit well with me. I blurted out to my dad, "Inerrancy
doesn't matter anymore. Your generation tried to prove inerrancy, but
that question doesn't matter to my generation. Everything is an interpretation now." As a third-year philosophy student, I had come to
realize that even if we claimed that scripture was itself inerrant, this did
not help us know how to properly interpret scripture. Trained in the
hermeneutics of suspicion and having talked with my friends, I knew that
no one my age cared about inerrancy because they were always questioning the authority of the interpretation rather than the authority of the
text. My friends all assumed that a hidden bias was always controlling
the supposed objectivity of an interpretation.

My friends distrusted any claim to an authoritative interpretation
because there could always be an additional meaning to a poem or an alternative rendering of a book. "Who does this benefit?" they would ask of
any interpretation. "What oppressive power structure does this support?"
they might inquire. "Does this dominant interpretation suppress a minority
perspective?" they would wonder. In their minds, every interpretation is an

imperialist act, seeking to control other perspectives. In that conversation with my dad, I realized inerrancy was out and interpretation was in.

The Bible as a Library

So if the scientific proof of inerrancy subcontracts authority to human sources and turns discipleship into a mostly cognitive process, and if our culture doubts the truth of every interpretation, how can we move forward with Scripture? Within a culture suspicious of all attempts to establish authoritative interpretations, the emerging church sought a new understanding of Scripture.

Brian McLaren, an early thought leader in the emerging church, talks eloquently about the ways we have failed in our approach to Scripture's authority in his important 2010 book, *A New Kind of Christianity*. He labels the traditional ways of upholding scripture's authority the "Constitutional approach."[7] This approach sees scripture as similar to the U.S. Constitution, a document that directs us how to live and what happens if we break the rules. McLaren shows how this approach to the Bible often hardens into a single "authoritative" interpretation of Scripture governed by an imposing authority figure (the pastor or the denomination, for example) who controls the text with few checks and balances. He claims that often the resulting interpretation of the Bible can be arbitrarily tied to certain power structures: racism, sexism, or something else. For McLaren, this approach saps the Bible of its authority. Based on our experience, we agree very much with him.

McLaren proposes we instead see the Bible as "a library of the culture and community of people who trace their history back to Abraham, Isaac and Jacob." This library was collected and passed on; it was inspired (by the people's experience with God in the Spirit) and was "intended to stimulate conversation, to keep people thinking and talking and arguing and seeking." McLaren asks that "as we listen and enter into conversations ourselves, could it be that God's Word, God's speaking, God's self-revealing happens to us, sneaks up, surprises and ambushes us, transforms us, and disarms us—rather than arms us with truths to use like weapons to savage other human beings?" The Bible, for McLaren, is "the portable library of an ongoing conversation so that we can actually encounter and experience the living God."[8] He sees it as a story "we find ourselves in" whereby we navigate our experience of the living God.

McLaren's proposal is a significant step forward. Rather than a distant set of static propositions, scripture engages us and draws us into an ongoing conversation based in scripture itself. Rather than being distanced from scripture, we engage in the new reality God is making. We are invited into an encounter with the living God through the "portable library" in our prodigal journey within the world, the missional far country. On this journey, no dominant interpretation can control the conversation, so we need not be concerned about ideological domination. Rather we must all be open to new experiences of God, adding them to the experiences catalogued in scripture.

But Which Library?

But is it fair to ask who gets to choose what goes into this library? Who is the librarian who has the "authority" to add books? And why this library versus another? There is a great deal of spiritual literature out there from numerous other religious traditions. Furthermore, even if these questions were answered concerning the library model, would not Scripture get lost in conversation just like witness (in the previous signpost), unable to truly lead us in a concrete direction?

If the ones who emphasize propositions are overly focused on the divine nature of the words in the Bible, thereby distancing us from both God and culture, McLaren's approach can overemphasize the human nature of Scripture and the importance of personal experience. But the prodigal God refuses to separate God's own coming fully (as God) from being fully present with us (as human). Neither of these two approaches therefore approximates God's prodigality. Neither approach to Scripture allows God's presence to enter human life in authority and power in a way we could call prodigal. Instead each approach accommodates to different cultural attitudes. One side capitulates to scientific rationality and the other to a "hermeneutics of suspicion." But as we will see, the authority of scripture is something we receive, not something we control. The Scriptures themselves possess (in Christ) a prodigal authority, recklessly beyond our power to manage but concrete enough to lead us into life with God in the far country.

From a Text We Cannot Control . . .

That we should receive scripture rather than control it was something I (Geoff) have slowly come to learn. I've always been a slow reader, and this influenced what major I chose. Torn between literature, history, and philosophy, I decided against the first two thinking they would have too much reading. Gladly I found that studying philosophy did require less reading, typically only a couple of books for a course. But I soon realized that I had to read these books two, three, four, or even five times just to understand them. Philosophy required a much more focused kind of reading. But as difficult as it was, I learned the art of reading carefully, mining a book for all its riches.

These skills later came in handy when reading the Bible. Going off to seminary, I began the long process of learning Greek and Hebrew, along with the proper tools of biblical exegesis. I was learning how to read the Bible closely, asking the right questions of the text, following the grammar of the sentences, and mining the depths of each passage.

But I soon realized a problem: with all this focused reading and all these new tools (new languages, new questions for discovering the context, new ways of analyzing grammar), I was losing the ability to listen to scripture because I was so busy trying to read it. I was attempting to master and control the Bible though *my* exegesis of it. When I sat at a worship service reading along in my Bible I often found myself trying to guess the underlying Greek sentence or diagramming the passage for its structure, looking for the main verbs that carry the meaning. I was no longer receiving Scripture as the revealing of God to me (to change and transform me), but treating the Bible as if it were a code I was to break. The center of gravity had slowly shifted from God's word spoken to me to God's word understood by me. I was subtly exercising control over Scripture.

Because of this, during my second year in seminary, I committed to just listening to the Scriptures without reading along when they were read aloud in a worship service so that I would learn again to receive them as a gift from God. I had to stop looking at the opened text so that my heart could be open to the words of God. I stopped reading the Bible so that God (through the Bible) could begin speaking to me again.

. . . to a Text We Must Proclaim

Exercising control over Scripture, doing "foolproof" exegesis of the text, is often expected of preachers. It is the basis for the authority of Scripture in some churches. Let me explain.

Early on in the planting of our community, I (Dave) met with someone who had known me when I lived in Chicago. He was in the process of finding another church. He mentioned a large church in the area and said the reason he would probably attend there was that "they preach the Word." When I asked him what that meant, he said the pastor preached through a biblical text line by line and explained the words right off the page. Then the pastor would give an application point to help the believer apply it to his or her life. The pastor stuck purely to the text: word for word, sentence for sentence. Here was the pure authority of the Bible. For this man, this was a big deal.

Both of us certainly think the Bible should be studied closely sentence for sentence, word for word, but is this biblical preaching? This approach certainly works for teaching and explaining information about the Bible, itself very important. But this kind of preaching can turn the Bible into an object for our own personal control. It makes the Bible into information for us to use at our discretion. It can actually cultivate a new "works righteousness" because each Sunday I've got one more thing to work on to live the Christian life. After a few months of getting a new application point every week, I'm exhausted! As we began gathering at Life on the Vine, I did not feel this way of preaching could address the need to hear and see the kingdom of God breaking out among us.

At the Vine's Sunday gathering, we shifted from teaching the Bible to proclaiming God's victory over the world in Jesus Christ as found in the Bible. We would still teach the text at the 9:00 a.m. hour each Sunday morning. But then we would gather together at 10:15 a.m. to hear Scripture proclaimed. We would listen to four texts read aloud, allowing ourselves to be immersed into the entire story of what God has been up to in ages past and will do in ages to come. Then the preacher would lead us into that reality of who God is, what he has done, what he is doing in Christ in our lives, our neighborhoods, our world. Then we were invited to respond in repentance, obedience, and faithfulness.

Over the years at the Vine, the sermon has become the time to proclaim the gospel over us. It declares the reality of Jesus's reign over all things. Each Sunday we gather to submit to that reality so as to respond to it and live into it by the Spirit. It is from this place that Scripture receives its authority—the authority of being connected to God's mission.

The Kingdom of God in Scripture

The approach to Scripture that Life on the Vine adopted makes sense once we see how authority operates in God's kingdom, in God's mission in the world. The kind of story that Scripture tells, from Adam to Abraham to Israel to David and ultimately to Jesus, reveals God's authority as it unfolds in God's mission, the kingdom of God.

Adam

God begins the story with the creation of Adam and Eve surrounded by blessings. On each of days 5, 6, and 7 of the Creation story, God gives a blessing. The first two blessings are accompanied by the command to be fruitful and multiply, first to the fish and birds (Genesis 1:22) and then to humanity (1:28). The third is the blessing of the Sabbath. God calls all of his creation into a fruitfulness and abundance within creation and a restful and harmonious relationship to the Creator.[9] Within these blessings, humanity is given the task (or mission) of "ruling" over creation by caring for it. This is not a dominating exploitation (as some would say based on Genesis 1:26), but a tending, serving, and caring for creation as if it were a beautiful garden entrusted to humanity (2:15). We could say that in Genesis 1 and 2, God charges humanity with "the great task of ruling over creation through keeping and serving the earth in which God has placed them."[10] There's an authority given to humanity out of a harmonious relationship with God that serves creation.

But in Genesis 3 we see that humanity abdicates its mission to serve and trust God and instead seeks to usurp God (3:5). Genesis 4 through 11 charts the course of escalating sin, violence, and destruction, all presenting the universal alienation of humanity from God. The intended rule of God (kingdom of God) through humanity fails with Adam, and the blessings are replaced with curses.

Abraham

And yet God does not abandon humanity or creation. God launches a redemptive mission to bless the nations again, spearheaded by a single individual, Abraham.[11] Genesis 12 tells of God calling Abraham to leave his culture and go to a land where God will make him and his descendants into a great nation in order to bring God's blessings to all nations (12:1–3). The word *blessing* occurs five times in these three verses. God had not given up on the original intent to bless all peoples, all nations. But this return to universal blessing is inaugurated through a particular family, a barren family at that, who must be totally dependent on God for their future. This blessing first falls on Abraham and then extends to the nations. In this way, "Abraham is first of all a recipient of God's blessing and then its mediator."[12]

We could say that the state of blessing is creational (what God intended), but the act of blessing is missional (how God is renewing all things).[13] This is God's (kingdom) mission extended through Abraham. The authority (rule, reign, kingdom) of God that brings flourishing and renewal is being extended through Abraham as long as Abraham submits himself in trust to God's rule. God is shaping a people to bring this new harmonious life to the world.

Israel

So if "Genesis singles out Abraham, the book of Exodus singles out Israel, the great nation promised to Abraham."[14] In Israel God is continuing to fulfill the promises made to Abraham. But just as Abraham was blessed in order to extend blessing, so too with Israel. This is why God says that Israel will be a "kingdom of priests" and a "holy nation." Israel will mediate or channel God's blessing as a priestly kingdom (among kingdoms) and a holy nation (among the nations). This will be a new way of living together, trusting in the faithfulness of God. In this new way of living together, God shall reign in peace, harmony, and the renewal of creation. God's authority will be made known.

Through this priestly mediation, God will become known among all the nations. As Richard Bauckham says, God "delivered Israel from Egypt at the exodus, with acts of awesome power, in order . . . to make his name renowned through all the earth, to make an enduring name for himself among the nations."[15] This knowledge of God is meant to flow through Israel to the nations, sometimes in judgment, sometimes in hope. God delivered Israel from the hands of the Egyptians, then later the Assyrian, Babylonians, and Persians, so that the nations would know the mighty salvation of God and would know Israel as a place of blessing and flourishing amid destruction.

David

Israel did not always desire to be a holy nation, wanting instead to be like the other nations. Specifically, rather than having God as their king, Israel longed for a human king (1 Samuel 8:5, 19–20). God reluctantly consents to this request, but the fortunes of Israel under its kings are highly divergent, as God had predicted. God's way of authority and blessing is never really accomplished (Deuteronomy 17:14–20). More often than not, the kings usurped God and brought destruction on their people. Whereas the ideal king for Israel was meant to protect and promote the true worship of God, thereby functioning as a symbol of the gracious rule of God over all the nations, Israel's kings failed miserably at obeying God and instead ruled out of their own egos with violence and for personal gain.[16]

And so Israel, via the prophets and poets, began to envision a coming king who would perfectly unite the kingship of God and the human king from the line of David. God's mission to bring the world into reconciliation would be fulfilled this way. This promoted a messianic hope within Israel (reflected in texts like Psalms 2 and 72, Isaiah 9:6–7, and Zechariah

9:10) that a future king would restore the peaceful rule of God to the entire world, not merely to Israel. This would be a renewal of the peace, rest, and abundance of creation and its original blessing.

Jesus

With Adam, Abraham, Israel, and David, we have a picture of God's working in history to extend the reign and authority of God across the whole earth for the blessing of humanity and the care of creation.[17] Of course, in the Old Testament there are many twists and turns, many smaller narratives, some of which reach resolution and others that are left hanging. But in one way or another, the Old Testament outlines a multi-stranded trajectory of God's kingdom coming, which the New Testament sees as culminating in the life, death, and resurrection of Jesus. This is why (as we saw in signpost 2) the fulfillment of God's mission in the world, centering on Jesus, begins with Jesus announcing that the kingdom of God is at hand (Mark 1:15). This is why Paul describes Jesus as the second Adam who restores blessing (life) out of curse (death) (Romans 5; 1 Corinthians 15:45) and as the fulfillment of the promised blessing given to Abraham (Galatians 3:7–9). It is for this reason the gospel of Matthew begins the genealogy of Jesus with Abraham (1:2). Matthew is telling us that Jesus is the climax of that initial mission of redemption begun in Genesis 12. And the gospels repeatedly paint a clear picture of Jesus ful-filling the mission of Israel as the coming messiah (the coming king). In this diversity of ways, all of Scripture paints a picture of the coming of the kingdom of God, culminating in Jesus. And it is within this kingdom that the authority of Scripture must be placed.

The Least of These

But something else must be said clearly about the authority exercised in God's kingdom. This is a kingdom unlike any other. Most successful king-doms in world history have been sprawling empires that subjugated inno-cent people. Conquering kings or, worse, dominating tyrants led them. But God's kingdom is the opposite of this. It comes through the "least of these."

God called an old man and his barren wife in Abraham and Sarah to birth this kingdom. God called Israel, the least of the nations (Deuteronomy 7:7), to be a blessing to the nations. God anointed the youngest and most overlooked of Jesse's sons to be king (1 Samuel 16:6–13). And God used a humble carpenter's family as the place for the Son of God to be born. God, the rightful king over all things, "not only inhabits the highest heaven, but comes among the humblest of . . . servants on earth" (Isaiah 57:15), even submitting to the cross. This is the prodigal God we have been talking about all along, who does not remain aloof, lingering among the eternal praise of the heavenly hosts. Rather, God forgoes the highest places and enters the lowly realms of the least of these: the elderly, the barren, the forgotten, and the despised.

In the same way, Scripture is not some great ideological document that seeks to dominate or control. Rather, it tells the story of the prodigal God who comes among "the least of these." It is for this reason that Paul, a faithful servant of the kingdom of God, could remind the Corinthians that although

> not many of you were wise according to worldly standards, not many were powerful, not many were of noble birth. But God chose what is foolish in the world to shame the wise, God chose what is weak in the world to shame the strong, God chose what is low and despised in the world, even things that are not, to bring to nothing things that are. (1 Corinthians 1: 26b–28 ESV)

This is the great reversal of the kingdom of God, which brings down those who are lofty and arrogant, raising up those who are weak and foolish (see the songs of Hannah and Mary in 1 Samuel 2:3–8 and Luke 1:51–53). This is the way God's authority is manifested among us.[18]

This, then, is the mission of the prodigal God: to restore blessing where there is cursing, to restore peace among humanity, creation, and God, to bring salvation to the whole earth. And it is only within this story, the mission of the prodigal God, that we can understand the authority of Scripture. Any other alternative is not prodigal enough, seeking instead to control and manage scripture.

Scripture in the Kingdom of God

So we have seen that Scripture portrays the mission of God as the in-breaking kingdom of God. Because of this, we must understand Scripture's authority as a principal component through which the kingdom comes. Therefore, it is not so important to find the kingdom of God in Scripture but to submit to Scripture in the kingdom of God. What could this look like?

I (Geoff) met Shannon a few years back before beginning my morning shift at Starbucks. She was on her way home from work as a night shift dispatcher and having her combined dinner and breakfast at the local IHOP (International House of Pancakes) at 5:00 a.m. Shannon did not really want to bare her soul, but she seldom had anyone who would listen to her. The daughter of an alcoholic, Shannon had been in a verbally and emotionally abusive relationship with another alcoholic for twenty years. Sitting dejected and discouraged, pain and loneliness bubbling out of her, she spoke of her simple desire to give her daughter a loving and caring home, something she had never had. But, she told me, her life was just repeating itself: her daughter was subject to the humiliation and danger of an alcoholic father and an impotent mother. On top of all this, Shannon no longer felt connected to God now that the early hope and joy of following Jesus had faded. The loudest voice in her head was that of her ex-husband telling her she was ugly, worthless, and a failure.

In that moment I proclaimed the kingdom of God to Shannon again. I declared humbly the truth of God over all the lies coming from her ex-husband, coming from her childhood abuse. I proclaimed that she had a Father who loved her, who valued her, who knew what she was going through. I reminded her that God cares especially for the widows and orphans (and Shannon is just one of many orphaned by alcohol), that God longs to be her Father in a way that her alcoholic father never could be, that God longs to be the Father that her daughter never had. I declared the story of God's kingdom again, for if Jesus came declaring the kingdom of God, he did this just as much by declaring the fatherhood of God against all abusive and abdicating fathers.

When I told Shannon that this is what the Bible is all about, she meekly responded that the Bible was confusing. She found the Bible hard to read and difficult to understand. I explained, "That doesn't really matter . . . what matters is that God is working in your life."

Perhaps saying "the Bible doesn't matter" is scandalous to some. But at that moment, the authority of Scripture was revealed through God's kingdom breaking into Shannon's life. It is the authority of truth breaking through the lies and deceit of this world. As N. T. Wright claims, "The authority of Scripture thus makes the sense it does within the world of God's kingdom, at every level from the cosmic and the political through to the personal."[19] If the authority of scripture becomes disconnected from God's mission in the world, it becomes disconnected from God. It becomes a disincarnate collection of facts or feelings, lacking the ability to participate and extend the incarnation of God.

Signpost Five: The Journey with, by, and in Our Story

Following this signpost, prodigal Christianity affirms the authority of Scripture as the product of God's mission in Christ by the Spirit.

In a world where the church has lost its position of authority and influence, where people do not readily understand the world of the Bible (signpost 1), Scripture comes alive as it becomes the means to participate in God's life and *missio* (signpost 2). As given to us through Jesus Christ and the apostles, Scripture is an extension of Christ's very authority in our midst. It is incarnational (signpost 3). And so it is ultimately within our life together under Christ's rule as witnesses (signpost 4) that Scripture's authority is revealed in a way that cannot be denied, only submitted to or rejected (2 Corinthians 2:14–17).

There is a time in every Christian's life when we must come to embrace the Bible as our own story, as the story of the kingdom. By the Spirit, the full authority of Christ is revealed to us, and we submit to this book as the one and true story in Christ. To follow Jesus, the apex of God's mission in the world, requires embracing the Old and New Testaments that witness to Jesus beforehand and after.

And so we approach Scripture first not to analyze it or subject it to study as an object, but rather to allow ourselves to be immersed in it. There will always be times when we will need to study commentaries, look up texts, and ask about the Jewish, Greek, and Roman backgrounds. "What does this word mean?" will be part of the study. But all of this will be a labor of love as we delve deeper into Scripture, allowing ourselves to see the whole world as it really is under the Lordship of Christ and where he is taking it. In a sense, the authority of Scripture comes from bringing us into contact with the reality of God and God's mission.[20]

It is for this reason that at Life on the Vine, we proclaim the gospel from Scripture in our preaching on Sundays. On Saturdays when we have spiritual retreats, we follow the classic *lectio divina* approach to reading Scripture together in silence, listening for God and the work of the Spirit. At Friday night town hall meetings, when we are discerning difficult challenges among us, we grapple with the texts; those who are gifted in biblical exegesis are listened to, the theologians among us contribute, all the other gifts speak as well, and we seek unity as we listen to Scripture through the gifts of the Spirit (we will come to this more in the signpost 7 on the church). Because Christ's authority is manifest in the gifts of the community (Ephesians 4:8), Scripture is read in mutual submission one to another under the Lordship of Christ. We join together under his Lordship to discern God's mission through Scripture (as in Acts 15). We do not battle over the exegesis of a text but learn to submit to God's kingdom as we listen to Scripture and one another. Through it all, the authority of God in Christ manifests itself among us. Jesus's Lordship becomes embodied in a people for this time and place in the story of our lives.

Discerning the Kingdom

One night a man in our church asked to speak with the pastors about his concerns with the direction of the church toward accepting women in pastoral ministry. Steve explained he was struggling with what had been going on. Two years earlier, our church had spent nine months reading Scripture together, listening to all sides of the issue and submitting to one another's gifts in order to discern how God was leading us in regard to calling women into pastoral ministry. We ended this time with a two-month-long church council to decide the issue for our congregation. But Steve had missed the entire process. He said he didn't agree with our openness to call a woman pastor (which at that time we hadn't actually done).

He gave us a text that he felt explicitly argued against women in ministry. He offered 1 Timothy 3:2: "Now the overseer . . . must be husband of one wife." This obviously meant, for Steve, that no overseer, elder, or pastor in the church could be a woman. The church had already discussed this text and came to an understanding that the passage meant leaders should be monogamous and not serial divorcers. Because it seemed that all the pastoral leaders were men at that time, the author of 1 Timothy articulated this principle in terms of male leadership. But in itself, this text did not address whether only men should be in leadership.

Despite this disagreement, the pastors did not just lay down the law and tell Steve to follow our decision. We were committed to truth being witnessed out of Scripture as we mutually submit to it in Christ. The prodigal God works in humble listening and places of mutual submission to Christ. So we invited Steve to submit this before the entire church body. We explained that if there was a disagreement, we should together follow Matthew 18:15–20 to see if we had been leading our congregation in sin. We were open to being challenged on this issue if he felt it was a serious enough issue. Although we had already been through an extensive process of prayer, study, and communal discernment; had had many discussions with our denominational authorities; and had come to a consensus on this issue, Steve still was not satisfied. For him, Scripture was clear, and it should be followed. Discerning the kingdom of God with the people of God guided by the Spirit of God is not what Steve wanted. He just wanted the "authority" of the Bible. Not finding it, he left.

But we are committed to the authority of God's kingdom in and through Scripture, even if it looks different from what Steve was thinking. Scripture is an extension of Jesus's person and work in the world. And his rule is extended through good communal reading habits: prayer, mutual submission to the gifts, including those recognized as gifted preachers and teachers of Scripture, the history of interpretation, and of course, patient deliberation.[21] When we submit together in these ways, Scripture's authority is made manifest among us. As we live together in Scripture as "Our One True Story of God for the Whole World," we come to know its authority in and through Jesus Christ.[22] Anything less reduces Scripture to a collection of facts or feelings.

The Kingdom of God—the Gospel of Jesus

As prodigal Christians, we should rarely find ourselves defending the Bible's authority. Rather, its authority becomes undeniable when its compelling reality becomes visible among us. The story of God as displayed in a people speaks for itself.

But what exactly is the story of God? And how do we participate in it? How is sin's curse lifted exactly? How does a renewal of blessing come? And what is it about the life, death, and resurrection of Jesus that accomplishes so many wondrous things? To ask these questions is to ask about the gospel, the journey of the Son into the far country that is the center of God's mission. From the journey into the book that is more than a book, we encounter the journey of redemption in Christ. This too is at the heart of prodigal Christianity. And so to the gospel we now turn in our next signpost.

GOSPEL

MAKING ALL THINGS RIGHT: THE JOURNEY
INTO REDEMPTION

IT WAS A TYPICAL SUNDAY MORNING, and our worship gathering had begun as usual with the announcements about what is happening among our communities. What normally follows is what we call "a story of wonder" about what God had been doing among us. This morning, however, the story of wonder took a different turn.

Dustin stood up and told us about his job at Starbucks. He had been working there for two years cultivating relationships. He'd been praying for months asking to see what God was doing at Starbucks. He was submitting himself to God's kingdom and how he could be used as an instrument of the gospel. This past week, a woman he'd known for two years asked him if they could talk. Sarah sounded serious and downcast. Dustin said they moved to a table away from store traffic and she began to open up to him about her life. She told Dustin that her boyfriend, a heroin addict, had left her. Her parents had split up. She had been denied admission to a graduate program. Everything in her life, she told Dustin, was imploding. As she looked to the future, she couldn't imagine anything to live for. She was spiraling downward, isolating herself from the few people she knew. In fact, she said that for two nights, she was having thoughts about killing herself.

As Dustin was telling his story, the room became still. The congregation was glued to their seats. Many just stared sympathetically. And then Dustin admitted he did not know what to say or do in that moment at Starbucks. His conservative Protestant upbringing told him that he should present the gospel, which for him meant "the four spiritual laws": "God has a wonderful plan for your life. . . . But we are sinful and separated from God. . . . Jesus Christ made provision for our sin. . . . And if you will just receive Jesus as Savior and Lord you can know his love and plan for your life." But he didn't share this because he didn't see how the four spiritual laws were going to connect with this friend in her crisis. She needed hope. None of those teachings seemed to fit her situation.

We asked ourselves a lot of questions that day as a community. Was our understanding of the gospel too small? Does it address only one problem (moral guilt) without dealing with others (relational devastation or cosmic rebellion)? Is our gospel limited to a "decision" that means little for the everyday lives of those around us? For years, a theme in our church was the need for a "bigger gospel," yet it seemed we knew little about how to bring that to bear on people's lives. And really, what is that "bigger gospel" anyway?

Where Are We Going? How Do We Get There?

There is a sense that in asking about the gospel, we are reaching the climax of the prodigal journey. Whenever we have discussed in the previous signposts about the kingdom of God breaking in through Jesus's ministry, we were in fact already talking about the gospel. When we noticed the Father sending the Son and Spirit into the far country, we were already in fact talking about the gospel. And when we outlined the coming kingdom authority that reestablishes the blessing of creation to all people in the signpost on Scripture, we were reciting the foundation of the gospel. But as we saw, Abraham, Israel, and David ultimately failed to bring the kingdom blessing to fruition and the curse remained. The gospel, then, is the good news that God has finally dealt with our sin-plagued and evil-cursed world in the sending of the Son, Jesus Christ. In him, the in-breaking of the kingdom—God restoring and reconciling all relationships—has begun.

But how does this kingdom of God actually deal with sin? How does it overcome the relational strife of a broken world? How does it heal the alienation of a rebellious humanity? Answering this gets at the heart of the mission of God. The sixth signpost leads us into the center of what God is doing in the world by leading us into the radical gospel that "Jesus, the crucified and risen Messiah, is Lord."[1] But how we unpack this makes all the difference in determining whether we will fully enter into the mission of God or merely circle it within our tidy cul-de-sacs.

Martin Luther in Starbucks

How did we Christians end up like Dustin at Starbucks? How did we come to a particular version of the gospel that left Dustin with so little to offer in the midst of his friend's crisis?

Growing up in an evangelical church, Dustin was taught a particular gospel that grew out of the split the Western church experienced in Europe during the fifteenth-century Protestant Reformation. Until that time, European towns and villages had formed their life around the Roman Catholic Church for centuries. In this time and culture, there was a strong sense of the justice of God seeking out and punishing all sin and unrighteousness. And much of European Christianity was trained within the penitential system of the church (confession, penance, absolution), which served to order their lives according to God's righteousness and alleviate their guilt. In the medieval world of Christendom, guilt was a major issue for Christians. Some of the church even became corrupted and used guilt to extract money for pardon and forgiveness (the indulgences that Luther protested against).

Like many others, Martin Luther labored under the heavy burden of guilt. For him, God was to be feared, not loved. During a prolonged reading of Romans, he made a critical discovery: that God is not only just (condemning the sinner as unrighteous) but also the justifier (making the sinner righteous). Luther discovered that Paul was proclaiming that all who would put their faith and trust in Christ were made right with God. We are justified, he declared, by faith alone through grace, not by any works, by which he meant the penitential system of the church. For Luther, this was the key to the gospel. It was a singularly revolutionary moment in the life of the church. This recovery of a dormant doctrine literally set Europe ablaze.

Today this great truth of the gospel is as true as ever before. But in a post-Christendom culture no longer dominated by guilt, can we assume that justification by faith answers all the problems of sin as effectively as it did five centuries ago? Dustin ran into a wall because he was thinking of the gospel within a fifteenth-century mind-set. Dustin may have been sitting in Starbucks, but his mind and soul were stuck in the world of Martin Luther, where personal sin before a Holy God was the all-consuming problem.[2] Being able to answer the question, "Will I be forgiven by a just God when I die?" did not speak into the reality of the brokenness of sin in that moment in Starbucks.

Dustin was equipped with a (personal) "plan of salvation" when what he really needed was a robust (communal) "story of salvation."[3] As Scot

McKnight outlines in his book *King Jesus Gospel*, a "plan of salvation" focuses on the personal moral aspects of sin, offers Christ as the solution, and pleads for a "faith" decision to trust Jesus for forgiveness when we die and face God the Judge.[4] We do not want to deny this part of salvation in Jesus, but it is only a part of the story of salvation. Sin is also the destruction of community, between God and humanity and within humanity.[5] It results in both personal and social brokenness. Sin brings darkness, isolation, and death. The gospel proclaims good news over all these ills. What Dustin needed in that Starbucks, what we all need today, is a bigger gospel.

Bigger Than "Not Burning"

Remember Richard from an earlier signpost? He was the man who was falling behind in rent because he couldn't keep his violent temper in check and kept losing his job. It was also normal for him to live in unreconciled relationships. It seemed he preferred it that way. Once the two of us had a meeting with Richard that gave us a window into his lopsided view of the gospel. He was discussing his problem of keeping a job, blaming his employers for being "idiots." He told us that he could get so mad at his bosses that he just wanted to beat them up. The only thing that kept him from doing it, he said, was that he knew he was saved from hell but they were all going to burn. He said, "I just flip them the finger in my mind because I know they are going to hell."

It seemed that because God loved him, he didn't need to love anyone else. In fact, he was positively excited by the prospect of his antagonists "burning in hell." The disconnect between his understanding of being forgiven for his sins, that is, "justified by faith," and the call to forgive others and live in reconciliation and love was stunning.

When the gospel is one-sidedly associated with God forgiving our personal sins, we end up laying the groundwork for people like Richard to disconnect salvation from life with others. Conservative Protestant preaching often perpetuates this duplicitous orientation toward the gospel. As a result, the altar call (an individual response of faith to receive pardon from personal sin) is the one response to the gospel we know. When this happens, faith in Jesus becomes disconnected from community with others. And when we are faced with those suffering in alienated and abusive relationships, speaking of personal sin before an angry God is not good news.

But the prodigal God chooses to enter recklessly into the sin and struggles of our everyday lives. The Son does not come as a distant judge, but as one who is reestablishing a kingdom of renewal, reconciliation, and blessing. The gospel that only addresses a person's guilt before a detached

God is not prodigal enough. The entire person, the entire human existence, is being renewed in what God has done in Jesus Christ.

A Way of Life in God's Kingdom

Dustin needed a bigger gospel in order to address the many-sided brokenness of sin: spiritual separation from God, relational alienation from others, physical and emotional estrangement from oneself. Brian McLaren has voiced similar concerns about the Protestant conservative version of the gospel. He challenged the consensus that centers salvation on the substitutionary view of atonement—the idea that Jesus died to take our punishment on the cross, thereby giving us a pardon from or forgiveness for sin. That version, he claimed, often makes the gospel into a selfish and trivialized transaction with God. It leads to the Christian becoming preoccupied with the afterlife and treating day-to-day living as an afterthought. McLaren has called for a return to the forgotten (or ignored) message of Jesus in the gospels: "the kingdom of God has begun."[6] For McLaren, Jesus brings a new way of life with God in God's kingdom. By following in the way of Jesus, we too can move into what God is doing for justice, peace, and renewal in the world.

McLaren makes the kingdom of God central to the gospel. He helps us all gain a deeper understanding of what God is doing in Jesus Christ. But there's a subtle danger here as well: McLaren is prone to reducing the kingdom of God to the practice of following Jesus as our model. Whenever we do this, we open ourselves up to making God's mission into something we must do. Even if we seek the Spirit to "help" us in the same way Jesus did, the Spirit can become something we do (or access) as well. And so if we're not careful, building the kingdom of God, bringing peace and renewal, and overcoming sin become our task, our job, and our mission. The kingdom is no longer the gospel; it is a new legalism.

Separating Kingdom and Cross

Imagine Dustin telling his friend at Starbucks that if she would just follow Jesus, she can help build a renewed society of justice and peace. Although she is hurting and depressed, suffering the brutal effects of sin all around her, now she hears that the gospel is calling her to go out and seek peace and justice for all! Surely this is going to further overwhelm an already overwhelmed person.

Talking about Jesus as merely a new way of life can sound like a distant promise to those already in the throes of sorrow. It can easily sound like another exhausting self-help method. The problem is not in seeking peace and justice. The problem is becoming convinced (and telling others) that we are the ones who do it. Being told, while in the midst of despair, that if we would just act like Jesus, then everything would be better in the world is like trying to teach someone to swim while he or she is drowning. Instead, this person needs to hear that Jesus has saved and is saving him or her from (drowning in) sin.

The question, then, is whether God has come to us only to reinvigorate our imaginations toward a better world. Has God walked among us merely so that we could learn to implement plans for a more just society? If you are already socially aware and engaged in activism, then this is compelling. If you are frustrated with a church locked up in a private religion without caring for the public world, this is convincing. But if you are already among the lowly, oppressed, and downtrodden, emphasizing the kingdom of God as a social strategy feels like just another burden to bear.

What we need is a radical encounter with God's kingdom breaking into our lives. We need to experience relationships being rearranged, brokenness being healed, and evil structures being brought down in and around us. We need to see that Jesus conquers the addictions of sin (be them chemical or relational) and that God is at work in the darkest places because God has already been to those places (on the cross). This is what Dustin's friend needed. This is what we need. Anything less is not prodigal enough to match the extravagant actions of God (in Jesus, by the Spirit, for the world).

Often the justification-by-faith gospel has focused entirely on the cross as the place where our personal sin is taken away. Equally often, the "kingdom of God" gospel has focused on our role as workers in establishing the kingdom. Meanwhile, the cross has been ignored as the place where God's final victory is accomplished. The prodigal gospel (of the Son sent into the far country) affirms God's victory in the cross and the resurrection as the inauguration of the kingdom, new creation, a kingdom of love and justice. Here, on the cross, God has definitively dealt with sin in such a way that not only are our sins forgiven but the power of sin and death has been overcome. The gospel holds together both the cross and the kingdom.

Signpost Six: The Gospel of the Kingdom Through the Cross

The gospel is the good news that "God has become King in Jesus Christ." In and through the victory at the cross, Jesus is now reigning over the whole world, drawing it into his salvation, including you and me.[7] In Christ, God has begun the new creation, reconciling the world, and making all things right (2 Corinthians 5:17–21).

New Testament scholar Scot McKnight makes this point by starting with 1 Corinthians 15:1–5 as the defining text for the gospel:[8]

> [1]Now, brothers, I want to remind you of the gospel I preached to you, which you received [2]and on which you have taken your stand. By this gospel you are saved, if you hold firmly to the word I preached to you. Otherwise, you have believed in vain.
> [3]For what I received I passed on to you as of first importance: that Christ died for our sins according to the Scriptures,
> [4]that he was buried,
> that he was raised on the third day according to the Scriptures,
> [5]and that he appeared to Peter, and then to the Twelve. (1 Corinthians 15:1–5 NIV)

What does this ancient expression of the gospel tell us? In a condensed fashion, it tells us the story of Jesus. It focuses on the main events of his life: Christ died for our sins, was buried, was raised, and appeared to the disciples. The gospel many of us have come to know is a three-point presentation of (1) God loves us, but (2) we are sinners, but (3) Jesus died to fix our sin problem. But here in 1 Corinthians we have a different gospel summary: (1) the death of Jesus, (2) his burial, and (3) his resurrection and appearances. As McKnight says, even in this condensed form, the gospel is not the plan of salvation (although it affects salvation); it is the story of salvation. And as N. T. Wright puts it, the gospel is the story of "how God became King" in and through the cross.[9]

But how is this the gospel? What is the good news here? How does this connect with our common ideas of salvation? Here it is helpful to look at Paul's famous letter to the Romans. As New Testament scholars like Wright and McKnight have emphasized, the story of Jesus fulfills the story of Israel. When we look at the first five chapters of Romans, we notice Paul thinking through the same story of scripture from the last signpost, but now in reverse, going from David to Israel to Abraham and back to Adam. In this process, Paul reveals how kingdom and cross fit together.

Paul opens Romans in 1:2–4 with a statement of the gospel. He tells us how he was set apart for the gospel of God (v. 1), which was promised through the Scriptures (v. 2). And what is this gospel? It is that God's Son "was descended from David according to the flesh and was declared to be the Son of God with power according to the spirit of holiness by the resurrection from the dead, Jesus Christ our Lord" (vv. 3–4 NRSV). Right out of the gate, Paul is telling us that Jesus is the Messiah (the Christ), the true king of Israel of which David was a foreshadowing. Paul is gathering up the last main theme of the Old Testament story: that a king (Messiah) like David, only greater, shall come to reign over the people of God and bless the nations. And this Messiah has come in Jesus. He is not merely the king of the Jewish nation but Lord over all the nations (v. 5). This is the gospel, and it stands in direct opposition to Caesar (who also declared himself to be lord of all).

Thus, Paul's gospel is the gospel of the kingdom of God coming through Jesus, the crucified yet resurrected Messiah. In proclaiming this gospel and calling it the "power for salvation" (Romans 1:16–17), Paul is proclaiming both the kingdom and the cross.[10] Jesus, through the cross, has fulfilled Israel's hopes for the (Davidic) kingdom, albeit in ways they did not expect.

Jesus came to fulfill Israel's hope because Israel had failed in its mission to be a blessing to all nations. This is Paul's argument throughout Romans 1:19–3:20. Instead of being part of the solution, Israel had become part of the problem (just as Adam did).

If Israel failed, does that mean that God's plan has failed? Is God going to renege on the promises to Israel? And if so, does this mean God is unfaithful and unrighteous (Romans 3:1–5)?

The answer is that in Jesus, God has been faithful to the promises to Israel while at the same time dealing with the sins of Israel and the whole world. God is faithful to Israel because Jesus, as the Messiah, is the faithful Israelite who does what Israel was supposed to do. In other words, the righteousness of God is revealed through the faithfulness of Jesus. This is the whole point of Romans 3:21–22:

> But now the *righteousness of God* has been manifested apart from the law, although the Law and the Prophets bear witness to it—the *righteousness of God* through the faithfulness of Jesus Christ for all who believe. (ESV; emphasis added)

As N.T. Wright explains it, "what was lacking . . . was *faithfulness* on the part of Israel . . . a faithfulness to God and his covenant purposes that would enable Israel to live up to its calling as the light to the dark world." Therefore, to fix this problem and remain faithful to Israel, "God's righteousness is unveiled *through the faithfulness of Jesus the Messiah* on the one hand, and for *the benefit of all who believe* on the other."[11] This is the gospel; God has become King in Jesus. Jesus, the Messiah, has done faithfully all that Israel could not do and now has begun the salvation of the whole world. The kingdom has begun.

Jesus is the faithful Israelite because his death is an act of faithfulness to God's covenant with Israel. In Romans 3:24–26, Paul piles on the language of God's covenant faithfulness through justification (a legal word about declaring righteousness), redemption (a military word about freedom referring to the exodus), and propitiation (a sacrificial word about forgiveness referring to the "mercy seat"). In these short, compact, and complex verses, Paul explains how the righteousness of God is demonstrated in Jesus to fulfill the calling and mission of Israel.[12]

As we keep moving backward in Israel's story, we remember this calling and mission was first given to Abraham, which is exactly where Paul turns next in chapter 4. If the blessings of God were to flow to and through Abraham's family, then how do we get to be part of his covenant family? Through faith. As Wright says, the faith of Abraham was a *"sign of a genuine humanity, responding out of total human weakness and helplessness to the grace and power of God, and thus giving God the glory."*[13] Through a faith like Abraham's, we enter the family of faith, which is really to enter the true humanity God always intended. And the fulfillment of these promises to Abraham ultimately solves the problem of Adam (which was the plan all along).

And so all of this brings us back to the beginning with Adam, the focus of Romans 5. In Adam, we finally see how kingdom and cross unite. The problem of Adam, the problem in us all, is that sin and death reign (Roman 5:12,14). In other words, sin and death have their own kingdom. Paul reminds us that the kingdom of death comes through Adam (physically, socially, and spiritually). But now, through Jesus, comes a kingdom of grace (God's blessings toward us) that brings life (5:21). This kingdom of life and grace comes not just because Jesus is a good example of "kingdom love," but because although we were still sinners, Christ died for us (5:8). All this comes through the Lord Jesus Christ, in whose death and suffering God has overcome sin and death.

It is telling that Paul uses the phrase "Lord Jesus Christ" here in chapter 5. He hasn't used that title since the first chapter, but now he uses it three times (vv. 1, 11, 21). Only when Paul has reached back to Adam and shown how Jesus overcomes the kingdom of sin and death by bringing peace and reconciliation does Paul again remind us that Jesus, the Messiah, is Lord. It would be safe to say that when Paul says "Lord Jesus Christ," he is uniting the entire story of the Bible. "Jesus" names the particular human person (human like we are all human) who is also the "Christ," or Messiah, of Israel through whom the blessings of God flow to the world. Because of God's work in the Messiah, this Jesus is "Lord" of the whole world, bringing the kingdom of grace and life Adam was supposed to do. In all these ways, Jesus is the second Adam, the new beginning.

The gospel is the good news that in Jesus, God has fulfilled the story of Israel for the nations. God is now reigning over the whole world, making the world right. In the victory of the cross, he now rules over all sin, death, and evil. Wherever his rule is extended, the world is reordered and restored. In Christ, the promised blessings through Israel are now making their way to all nations. And in this way, God is making all things right.

On-Ramps into This Kingdom

At the end of a traditional evangelical gospel presentations, we often ask, "Have you made a decision to receive Christ as your personal Savior and Lord?" It has been the one question we thought everyone needed to answer. But now that we see the gospel in the cosmic terms of God "making all things right," we need a new question. We need a new way to invite people into God's good news. We should be asking something like, "Have you entered the salvation already begun in Jesus Christ that God is working for the sake of the whole world?" Of course, how we ask that question, how we invite people into this new world, is different for every person and situation we find ourselves in. And that is the point. This is the prodigal nature of the gospel itself. We have moved quite a distance from that one simple gospel question Dustin hesitated to ask at that Starbucks. We have moved from, "Have you asked Jesus into your heart?" to, "Have you entered God's kingdom with your life, your circumstances, your very soul?"

But will this work? We admit we have found it difficult to do this kind of evangelism at Life on the Vine. We had deconstructed the former "evangelism" for all its theological and contextual problems, but we had offered no way forward. We decided therefore to just sit down and chat with all interested people about what it meant to proclaim the gospel in our culture with the people in our daily lives. We met for about eight Sundays at 9:00 a.m. to talk, study, and pray. We listened to stories, analyzed our culture, and searched the Scriptures. After several weeks, we discerned four central ways of proclaiming the gospel for our culture in the northwest suburbs of Chicago. We called these "on-ramps to the kingdom."

ON-RAMP 1: "GOD IS RECONCILING YOU IN ALL YOUR RELATIONSHIPS" Around us we see enormous isolation: relationships that are disconnected, broken, or abusive. We see it every day in families, marriages, and friendships where one has sinned against another and alienation reigns. So we talked about how, if we are no longer enemies of God but are now reconciled through Jesus, we are called to be ambassadors of reconciliation (2 Corinthians 5:17–21). We must therefore proclaim into people's lives, when the occasion arises and the Spirit prompts, that God is at work reconciling all relationships, including our relationships, in Jesus Christ. Sometimes this means calling one another to receive forgiveness in Christ, and sometime it is a call to ask for forgiveness. Sometimes it is seeking reconciliation between businesses or political organizations that have done harm to people in a neighborhood— repairing wrongs done. Through this, we are entering into the righteousness of God, restoring relationships. This on-ramp into the kingdom focuses on reconciliation between people, inviting all those around us into right relationships. This requires the cross and the kingdom. If the invitation is accepted, people enter the kingdom, and this salvation spreads into all areas of their lives.

ON-RAMP 2: "GOD IS AT WORK" Everywhere around us is busyness and emptiness. Many are losing faith in the American dream. We have failed at a job, a marriage, personal or moral health. We are financially trapped. We have no vision for the future. In response, we can proclaim that Jesus is Lord and at work renewing all things—making a new creation (2 Corinthians 5:17). As we listen, we can point to places where by the Spirit, we see God at work. We can proclaim the gospel: Jesus is Lord and King over that place or person bringing his purposes into being. We need to help people see that God is at work in this job situation, or this marital strife, or this financial breakdown. God is taking us somewhere. We must learn to ask, "What is God saying to you? What is God doing?" and believe that God is really at work, taking us somewhere, building the kingdom. This on-ramp into the kingdom asks, "Can you take steps of faith and obedience in response to what God is doing? Can you enter in?" Again, if the invitation is accepted, people enter the kingdom, and this salvation spreads into all areas of their lives.

ON-RAMP 3: "GOD HAS PUT THE POWER OF SIN TO DEATH AND IS CALLING YOU INTO LIFE" Our culture is a place of addictions. People find themselves powerless, trapped, and overwhelmed. They ask if things will ever change and believe they never will. The gospel is that Jesus has defeated the powers of sin and death. The kingdom of death (the first Adam) is crumbling, and the kingdom of life (the second Adam) is coming. Jesus reigns in victory over the powers that enslave us, be it addiction or abuse. We must learn to invite one another to put these desires to death on the cross with him in order that new life might be resurrected in and out of us. We must call each other out of the evil powers of lies and falsehood by asking, "Can you enter in?" Again, if the invitation is accepted, people enter the kingdom, and this salvation spreads into all areas of their lives.

ON-RAMP 4: "GOD IS CALLING YOU INTO MISSION" Our neighborhoods often lack purpose. We work sixty or seventy hours a week, have nice things, and yet our lives feel empty. Or if we're younger, we have none of these things and find the pursuit of them empty.

At the Vine, we thought it important to proclaim God's mission in these cases among us and around us. The great mission of God is to bring the whole world to God's own righteousness, justice, new creation, and reconciliation. God is already at work doing these things. Let us then proclaim this reality among us and invite those around us into God's mission, even if they have yet to recognize God in their lives. Some might not yet even fully know or trust God in Jesus Christ. Nonetheless, there is a point of entry in the proclamation that over all the injustice, hate, and emptiness in the world, God is at work to redeem it all. So we issue the invitation: come discover it with us; join us in meeting with the poor. If the invitation is accepted, people enter the kingdom, and this salvation spreads into all areas of their lives.

There are numerous variations of these on-ramps. And we must never forget the most familiar on-ramp into the kingdom of them all: *the forgiveness offered in Christ's work on the cross from the guilt and shame of sin. The gospel still includes the fact that God is at work in making all things right, and our guilt and sin before a just and righteous God are forgiven in Christ. This is inextricably part of the gospel that Jesus is King.* Yet we must see that the gospel of Jesus Christ is multifaceted and there is no limit to the ways we live and proclaim the gospel in and through our lives to others.

Beyond Starbucks

It is impossible to know precisely what Dustin should have said to Sarah at the Starbucks that day. We can imagine Dustin listening intently, being patient and present. We can imagine (indeed, we believe) the Spirit prompting Dustin to say something, pressing into this issue or that question. When the time was right, we can imagine Dustin sharing how God's kingdom had broken into his life, or exploring with Sarah how God might be breaking into her life. If and when she could hear it, we can imagine Dustin saying clearly, "Jesus is Lord here in this circumstance. He's working for your flourishing in his kingdom. Can you enter in?" There's no way to know when or how such a gospel moment might take shape.[14] But no matter what Dustin might have said, we believe the Spirit is already working to land Sarah's life firmly in the gospel. There is no script for this, no checklist of scriptures or spiritual laws to cover, just Dustin's story intersecting with Sarah's story through proclaiming the gospel story of Jesus guided by the wisdom of the Spirit.

This signpost must take us beyond being "justified by faith" before God. And it must take us beyond the "kingdom way" of God in the world. Signpost 6 points us into new territory that is the very center of the world's hurting and lost places. Here we are freed to proclaim that Jesus, the crucified and risen Messiah, is Lord. Here Jesus comes into our dirty, confused, and troubled lives and seeks to establish his kingdom of life through the Spirit. In a very real sense (which the gospels vividly portray and we looked at in signpost 2), Jesus invades the world of darkness, sin, and death and is setting the world free.

But if people like Dustin go out individually, how will people understand reconciliation having never seen it concretely at work among people? If we go out individually, how will other people see forgiveness enacted before them? Reconciliation, forgiveness, and peace are things that you cannot encounter as a concept. Nor can you pass them along to someone else entirely by yourself. These ideas need context and must come to life among real people. We must therefore live the gospel in communities that share and live the kingdom of God together. Every journey into the gospel is a journey in and through communities of the kingdom. And this is where we go next on the prodigal journey.

CHURCH

IN KINGDOM COMMUNITIES: THE JOURNEY
AS THE BODY OF CHRIST INTO THE WORLD

FOR MY WIFE, CYD, AND ME (Geoff), everything we had been thinking about church changed halfway through seminary. We were thoroughly dissatisfied with the church we had been attending, but it wasn't just that church; it was church in general. So we began looking for a new one. We wanted more than just a church to attend, more than just a couple new programs. We wanted to actually believe in what was happening, believe that it (that they, the people) was actually there to be a part of God's mission rather than just receive a nice sermon and sit comfortably with settled answers. We were not looking for a place to *go* on Sundays but a people to be with all week long (in mission). We longed for community. In retrospect, we did not really know what we were looking for. We just hoped we would know it when we found it. After six months we were still looking.

Then it happened. Grace. Sovereignty. Providence. Luck? Our upstairs neighbors, seminarians who were also looking for a church, told us they had visited a new little church that Sunday. They had gotten a flyer in the mail, decided they would check it out, and they loved it. Grabbing the flyer, I scanned the sales pitch. It looked horrible. The graphics were just one step better than clip art. The fonts and spacing were bad. And the ink was running (away from the graphics, I think). It was made on the cheap, and I wasn't impressed. Still, I read on. The flyer said the church was centered on four activities or emphases, but I remember only the last one: "Evangelism: Invite someone over for a meal." Not a program, not a packaged message, just a meal: that was all I needed to read. The suggestion that evangelism could be as simple as hospitality struck a chord with us. It spoke to our need to connect with others rather than be anonymous individuals; the reality that evangelism is about relationships, not just information; and community being the center of God's mission. We were sold.

Once we started attending services, we noticed another strong emphasis, but one that was not on the flyer. This little church made a big deal about the Lord's Table (or Communion, or the Eucharist, depending on your background). I had been raised in a typical evangelical community where the Lord's Table was purely incidental—something you did at the end of the service. With a piece of wafer and a cup of juice, you took five minutes (with accompanied music) to remember what God had done for you through Jesus's death (the resurrection was often forgotten). When I was a kid, Communion felt to me merely like an object lesson (ordained by God of course). But at this little church, celebrating Communion actually did something to us. They would say things like, "God's kingdom flows out from the table," or, "At our Lord's Table the kingdom comes to us and the world." It appeared as if they believed that Jesus was actually doing something in and through us when we practiced Communion.

This little church believed that Jesus was welcoming us at his table. I was learning that the pastor is not the host at that table. It is Jesus who extends hospitality to us, who welcomes sinners and embraces the downcast. After a couple of months, I finally realized that at the Lord's Table, I was receiving the gospel again, that I was being evangelized again. This hospitality enabled us to go out and evangelize others, not through slick programs or clever presentations but through sharing a meal, just as Jesus had done with the disciples and just as he was still doing through his table. That little church was Life on the Vine.

In the fourth signpost, we saw that *witness* refers to someone's entire way of life—a way of life that embodies (makes visible in the flesh) the reality of God's kingdom in the world. Christians live as witnesses when our lives exhibit the reality that Jesus is the Lord who is bringing God's kingdom. This way of life is shaped around the story of Scripture (signpost 5) and centered on the gospel (signpost 6). But this way of life is not an individual activity or accomplishment: it is something expressed in social relationships and inevitably shapes all Christians into communities of God's kingdom.

The prodigal journey into the far country cannot be traveled in isolation, undertaken for our individual benefit. And so the seventh signpost points us toward the journey into church as the inescapable place of community with Christ. This journey reveals that our very life together is the sign that God's kingdom has entered into the far country.

Does this mean the church owns the kingdom? Does this mean the church is identical to the kingdom? Many will rightfully resist. "No way!" they say. "The kingdom is not the church because the kingdom is bigger than the church." Others will simply claim, "The church is not the kingdom because the kingdom has not yet fully come." Both sides know well the (colonialist) mistakes of the Western church when the church claimed to possess the kingdom, and they worry about making the church too central to the mission of God. And yet all previous signposts point to the conclusion that local communities are where God's kingdom will be found. Our life together reveals the prodigal life of God to the world. How do we inhabit this kingdom without falling into the mistakes of the past?

The Mission of Proclamation?

I (Dave) have been in men's groups for years. Typically we gather midweek to submit together to the Holy Spirit's presence in prayer and discernment. Amid our struggles, our work, and even our sins, we discern the kingdom and God's victory in and among our lives. In a group I was in a few years ago, one of the members revealed to the rest of us that he had no passion for God. Greg said he felt disconnected from God and saw no reason to go to church. He asked me why I go to church. I told him (among other things) I go to the weekly gathering for the Lord's Table where I encounter Christ. I connect with Jesus's offer of forgiveness and renewal in his person and work laid out there at the table. The table, I said, profoundly shapes me each week into my relationship with God and to God's work in and around me. Meeting Jesus there changes the way I relate to everyone, especially fellow Christians like him. Jesus's real presence makes present his kingdom. Greg wasn't convinced. He said, "That sounds like hocus-pocus."

It's not all that surprising that Greg might respond that way given our culture and its preoccupations. If you ask me, he didn't see how being part of a people is part of what God is doing in the world. He wasn't seeing how what happens between us and among us is an anticipation of kingdom life with God.

Kevin DeYoung and Greg Gilbert in their recent book, *What Is the Mission of the Church?* remind us that the true worship of God shapes us into God's mission for the world. Much like the famous Baptist pastor John Piper, who said "worship is the fuel and goal of missions,"

DeYoung and Gilbert teach us that the worship of God is the necessary precedent to mission.[1] They say that "the mission of the church is to go into the world and make disciples by declaring the gospel of Jesus Christ in the power of the Spirit and gathering these disciples into churches, *that they might worship the Lord and obey his commands* now and in eternity to the glory of the Father."[2] There is no mission apart from the worship and love of God that drives our passion and desire and to which all missions must lead. This is something that Greg needed to hear.

DeYoung and Gilbert also rightly tell us that the church is a sign of the kingdom.[3] Yet they caution us at this point: "The creation of the new heavens and the new earth happens when and only when King Jesus returns in glory, and not before." They warn believers against a false and "discouraging optimism about just how good we should expect to be able to make the world."[4] We should certainly strive to participate in bringing justice to God's creation, but we ourselves can never bring the kingdom.

For DeYoung and Gilbert, the key question for understanding the Bible in the present is not the kingdom. It is, "*How can hopelessly rebellious, sinful people live in the presence of a perfectly just and righteous God?*"[5] For them, from Adam to Abraham, from Moses to David to Jesus, the primary focus is the sacrificial system God puts in place to forgive sins. They acknowledge that the Bible does emphasize the coming king of Israel, which Christ will ultimately fulfill later.[6] But for them, this is the wide-angle-lens gospel, which they label the "gospel of the kingdom." The zoom-lens gospel is "the gospel of the cross" and the sacrificial system.[7] According to DeYoung and Gilbert, the "gospel of the kingdom" is by and large limited to the future, and the "gospel of the cross" is central for the church today. We therefore ought to keep to the main thing: the preaching of personal salvation in Jesus. Individuals in the present can receive and live into the promises of God's kingdom now, but the reign of God over the world is only for the future.

For us, the problem lies in what this view does to the gospel, witness, and the church. The gospel becomes about individual status before God, witness becomes limited to verbal proclamation, and the church becomes a collection of individuals who can get the right information about salvation in order to believe and follow. These believers then have a job to do: give this information about salvation to others. God's mission becomes something we do. The gospel becomes secret information. This approach to gospel, Scripture, and mission sequesters the kingdom of God to the interiority of our hearts. It can quickly turn defensive because it is based on knowing the right information. And because this Christianity focuses on our personal status with God, it can devolve into "being about me" and become narcissistic. For all these reasons, we suggest that DeYoung and Gilbert eventually lead us away from the prodigal way of life of the Son that leads us into the far country.

Our hypothesis is that Greg, in the story at the start of this chapter, is similar to DeYoung and Gilbert. He sees the church as a place where he goes to "get something" that will help him be a better Christian. As a result, when he is either not motivated to be a better Christian or decides the church isn't "giving him something he needs to be a better Christian," he chooses not to attend services.

And so we must ask DeYoung and Gilbert, Is the church only a place for proclamation to or teaching individuals? Is it only a training institution where individuals prepare to go out into the world and be better Christians, better evangelists, or is it something more? Is the church more prodigal than that? Does the church itself cross boundaries to participate in the mission of God?

The Mission of Transformation?

Once, on a trip through Buffalo, New York, I (Dave) stopped for a visit with my friend Austin who was founding a new church. This church was not a church in the traditional sense: it was in essence a large coffee house at the edge of a troubled urban downtown district. If there was ever a church that crossed boundaries, this was it.

Over a cup of coffee, Austin described to me how this place would become a "third space." Not a church, not a place of work, this would be a space where people could meet and develop relationships unencumbered by an agenda. Out of this space, this new church would offer a food pantry for the poor, computer tutoring to help the homeless and others in need develop the necessary skills to get a job, and counseling for domestic abuse. There would be times for local musicians and artists to share their work. And there would be a Sunday evening gathering for all the Christians participating in this work.

Fascinated by what Austin was doing, I probed further as to how this work was being supported. He had government grants, and some churches in the area were donating support. I asked if anyone who participated lived in or near the neighborhood. He said, "Just a few." I then asked what I thought was an innocent question: "How in your opinion is this different from a social service agency?" Austin hesitated. He thought long and hard, and then he said, "Jesus!"

I pressed further on the question, but it was unclear to Austin just how Jesus was a force in organizing this coffee house. Did Jesus motivate the support gifts? Did Jesus guide those who helped and served the coffee? Was Jesus's presence there whether we knew it or not? We applaud everything Austin is doing, but is there something more going on here that makes this church a church?

Austin is an example of those who have shifted from a gospel of personal salvation to one of social transformation. He is a practical example of some streams of ecclesiology coming from people like Brian McLaren and Tony Jones. For McLaren, churches should focus on forming people who embody and communicate God's kingdom beyond isolated religious subcultures. Churches should encourage people to live "in the world as it is and for the world as it could be, as agents of transformation."[8] Agents of transformation like these would offer the world compelling examples of love-shaped lives as an alternative to the violent society in which we find ourselves.

Tony Jones understands that this transformation works far beyond the walls of the traditional church. He sees the emerging church as crossing the boundaries between church and world, tearing down the dichotomies of clergy/laity and the sacred/secular. He notes that the emerging church seeks to "sacralize the world" by seeing God at work in all areas of life and "desacralize the church" by making it one among many institutions in our society.[9]

People like McLaren and Jones push us toward an understanding of God's kingdom that looks for its presence beyond the church. But it is hard to tell just how Jesus would or should make a difference outside the church. Has the church merely become another social service institution amid the many others in the world? And if it has, how do people like Austin and his volunteers keep from burning out as they try to do some good in the world? How do we keep such an institution from becoming just another thing we do? This kind of church, we fear, becomes a "kind of spiritual gas station from which all and sundry [can] draw energy for a great variety of worthwhile projects."[10] And it eventually runs out of gas.

Too Much Kingdom? Too Little Cross?

The problem seems to be too much kingdom and too little cross. McLaren sees the gospel primarily centered on Jesus's announcement of the coming of God's peaceable kingdom. Much like N. T. Wright, he reads Paul's letter to the Romans as the announcement of how this kingdom includes both Jews and Gentiles. He examines the whole story of Scripture, from creation marred by sin, to the Exodus liberation, to the prophets foretelling the coming peaceable kingdom, all as leading to Jesus coming to "launch a new Genesis, to lead a new Exodus, and to announce, embody, and inaugurate a new kingdom as the Prince of Peace."[11] McLaren brilliantly reveals that Jesus has a social agenda beyond individual salvation from hell: establishing the peaceable kingdom. Yet McLaren's account strangely lacks a place for the cross of Christ.

At each stage of his telling of the story, McLaren seems to resist the idea that the cross and the resurrection are God's ultimate triumph over sin and death. He recognizes that the cross is the consequence of living in a violent world. Yet in his account of the cross, there is no overturning of sin or cosmic victory over evil. One wonders how God is working in the world for the kingdom. Is God merely present in all the human acts of love? Are we somehow more inspired to do these works because of Jesus? If God is working only within the natural processes of the world for some sort of "creative transformation," if the cross is one more example and less actual victory, then the church as a community of love in and for the world sounds exhausting. The church sounds like a bunch of good people trying to do good work for God.

As a way out of these problems, Jones states that "the Spirit of God is available equally everywhere and to all because God is in all things, and all things are in God." And because of this, all of "life becomes a sacrament, and all endeavors become holy."[12] But as nice as this sounds, we know (and Tony knows) that all endeavors in the world are not holy. There are activities in the world in outright rebellion against God (child pornography and Hitler come to mind). How can we discern where God is and is not (need we remind ourselves that many German Lutherans believed Hitler was on the side of God in World War II)? As we learned in the second signpost, seeing God everywhere can lead us on a wild goose chase. And as we learned in the third signpost, God's mission (*missio Dei*) works through the incarnation. In our opinion, Jones has failed to distinguish between merely asserting *that* God is working in the world and showing *how* God is working in the world. All of this leads away from a local embodied mission and thus cannot lead us into a prodigal Christianity. We need a signpost that can lead us into the concrete, grassroots struggles and pains of everyday life where God's kingdom can become visible (incarnate) among us.

Mission and the Church

Alan Hirsch and Michael Frost are two prominent spokesmen for returning the church to the center of God's mission. They resist the consumerist impulses of someone like Greg and challenge attractional modes of church that encourage people to come to church "to get something." Instead they call for the church in North America to follow the incarnational model in which God sends us into local contexts, rhythms, and languages of everyday life. These are "the forgotten ways" of Jesus and his disciples, which birthed the first mission of Christ in the world.[13] As we already discussed in signpost 3, Hirsch and Frost push us further than anyone else we have discussed toward a prodigal way of being church.

For Hirsch, Christians are to enter the world by identifying with the people around us, getting to know, understand, and live in that context. Only then, after one's Christian life has taken shape in the culture, after redemption has taken hold in our community, can the church take concrete form. As they say, "missiology precedes ecclesiology."[14] True mission, they tell us, requires that we return to "a direct and unmediated relationship" between the individual believer and Jesus in order to get to the place where Jesus can be known in each context.[15] They tell us we must "debunk the many false images" of Jesus that have existed in the church down through the ages by going to the "Wild Messiah," "back to the daring, radical, strange, wonderful, inexplicable, unstoppable, marvelous, unsettling, disturbing, caring, powerful God-Man."[16] In amazing ways, they articulate a prodigal way of understanding mission and the church.

But all this prompts a very important question: Can we really seek Jesus all by ourselves apart from the practices of the church? Hirsch and Frost think that a fresh encounter with the living Christ can overcome stale forms of church.[17] But how do we avoid interpreting Jesus (even with the Bible) according to our own image? Doesn't Frost and Hirsch's "Wild Messiah" look suspiciously like them?

We believe Hirsch and Frost could unintentionally separate us from Jesus by separating us from his ongoing body, the practices of his church, in the world. Instead we believe that Jesus has given us those practices for shaping his people in his mission. Here is where we can encounter him in his presence and authority which illumines him at work in every context.

Signpost Seven: Communities of the Kingdom

I (Dave) am a blogger. I admittedly like to provoke constructive discussions, so in summer 2011, I wrote a post entitled "Stop Funding Church Plants and Start Funding Missionaries!"[18] I argued that church planting as traditionally conceived worked only to upgrade existing forms of church and then attract already Christianized populations. The church planter often had to be financially self-sustaining in three years, forcing the planter to focus on getting "butts in the seats" on Sunday mornings. I argued that time was running out on this approach because there were fewer and fewer Christianized people who would want this kind of church. We needed to rethink church as mission in our increasingly post-Christendom cultures.

The post made quite a splash. The venerable magazine *Christianity Today* carried an article about it.[19] What seemed a rather simple idea already in practice among many church practitioners I knew caused a stir because some worried I was giving up on the very idea of church.

But nothing could have been further from the truth. What I was advocating instead was the cultivation of church as mission. I was suggesting that churches send out three or more leaders (or leader couples depending on whether they were single or married) into a neighborhood context to get jobs, live relationally, and begin the rhythms of life in Christ there. This would require a commitment to a place, humble living in a neighborhood, and going to places on the margins, not the most affluent places where large churches already exist. It would require being sent as missionaries through a discernment process at a local church.

All this means that the church does not merely have a mission (either to proclaim personal salvation or practice public service). The church is not merely the product of mission. Rather, the church is mission. In the same way that Jesus's incarnation both proclaimed and made present the kingdom of God, so too the church proclaims and makes present the in-breaking of his kingdom. The church is nothing if not local, incarnational communities practicing the kingdom.

Church Practices, Not Programs

Instead of planting a church through starting programs, we must plant ourselves in the practices given to us by Christ that have been traditionally understood as "church." These practices shape a community of people into his kingdom within a neighborhood and enable us to come together and submit ourselves to the reign of Christ in any context. By leading one another in and through these practices, we are no longer church planters. We *are* the church.

These practices are much more than organizational tools. They are the means by which Jesus's presence becomes manifest among us, changing the way we live with one another in the world. These practices— the Lord's Table, proclaiming the gospel, reconciliation, being "with" the least of these, being "with" children, the fivefold ministry, and kingdom prayer—have defined the church in the past. Unfortunately the church of the past has sometimes turned them into mere maintenance functions (or programs) for existing Christians. But as we hope to show, these inherently missional practices can be recaptured. In them, the kingdom becomes manifest visibly as a foretaste of the future. They shape us as Jesus's body in the very middle of his mission.

The Hospitality of the Table

A while back, a number of us from Life on the Vine within the same geographical proximity started to gather at my (Dave's) house on Friday nights. We gathered together first to share a meal. We decided everyone who came had to eat together around one table no matter how many came. We each shared a dish out of our abundance.

This meal became unusual. We began the meal with the leader reminding us that in Christ, we have been given a kingdom. Just as we share the forgiveness and renewal of God's salvation in Jesus Christ around the table on Sunday, so we also share the same things around this table, an extension of Christ's presence and reign. In that we share reconciliation (in his broken body) and the renewal of all things ("the new covenant in my blood"), we have a bond. In this bond, we commit ourselves to each other every time we eat as members of one Body. After the leader says these things, we all just sit together and eat, listen to each other, and talk. The time around the table was rich.

Between dessert and coffee, someone usually poses an important question. One night someone asked everyone, "Why do you come here every Friday night?" The answers were telling. Some said they long for true communion, and this is the only place they've ever found it. Others said that amid all their personal crises and struggles, this was the only place they felt they could be known. As we sat around and committed to practicing table hospitality week after week (something that was unusual in the Chicago suburbs), we realized how our relationships were being rearranged by the reign of Christ. Every night at about nine o'clock, we would gather our children (who had scattered to play) to close with prayer for our needs and the neighborhood. A revolution was beginning in a way few of us understood.

In Luke 22, Jesus inaugurates the Lord's Table, a practice all Christians are meant to observe "until he comes" (1 Corinthians 11:26). Over against the disciples' jockeying for personal position in the kingdom (Luke 22:24), Jesus declares the founding of a kingdom that arranges our relationships differently. Unlike the Gentiles, who "lord it over" their subjects, Jesus declares this shall be a kingdom where we shall *live* among one another and serve one another (v. 27). As they sit around the table, Jesus says, "And I confer on you, just as my Father has conferred on me, a kingdom, so that ye may eat and drink at my table in my kingdom" (v. 29 RSV). The kingdom was breaking in among the disciples. And the kingdom is breaking in among us whenever we come to the table. Our relationships are reorganized (as the apostle Paul spells out clearly (1 Corinthians 11:17–20). There is a foreshadowing at this table of the future table (the eschatological banquet; Luke 22:30) when "the twelve shall rule." But they shall not rule as "the pagans" do but out of the new, healed relationships of the kingdom, the completion of God's plans to bless the nations through Israel.

As we submit to this essential practice given to us by Jesus, we submit to his reign and are formed as a people under his rule. The church has always believed that in some way, Jesus is present in the eating at his table, extending again his own practice of gospel hospitality (see Luke 24:30–31). In a very real way, we experience the welcoming hospitality of Jesus ever anew in Communion.

This hospitality from which flows forgiveness, reconciliation, and renewal in the Spirit does not end here at the table on Sundays (or whenever we practice it). Rather, this hospitality extends through us into the neighborhoods on Friday nights (or whenever we gather during the week). From here it goes forth into every meal with those with whom we share this wondrous hospitality. At the table, we receive the hospitality of Jesus so that we can then turn around and extend this hospitality to the world. It could mean sharing a lawn mower, bringing a meal to a hurting person, inquiring about a neighbor in foreclosure and discerning her or his next steps in Christ, visiting the sick in the local hospital, or serving meals at the local homeless shelter. The ways that hospitality spreads are too numerous to mention, but they are part of our everyday life and if the table does not lead there, then the table is incomplete. In this way, the Lord's Table connects us with God, each other, and the world. The Lord's Table and all of the practices listed below must always integrate these three: God, church, and mission.

And so I have come to understand that whenever I eat with anyone (or share hospitality in other ways), I am in fact sharing something that is beyond me. In my local McDonald's, when I am sharing a breakfast sandwich (with no cheese or breakfast sauce) with a friend who has not had a home in three years, I am conscious of a dynamic there that is not of my own making. God is extending reconciliation and renewal in ways I might not fully understand. Countless times, through prayer or proclaiming the gospel, I have seen the kingdom's hospitality break in across the table in a McDonald's booth. I have seen simple relationships change people's lives.

For many, the Lord's Table is something we do in a church. For others, to locate church in a practice like the Lord's Table limits the church. But what we have discovered is something completely different. Once released from the shackles of the maintenance structures of the church, the Lord's Table becomes one of the ways God shapes a people into the hospitality he is offering to the whole world. What starts out on a Sunday morning or any other time with a gathering of Christians around the Lord's Table, forms a new social reality in the neighborhood. It is a foretaste of the kingdom.

Six Other Practices

The Lord's Table is just one of the essential practices. Baptism precedes all the others by initiating believers into all the practices of the kingdom. In being baptized, we are leaving the old world (or kingdoms) behind. We have died and entered "newness of life," the new order. The kingdom has begun. Baptism initiates us into the new social reality of the body of Christ that is the first sign of the new kingdom on earth.

Beyond baptism and the Lord's Table are six other practices that function in much the same way as the Lord's Table. Each of these practices, has a long history that goes back to Jesus himself and his life with the first disciples. They are practices of his reign. Each practice comes with a promise of Christ's presence being extended in a specific time and place. However, whenever these practices are used in an attempt to control or possess the power and authority of Christ, they devolve into legalism and the kingdom is lost. But when we enter these practices submitting ourselves to his Lordship (which is what these practices are), when we become humble and vulnerable in service to the King, his kingdom breaks in. These practices become tools for organizing the kingdom in the neighborhood. Here are the six other practices.

PROCLAMATION OF THE GOSPEL In Luke 10, Jesus sent his first missionaries into the towns and villages to "proclaim the gospel"—that the kingdom of God is near! The authority of the kingdom (Christ himself) is released in this activity: "Lord, even the demons submit to us in your name," the disciples declare (v. 17 NIV). Jesus's very presence extends through the disciples in this practice. So Jesus tells them, "Whoever rejects you rejects me, and whoever rejects me rejects the one who sent me" (v. 16 RSV). It is our contention that we need to develop the same regular practice of proclaiming the gospel in our gatherings and in each other's lives and then to do the same in our daily lives in our neighborhoods.

Proclamation is the act of declaring a reality (or truth) that others have yet to see (the kingdom has come!) and doing so in a way that speaks into a situation ("every town and place"; Luke 10:1 NIV). Proclaiming the gospel in this manner has become a lost practice in our churches. More and more, Sunday morning preaching has become teaching information. But when done in submission to Christ, by the authority of the Spirit (it is often called "prophecy" in the New Testament), proclamation becomes the means for Christ's authority to break in and the believer to respond in faith and enter in.

Recently I was sitting in the back yard of a neighborhood friend who is not a Christian. He was pouring out his heart about being out of work and the difficult struggle he was having. He talked about some job interviews and his fear of not being able to provide for his family. He said he kept running into an acquaintance who was a chemist in his field but was too afraid to ask him advice. I listened carefully and perceived an opening to proclaim some good news into my friend's life. I felt led to proclaim, "Jesus is Lord over even job situations and he is working in this situation." I put in an occasional "we believe . . ." to explain what all this meant. Then I asked if I could pray and submit this to God's kingdom work in his life. I asked him, "What do you think God is asking of you in this time together?"

This is proclamation. We declare humbly the reality of his Lordship at work in people's lives. It looks different in each situation (see signpost 6). We do it together in our weekly gathering when the preacher proclaims the gospel out of Scripture. But we also proclaim the gospel one to another as people of God in everyday life. And then, when the right opportunity affords, when the Spirit prompts, we do it in the neighborhood as well. Each time the gospel is proclaimed and entered into (repent and believe), the kingdom breaks in.

RECONCILIATION Jesus teaches us to come together whenever there is a sin or disagreement against someone in the community (Matthew 18:15–20). We come together not to win an argument but to submit to his Lordship and thereby to one another. And so we discover that where two or more are gathered under Christ's reign ("in his name") and agree on anything, what is bound on earth is also bound in heaven and what is loosed on earth is loosed in heaven. The very authority of heaven breaks in when we gather under the name of Jesus (v. 20). Because Christ has reconciled us to God, we are working out this reconciliation with one another under his reign. As we practice this reconciliation in our lives together, we are then able to practice it in the neighborhood, bringing Christ's in-breaking authority to broken relationships and structures where we live. In this way, the kingdom takes shape in our neighborhoods.

Recently I (Dave) had the opportunity to extend the grace of reconciliation to a divorced man in the neighborhood who had not talked with his children for many years. They had said a long time ago that they would never talk with him again. I shared again the gospel that Jesus is working for the reconciliation of all things and invited him into the process of reconciliation found in Matthew 18:15–20 and said I would be glad to facilitate. I asked him if he could share the forgiveness in Christ with his children. We began the process that week.

What was going on in the neighborhood was the same practice of reconciliation that we had learned in our church body, but it did not stop at church. It spread to all the relationships within church (even our marriages) and then to the neighborhoods. Each time it happens, Christ's presence is there. The kingdom breaks in.

BEING WITH PEOPLE ON THE FRINGES Jesus says that when you are truly present with "the least of these," you are also in his presence and this is a sign of what the kingdom looks like (Matthew 25:31–46). The fact that the people in Matthew 25 who were actually with the hungry, thirsty, and naked were surprised when the King made a big deal of their actions shows this "being with" was very much a regular relational part of their lives, not a program they did at church. We need to help people practice being with "the least of these" as part of everyday relationships, not treating them as clients or as part of other programs.

Being with people who are hurting and in need is a practice that also has been lost in the church. As we will discover in the next three signposts, the practice of being with is as much about being as doing. It is about regular relationships and a regular presence in the lives of others. We will learn more about this practice in signpost 9. In this practice, we become aware of Christ's presence and his authority. His authority breaks in and does marvelous things in people's lives. At the Vine, we practice presence by having silence at the beginning of our gatherings. We practice being with God, listening for his voice, and making ourselves available. As we do this, we are leaning into the practice of this same presence in our neighborhoods. In each instance, we relax, take all agendas off the table, listen, and pay attention in order to listen for God and discover where God is working.

BEING WITH THE CHILDREN Jesus also says that when we welcome children, when we are present with them in love and hospitality, Jesus becomes present with us. We welcome Christ's in breaking presence in that place (Matthew 18:5; 19:13–14). Jesus even makes the strong statement that only by welcoming and becoming like children can we enter the kingdom of God (18:3). This practice of being with children is a special tending to the in-breaking kingdom in our midst. When we spend time being with children, loving them, and teaching them, we in fact participate in the kingdom.

Often churches have made their children's ministries into programs. Yet when we refuse to make children into a separate program or ministry, instead inviting them into our presence, allowing them to worship with us, making space for them in our community, we find ourselves being transformed by the love of children and the things they teach us. And so more than once, we've had adults tell us how their lives were changed by being with the children on Sundays. Indeed, we see whole families changed. In the same way, we are called to enter into our neighborhoods, paying special attention to the children there. In so doing, God's love reorders people's lives. His kingdom breaks in.

THE FIVEFOLD MINISTRY AND GIFTS In Ephesians 4:7 we learn that Jesus ascends to the right hand of the Father to reign over the world. And yet he is not distant in his authority and power. Rather he offers gifts (v. 11) for equipping the church: apostles, prophets, evangelists, pastors, and teachers.[20] These are the five main equipping roles of the church. Every community needs these gifts of leadership to flourish in the kingdom. Elsewhere we learn that these gifts carry the authority of the Lord himself by the Spirit (1 Corinthians 12:3–6). When the apostle, the pastor, the teacher, the evangelist, and the prophet together function in mutual submission one to another in dependence on God (Romans 12:3,6), the authority of the Lord is made manifest in a community (1 Corinthians 12:3–6). However, anyone who uses this newly found authority selfishly for the purpose of gratifying his or her own ego loses it ("they are to sit down and be silent," 1 Corinthians 14:26–34).

We do not think that these gifts are only for the internal organization of the church. They are not to be practiced only for Christians. Rather, they are necessary for forming the kingdom in each neighborhood. Each neighborhood gathering needs to discern God's working in the giftedness of its leaders. Wherever they are practiced in submission to the King, the kingdom breaks in.

Once we had a missional community that had been meeting in a neighborhood for a year and a half, and some of its leaders were worried that they were not reaching out to their community. They had plenty of pastoring, teaching, and even prophetic ministry going on. People were growing in Christ, but they had no outreach in the community. As we looked at their leadership, it was obvious they lacked an evangelist to lead the community outward. We noticed that someone in the group who was always talking about neighbors showed leadership ability. We recommended she be put before the community to be recognized as a pastoral leader in her evangelistic gifting. This all happened rather quickly, and she was affirmed. The next time I visited this group, they were sitting at a local park pavilion having a neighborhood picnic. The evangelist was talking at a table with three other people she had never met before, and approximately fifty people were mixing together, talking about the neighborhood with people from the missional community. The kingdom was breaking in.

Each neighborhood needs leaders leading out of the fivefold gifting. The five gifted people (or it could be three people with the five gifts) help encourage and facilitate the flourishing of the rest of the gifts. In this way, Jesus's authority is set loose in the neighborhood. In bigger churches, this leadership structure must be modeled at the larger level of the church and all the way down to each local neighborhood. Leaders must act out of their recognized gifting in submission to one another at all levels of the church. There can be no pure hierarchy in the church, for this stifles the authority of the kingdom from fleshing itself out in the local places where we live.

KINGDOM PRAYER Jesus teaches us how to pray the Lord's Prayer (Matthew 6:9–13). This prayer teaches us that prayer to the Father, in Christ, through the Spirit is first and foremost about submitting our lives, circumstances, needs, wants, and struggles into God's coming kingdom ("Thy kingdom come . . ."). Prayer in this way opens spaces for the kingdom to break in as Christ enters in power, presence, and healing. Yet whenever we pray to secure our own designs, Christ's kingdom cannot be present. Presenting our own needs is certainly part of prayer, but we learn through Christ that we are to come together ("our" Father) and submit our lives, circumstances, and neighborhoods to God's incoming kingdom. We release our egos, wants, and desires and instead submit to the King and pray for his purposes and righteousness to come right here in this place, whatever that might mean. Only then do we submit our needs and wants for God's filling.

This kind of prayer goes beyond our personal prayer lives. Praying for the kingdom in this way goes to places where warfare is going on in the neighborhood, where drug trafficking, domestic violence, or other ills pervade a community. Christ reminds us that his kind of evil can be overcome only by prayer (Mark 9:14–29). So we gather to pray in the kingdom in our neighborhoods over injustice at our schools or social service agencies, over our families, jobs, and marriages. And when we gather to submit these places and problems to his kingdom, then indeed, his kingdom breaks in.

Reclaiming the Practices for Mission

These six practices, together with the Lord's Table and the founding practice of baptism, shape our life together in neighborhoods. We bring these practices as ways of entry into every situation of our everyday lives. Whether it be the local Boys and Girls Clubs, athletic competitions, public schools, engagements in global mission, local homeless shelters, hospitals, neighborhood book clubs, or other places too numerous to mention, these practices lead us into the in-breaking kingdom. This is not a shapeless church that joins in with whatever is going on in the world. It is a church that extends the presence of Christ from the times we gather in worship, to the times we gather in our homes, to the everyday interactions we have in the neighborhood. This is the church that extends the in-breaking kingdom: the prodigal church.

If these practices sound familiar, it's because we also see them in Christendom churches. Too often we know firsthand how the Lord's Table has become a quick five-minute cognitive exercise squeezed in at the end of the Sunday morning service. Rarely does it shape the way we live in our neighborhoods. We need to reclaim it as an organizing tool for the kingdom in the neighborhood.

Likewise, our preaching often looks like slick packaging of information with an application added at the end. We need to reclaim the proclamation of the gospel in the pulpit, our everyday lives, and our neighborhood conversations as an invitation into God's transformative kingdom.

In the same way, we have made "being with the least of these" and "with children" into mere programs. We have programs for the poor that make them into our clients. We have programs for our children that make their parents into customers. We need to reclaim being with the least of these as a way of life in the neighborhood where God's kingdom breaks in.

We could go on about how the fivefold ministry got organized into the more efficient (and highly overworked) senior pastor, or how kingdom prayer got organized into Wednesday night prayer meeting, or how reconciliation got organized into conflict management where the pastor-authority figure intervenes and arbitrates in a way that does not represent true reconciliation. In all of these cases, as we look back, we see how the church has managed these practices for efficiency and its own maintenance. They are no longer practices for living everyday life in our neighborhoods. Mission and kingdom were lost. The prodigality of the gospel could not take shape. We need to reclaim these practices for mission.

Becoming Communities of the Kingdom in the World

Jesus gives us these practices for the shaping of the church into God's mission. Wherever a group of people is led together into submission to Christ through these practices, a church is planted. Because of this submission in these practices, each one of these communities will necessarily be the humble, vulnerable, and incarnational expression of God coming into the world. They will extend Christ's very presence and rule into the margins. This is why John Howard Yoder calls his version of these practices social "sacraments," activities where God is especially active inhabiting the world for his rule.[21] Instead of a volunteer association sending well-trained professionals out into the world to do God's mission, communities are shaped in a way that incarnates Christ in the world for God's mission. Wherever such communities come into being, sin is overcome, evil is defeated, and death no longer holds power. The kingdom is breaking in.

This is what witness looks like, and we contend that these communities will engage the most difficult issues of our day. They will not shrink back. This is prodigal church. Let us now turn to some of these issues—sexual abuse and confusion, injustice, and religious pluralism—and explore where the signposts take us now.

PRODIGAL RELATIONSHIPS

WITH OUR BROKENNESS: THE JOURNEY
TOWARD SEXUAL REDEMPTION

IN NORTH AMERICA, ALTERNATIVE sexual lifestyles are a fact of everyday life. Many are confused by various gender roles and alternative sexualities. The casual crossing of sexual boundaries is now everywhere. And sadly, sexual abuse is a fact of everyday life. Yet God has come recklessly into the far country to heal, renew, and redeem, and so we must follow God into places of hurt, confusion, and brokenness.

Among Christians in North America, the issue of same-sex sexual relations has become the test case for what kind of Christian a person is. "Are you an evangelical who hates gays?" one side asks. "You must be a progressive who stands for nothing," the other side responds. No matter what position you take, you are immediately shoved into one of these two groups and ostracized by the other.

Of course, this happens beyond the issue of same-sex relations. Christians have become a people with whom it is unsafe to talk about any sexual issues. Amid the sexualized cultures of North America, we have become an inhospitable and dysfunctional people.

All this is tragic because most everyone we know has a family member (or *is* this person) who has come out as gay or lesbian or is struggling to make sense of a same-sex attraction. Many more are recovering from sexual abuse or struggling with some form of sexual addiction. Once we open our eyes to these realities close to home, it is no longer easy to make grand pronouncements or possible to ignore these complex issues.

The Case of the Young Seminarian

A few years ago I (Dave) read a compelling story of a self-described "pedophile" on the website of my friend Drew Marshall. Drew, a radio talk show host in Toronto, broadcasts his show nationally in Canada on Christian radio. A young man, struggling with pedophiliac desires, wrote him a letter. Drew rarely shies away from controversy, so he put the letter on his website and asked his audience what they would do. The letter reveals the situation of everyone and anyone who struggles with a sexual issue of any kind (not just pedophilia) in the church. Here it is:

> I am a 23 year old guy and a seminary student. For as long as I can remember I have felt called by God to enter the ministry. Growing up in a home where my father was an abusive alcoholic who verbally and emotionally abused my mother and his 3 children has given me a deep empathy for those families who struggle with painful secrets like mine has. Having been an overweight kid who was picked on at school and who was abused emotionally, physically and sexually in the home, it has given me a deep sense of compassion for those with pain that runs deep. Because of my past, the ministry that I have chosen to focus on is pastoral counseling. After earning my honors BSW [bachelor of social work] I selected an MDIV [master of divinity] program that offered a counseling focus.
>
> Over the summer I am required (as a part of the program) to work at a child/youth camp, working with young people between the ages of 6 and 16. The thing that gives me pause, is that I am a pedophile. I am a celibate pedophile. For as long as I can remember, I have been attracted to young children. I have thought about asking for another work assignment this summer, working with adults for example. However this would only delay the problem, since one of the requirements of graduation from the MDIV is that one of the placements be with children and youth.
>
> While my therapist and I are confident in my commitment to celibacy in regards to my pedophilia, I find that I struggle with increased lust and temptation when I am around children. Given that pedophilia is such a hated and maligned condition, which I am thoroughly disgusted with as well, when I am feeling lust and temptation I go on extreme guilt/shame cycles. I hate myself for struggling with these urges, and often drown this out with either food or booze . . .

I guess my question is, what should I do? Can I be an effective minister with these urges? Can I be a celibate pedophile? I feel so alone and isolated with this. I would love to have friends that I can share this secret shame with, but I am wondering if I have been cursed with the one sin/condition that cannot be shared. Should I live in the light, or lie my way into ministry? I am confused and doubting the path I have felt called to. Help![1]

"Your work is my work" is a common saying in our spiritual formation groups at Life on the Vine. This man's dilemma is that of everyone who seeks sexual redemption in Christ: "his work is our work" in that we all have desires that we do not know what to do with; "his work is our work" when we do not understand how these desires got there or what they mean; "his work is our work" when we are tempted to turn to destructive behavior; "his work is our work" when we are confused and isolated in our struggle, unable to talk about our sexual issues for fear of drawing attention to ourselves. And when we're judged by people who don't know anything about what we're going through, who have never experienced any of the things we are experiencing, it is easy to deny and abuse all over again. And so this person is every man and woman who sits in the church pew dealing with a sexual issue in his or her life.

The bottom line, then, is how we—the local church—are to receive this pedophilia-oriented person into our community of the kingdom. How do we nurture a discipleship together toward God's redemption of all things sexual? The pedophile is the "least of these" in our society, the most despised among us, and yet God has come to redeem him or her. How we engage this person is a test case for how we will engage everyone.

We Need a Place That Is Safe

We need a place where all people can come and feel safe, however and wherever they are in their sexual lives, where we can gather together in Christ's kingdom to give witness to and discern the sexual redemption God is working in and through Jesus. This place would invite anyone who seeks the work of redemption and renewal in their lives no matter the sexual struggle or concern. In this place, we would come willing to mutually submit to the authority of the Risen Lord as he speaks through scripture, guided by the gifts of the Spirit that are active in his people. The practices described in signpost 7 would be lived out (contextually) in this place. In the midst of such a place, we submit all our desires (whatever they are) to the way of cross and resurrection. But above all, this place would have to be safe.

This is what the local church should be: the place of Christ's in-breaking authority, the foretaste of God's kingdom, an incarnational community, the place where we gather to participate in God's healing and renewal of all things sexual. But, sadly, the church has rarely been a safe place to talk about sexual issues, and we have offered no ways of orienting our sexual drives and desires toward created purposes. We just give out decrees and expect people to get in line. And so the church has often left everyone in the pedophile's shoes (or with any other sexual issue) in his or her own silence. It would have been easier if they had never been part of a church (and so many leave quickly and angrily). And since the church is unsafe for its own people regarding sexual issues, the rest of the world is even more repulsed. In many ways, in the midst of the greatest sexual upheaval in our history, North America has been left without a witness to what God has done in Christ Jesus for the sexual redemption of us all.

A Missionary Point of View

The church's current situation with regard to sexuality reminds us of the experiences of nineteenth- and twentieth-century Western missionaries in Africa. When missionaries from the West arrived in Africa, they discovered that polygamy was deeply entrenched in some of the cultures where the gospel was taking root. In response, these missionaries took colonialist (or Christendom) postures and made quick and decisive judgments: they quickly imposed orders that they believed would rectify the problem and required married male Christian converts to disengage from all wives except one.[2] This left many women and children out on the street. In some cases, entire villages became unraveled because nothing replaced the social structures of polygamy. Many children starved, and many women were forced into prostitution. Rather than being known for the gospel, local churches became known for breaking up families. Ironically, people began to see the Christian faith as in favor of divorce. Try as they might, these missionaries had no cultural language or social capital to communicate God's purposes for marriage and sex through monogamous relationships. They hadn't been present in these contexts long enough to communicate in the culture's own terms.

As a result, miscommunication went in both directions. Not only did the Africans not understand the profound meanings at the core of Christian marriage; there were also larger African social meanings and nuances related to the practice of polygamy that the Christian workers completely missed with their "Western" solutions. In some parts of Africa, women were owned and therefore not viewed as mutual complementary partners in a God-ordained union. Simply disbanding multiple wives bypassed this important issue entirely and did nothing to change the debasement of women. In fact, polygamy in Africa was also a way for women to enter a household when there was a perpetual shortage of men. Given the context, divorcing every wife but one (as the missionaries taught) lent a cavalier attitude toward the marital covenant and created an underclass of divorced women without the means to support themselves. Imposing a sexual behavioral requirement on new Christians completely missed the redemption that God was truly working in that people.

And so despite there not being a single doubt that monogamy was God's intent for the Christian life, many mission organizations (including our own denomination, Christian and Missionary Alliance) retracted their practice of demanding monogamy of all baptized Christians. Instead, they had to navigate these difficult waters even while holding on to their convictions. They needed to be present and allow time for God, through the Spirit, to work sanctification in the churches. Eventually and unpredictably, sexual redemption did erupt in communities that submitted their lives to the Lordship of Christ. Today we desperately need to apply this lesson in other settings.

Let's Back Up a Bit

Can we learn from the past mistakes of these missionaries? Is it possible to open up a space for the in-breaking of the kingdom amid the sexual issues of our day and make way for sexual sanctification and healing over time? Is such a safe place even possible within the church? What has kept Christians from being this kind of place in the world? To get at such questions, let's back up to 2006.

In 2006, Brian McLaren wrote a post on *Christianity Today*'s "Out of Ur" blog entitled "Brian McLaren on the Homosexual Question: Finding a Pastoral Response." This post was an excerpt from an article Brian wrote in *Leadership Journal*. The readers of both the blog and the publication were decidedly conservative Protestants. Brian suggested in this post, in regard to the same-sex sexual relations debate, that "we need a five-year moratorium on making pronouncements." In essence he asked the church to take a five-year break from making any specific judgments on the issue and instead use this time in a different way:

> [to] practice prayerful Christian dialogue, listening respectfully, dis-
> agreeing agreeably. When decisions need to be made, they'll be admit-
> tedly provisional. We'll keep our ears attuned to scholars in biblical
> studies, theology, ethics, psychology, genetics, sociology, and related

fields. Then, in five years, if we have clarity, we'll speak; if not, we'll set another five years for ongoing reflection. After all, many important issues in church history took centuries to figure out. Maybe this moratorium would help us resist the "winds of doctrine" blowing furiously from the left and right, so we can patiently wait for the wind of the Spirit to set our course.[3]

What seemed like a rather innocent proposal set off a firestorm in the blogosphere. Seattle's Neo-Reformed pastor Mark Driscoll responded with a rant that ridiculed McLaren for giving a nonresponse to an issue that many are struggling with.[4] The exchange went back and forth, and the blog comments became vitriolic. It was easy to see how no one, no matter what side or sexual orientation, could feel safe entering into this discussion.

Four years later, in 2010, Southern Baptist biblical studies professor Denny Burk wrote an article entitled, "Why Evangelicals Should Ignore Brian McLaren: How the New Testament Requires Evangelicals to Render a Judgment on the Moral Status of Homosexuality." Burk argued that the debate over homosexuality in American culture had only intensified since Brian called for that moratorium four years earlier (maybe because no one had listened to him). Burk took notice that in 2006, only one state had sanctioned same-sex unions. Now, five states, plus the District of Columbia, have legalized same-sex unions. Burk seemed to imply that during these past four years, the churches had missed the opportunity to speak to this important issue in the culture. Then he proceeded to detail how McLaren broke his own moratorium on making judgments on the issue in his 2010 book, *A New Kind of Christianity*. Burk then spent the rest of the article methodically arguing for the absolute clarity of the Bible's condemnation of same-sex sexual relations and closed in this way:

> The Bible's verdict on this question is sufficiently clear for Christians to render a verdict on the moral status of homosexuality. For this reason, Christians must never shrink back from declaring the truth of God revealed in the Bible, even if that truth runs counter to the culture. Serious Christians cannot defer judgment on the moral status of homosexuality (as McLaren suggested) for at least three reasons: (1) the Bible's meaning is sufficiently clear in all the relevant passages; (2) faithful Christian discipleship needs clear norms for human sexuality; and (3) Christian witness to the lost world requires an accounting for human sexuality.[5]

For us, this McLaren-Burk exchange illustrates much of what has gone wrong in the debate over same-sex sexual relations among Christians.

Too Safe

We see, for instance, that McLaren genuinely tries to open up space for listening to each other and hearing each other's stories.[6] For McLaren, anything less would not allow us to echo the words of James from Acts 15:28 (NIV) that "it seemed good to the Holy Spirit and us." McLaren has been persistent over the years in pushing in this direction of open discernment, and we applaud him for that.

And yet something is missing. McLaren offers no serious process for having such a conversation that invites us to submit our lives to the Spirit's guidance for our times and context. Granted his was a small article. Yet there is no sense in his proposal of how we might gather to submit together to the Lordship of Christ, the Scriptures, the gifts of the community, and the work of the Holy Spirit in our midst. Instead, he suggests we listen and study "scholars in biblical studies, theology, ethics, psychology, genetics, sociology, and related fields." But when we make these modern experts the dominant voices (we are not saying they have no place, just not a dominant place), the conversation inescapably becomes conceptual. We end up discussing gay and lesbian issues as if they were about concepts, not people. And so we must wonder whether this conversation might be just one more futile debate over the merits of these sources (for example, scripture versus psychology versus biology).

The two of us see the need for the church to create local places where we gather to discern the kingdom. Here, we sit together and get to know each another, listen to each other, and submit to each other in Christ. In groups with as few as three or four people or as many as twenty, we learn to tell our stories, uncover our pains, reveal our motivations, submit all things to the cross, and allow the gifts of the Spirit to work among us as we listen together to the scriptures (at the end of signpost 4, we touched on this process from Acts 15). The layers of sin, oppression, victimization, and anger slowly get peeled away. We practice kingdom prayer, confession, forgiveness, communion (via the Lord's Table), the fivefold gifts, and being with those who are hurting. In these ways, we open a clearing for Christ's power to break in. Without such a process, discussions become merely research projects, exegetical debates, or scientific musings. They lack the breaking in of the incarnate Son into our lives for the sake of the world. They look nothing like the gathering of Acts 15.

And so the real question is whether the kinds of conversation that McLaren proposes are too safe. Have we removed the possibility of God's disruptive work? If the discussions are kept at a conceptual level and there are no practices of interpersonal submission to the Lordship of

Christ in our midst, then divine breaking in will be pushed out of these conversations. And like our churches, these places will ironically be safe from the presence and authority of Christ.

How do we keep the "safe places" that McLaren is calling for from becoming too safe? How do we keep from forming places that tolerate everything yet resolve nothing?

Too Sure

Someone like Denny Burk might wholeheartedly agree with our critique of McLaren, but we question whether he has accomplished anything more. He has of course has made the "truth" clear. He outlines his biblical position, choosing theologians who agree with him and dismantling those who do not. Yet what has he accomplished? Perhaps he has made those who already agree with him feel better about their own position. But has he entered into the world of those who are lesbian, gay, bisexual, or transsexual/queer (LGBTQ)? Has he encountered anyone who thinks differently than he does and asked what the real issues are? Has he proclaimed the good news in any way that relates to the issue of the LGBTQ person? Has he entered the far country?

Several things work against Burk's moving into the missional far country regarding this issue. For one, he approaches the question from a culture war point of view. He acts as if the church is still in charge of the culture when plainly we are not. He acts as if expert analysis of the Bible can help win the church's war with the culture. But where is he living? In few places, except maybe in the South (where he is from), do people outside the church readily bow to the authority of the Bible. And even within the church, interpretation of the Bible is not uniform. Burk is operating within the Christendom mentality we have been seeking to overcome throughout this book. He is not a missionary: he has not crossed the boundaries into the very lives of LGBTQ people who could care less about the church, especially in light of the way most churches have treated them.

In addition, Burk's exegesis, or anyone else's exegesis, offers little positive to shape desires or relationships. Information might win an argument, but it seldom draws a person into the kingdom all on its own. Instead Burk's posture, one that is all too common in today's churches, unconsciously assumes that all people have been shaped by the sexual mores of the church and only need to be reminded of what they need to do to get back on the straight and narrow. It's an approach that does not engage those who are hurting or confused in the sexual worlds of post-Christendom.

———————— o ————————

To sum up, the Scriptures are important, good exegesis is essential, and we must mine the richness of God's wisdom concerning creation and the ordering of sexual life. But all of this will mean nothing to those outside the church if we fail to cross boundaries. Getting the information right is insufficient to engage our culture. It is a posture that does not recognize God already at work in the hearts and minds of the sexually broken (which is all of us) if we would just come alongside and listen and discern as friends.

The polarized church of both Burk and McLaren must become unstuck. It either maintains a current position on sexual relations and defends it with all its might, or it offers those hurting or confused a place to talk while defending them from the other side. No one truly enters the far country to discern what God is doing because we are dug in on what we already know.

Meanwhile, those like the pedophiliac seminary student are left alone in their own personal hell. Burk would give him decrees from scripture and then encourage him to go out and do better, be celibate, pray for the Holy Spirit (with the admonition, "and, oh, by the way, we'll be watching you!"). McLaren offers him discussion with little hope for transformation and little guidance for a future. Through it all, the church fails to be a place for discerning the kingdom breaking in. The church fails to enter the far country of hurt, pain, and marginalization that is the sexual world of our day.

Signpost Eight: The Welcoming and Mutually Transforming Church

We need a signpost pointing us to the new places of the kingdom—spaces where we can experience God's rule breaking into our sexual lives, where the Son's work of transformation goes before us.

We need to open these spaces in the midst of our lives for sexual redemption. Such a space will invite everyone together with whatever sexual issues he or she carries. We will not consider sexual issues from a distance as if we could make a pronouncement on a single issue and have that somehow solve everything. Instead we will come together locally and commit to love one another, listen to one another, and submit to one another through the work of the Spirit and the word of the Scriptures. We will seek the presence of Christ so that his rule might break in and become visible in our lives. His authority will be made clear through mutually submitting to the gifts of the Spirit. We will ask what is going on in the depths of our lives, our sexual histories, our hurts, our pains. Then we will ask, What is God saying to us? What is God doing? What is God calling us to in these things? We will own sin, forgive victimizers, forgive others and be forgiven, submit to Scripture, and submit to the way of the cross and the resurrection. We call these kinds of communities "welcoming and mutually transforming"[7] rather than "welcoming and not affirming" or "welcoming and affirming."[8]

Here are a few directives for what we think these safe communities will look like in our neighborhoods as we go into the far country of our sexual culture.

No Labels

First, we will not publicly label our communities. We will, for instance, not put up a website that labels ourselves "welcoming and not affirming" or "welcoming and affirming" or, for that matter, "welcoming and mutually transforming." Sexual redemption can be witnessed only through the sharing of stories in humble listening and committed relationships. If we label our community according to who we are for or against, we will communicate that we really are concerned only about the mechanics of sex and body parts (like the Western missionaries in Africa concerning polygamy). Yet we know we can truly grow into a redeemed sexuality only within a context of living relationships. Saying that we affirm or do not affirm LGBTQ relationships can be heard only as rejection by those outside a community. We simply cannot communicate what we mean to say about sexuality through a label. It therefore makes no sense to broadcast public statements about what we are for or against before we have even begun to live with each other around these issues.

Some leaders at Life on the Vine were once asked to meet with a group of church planters who wanted to bounce some of their organizing tactics off us as they began to plant a new church in another city. We all gathered at the pizza joint across the street from our building and began to chat. In the middle of dinner, the conversation turned to the debate about same-sex relationships. These planters said they felt compelled to make space in their city for a church that would be distinctly "evangelical" while at the same time "welcoming and affirming" to same-sex sexual relationships and marriage. They felt there was a unique need in their city for this. God was calling them to offer a public place where religiously open gays and lesbians could come, worship, and feel safe. They felt strongly they needed to make their commitments very public on their literature and website. We definitely sensed among them a great love for gay and lesbian people.

Nonetheless, I (Dave) suggested that to publicly label themselves as "welcoming and affirming" was to foreclose missional engagement in their context. They would be setting themselves up to attract only people who already agreed with them and repel those who didn't. They were foreclosing the possibility of authentic sexual transformation because they would appear to be announcing a broad affirmation of many LGBTQ sexual behaviors. I pointed out that it is hardly clear what it would mean to say "welcoming and affirming" regarding LGBTQ sexual relations, just as no one would know what it means to be "welcoming and affirming" of heterosexual relationships. Indeed, they did not really know what they were affirming and what they were denying. It seemed clear they did not want to affirm all sexual behavior of any kind (certainly not behavior that was violent, abusive, or unfaithful), same sex or otherwise. As a result, we recommended not labeling communities in advance. Instead, we suggested preparing the way for a community to be present in the world and invite all who seek God's work in their sexual lives to come and discern together God's redemption in our sexuality, even if, and especially if, we don't know what that might mean.

In 1 Corinthians 5, the apostle Paul takes this position about not judging outsiders. He makes the distinction between judging those within the community and those outside it. He asks, "What have I to do with judging those outside? Is it not those who are inside that you are to judge? God will judge those outside" (vv. 12–13 RSV). We should not judge those we do not know and are not in relationship with in Christ. Yet for Paul, we do judge those inside ("the brother") the community (vv. 11). We are to mutually discern the character of our lives together under Christ.

At the same time, the writer of another epistle, James, warns against speaking evil of or judging a "brother" inside the community (James 4:11). Here we are told not to take the law under our own control and judge our brother, for "there is only one Lawgiver and Judge," who is God (v. 12 NIV). The apparent contradiction between Paul and James can be solved when we realize that James is encouraging the posture of submission and humility in discernment before God. James is speaking about the process of coming alongside one another in order to discern moral issues together. And so he encourages coming together to seek agreement in submission to God and humility with each other (vv. 7–10), resisting the pride and boasting that lead to slander and division.

There is a difference between judgment, whose goal is to condemn, and discernment in mutual submission to Christ, whose goal is the redemption of one another in love and humility (1 Corinthians 5:5). This coming alongside, being "with," is a practice of God's in-breaking kingdom.

This way of humility and vulnerability is an extension of the incarnation. It makes possible the crossing of boundaries to enter into the far country. This posture defines the welcoming and mutually transforming community.

A happily married Mormon man named Josh Weed came out in June 2012 and revealed on his blog that he was a gay man. He defined himself as gay: he had been attracted sexually to males since he was eleven years old. Nonetheless, he has been married happily to his wife for many years. According to Josh, they have an "enjoyable" sex life and three wonderful children. Despite being adamant about his gay identity, he describes his sex life with the woman he has married in stunningly orthodox Christian ways. In fact, he suggests the reason he and his wife have such a wonderful relationship is that they were able to get to know each other undistracted by the sexual libido that drives so many relationships early in their development. In my opinion, given the way he and his wife dated, have sustained faithfulness over many years, and grown together in oneness and mutuality, this gay man is more "Christian" in his married life than many heterosexual Christians I know. His life speaks to the stunning reality that sexual attraction (as he defines it) may have nothing to do with the proper ordering of our lives into the fulfilling purposes of God for our marriages and our sexual lives.[9]

And yet a community labeled as "not affirming" may never have met Josh Weed and his wife. They would have been unwelcome. The things that could have been learned about how God works in sexual life would have been lost.

There must be a delicate sense in which judgments cannot be made against the LGBTQ community, or any sexual issues, until we cultivate a vibrant, redemptive communal life into which we humbly invite people of all sexual orientations together into mutual discernment about what God is calling us to.[10] Until we become this kind of community, we are hiding behind sound-bite labels and prepackaged pronouncements. This kind of "welcoming and mutually transforming" space may be within or outside a church structure. It will be marked by the way we live humbly and hospitably among all people, including LGBTQ people. Once we are "with" people, we can invite those seeking sexual redemption to join us in the repentance and renewal of all desire (not just sexual ones).

We All Come Broken

Second, these spaces must invite all people to enter by owning that we are together in our sexual brokenness. Regardless of sexual orientation, sexual history, or sexual issues or addictions, all must confess their brokenness. We all must learn to admit (those who are straight, those who are lesbian or gay, those who are confused) that we are fundamentally broken in ways we may not even be aware of. This is a fundamental requisite for the formation of this space if we are to build a safe incarnational community in and among the sexual cultures of our day.

In such a community, governed by the in-breaking kingdom of God, there will be no sins targeted as more reprehensible than others (and if there is, it does not deal with sexual sins, but the spiritual sin of blaspheming the Spirit [Mark 3:29]). When it comes to sexual sin (or any other sin for that matter) we need to, in a sense, renounce "Lord of the Rings" theology. There is no "one sin to rule them all." Those who are called to extend the incarnational ministry of Jesus must be the first in line to model this brokenness. We go first by humbly confessing our brokenness, the way we have been hurt and hurt others, and submit our desires to the kingdom of God. When we come together in this way, Jesus can be Lord and his rule can become present. The kingdom of God will break in.

When we do this, we begin to recognize that many of our desires are formed and shaped within a society of sexual objectification and misogynistic commodification. We begin to discern different things that we had never before seen. We must submit all our desires to the cross and resurrection of Christ, taking nothing for granted. All desires are in view, not just sexual desire, including desires that express themselves as greed, lust for self-fulfillment, gluttony, vanity, and beyond. We cannot enter the radical transformation that Christ is doing in the world apart from admitting our brokenness and submitting our desires.

We must engage mission in a place that offers a look at the de-forming of our desires. If we cannot become such a place, we will have nothing to offer those caught in the dark side of sexual desire: deep patterns of behavioral abuse, patterns of objectifying and being objectified, pedophilia, and pornography. This is not a heterosexual or an LGBTQ issue. This is all of us. To enter into the redemption of Christ and minister incarnationally, we must be able to walk into the re-forming movement of death into life, of dying and being resurrected to new life (as Paul expresses this in Romans 6–8). If the postures of humility and vulnerability express what it means to be welcoming, the practice of all of us confessing our brokenness defines what it means to be a mutually transforming community. It is the entrance into the way of death and resurrection, the new creation, the coming kingdom.

We Gather to Discern God's Voice

For some of our readers, it might feel that a welcoming and mutually transforming community is a free-for-all where all come and confess their sins but forget God's mission as revealed in Scripture. But this is not so. A welcoming and mutually transforming community does not discard Scripture or the history God has worked in the church, as imperfect as our human response to that work may be. It does not discard the moral direction that comes out of these sources. But a welcoming and mutually transforming community comes together to mutually discern the Scriptures for our time and this place.

Such a place will still rely on those gifted in teaching the Scriptures in our midst. We will listen to the healers gifted in the care of souls, those gifted in prophecy who speak the truth of gospel into our lives. Only when all the gifts of the body work together (1 Corinthians 12 and Ephesians 4) will Scripture come alive for us and lead us into life. Together we will pray, listen, and seek God's wisdom as we navigate the waters of healing alongside one another. Scripture cannot be taken out of this place. Instead, from within this place of trust and safety, we gather to bow to its authority as revealed by the Spirit, the authority derived from the mission of God moving through us.

Scripture is not wielded as a hammer from above by a presumed expert, as is so often the case in Christendom, where authority works from positions of power. Instead, a welcoming and mutually transforming community will engage God's mission by searching the Scriptures in mutual submission. This will always include (and we must emphasize this point for those who assume a welcoming and mutually transforming community abnegates the authority of Scripture) submitting to those recognized and proven to teach among us (ordination is a helpful process here). Yet these teachers in our midst will operate in submission to the pastors and healers in the midst as well. All the gifts are used to edify (1 Corinthians 14:26) and build up the believer piece by piece into what God is doing, until we all become mature in Christ (Ephesians 4:13). Guided by the Spirit under the humble, powerful, and loving Lordship of Christ, we will become a prodigal community of transformation.

All this makes possible a place where we do not come to fight over exegesis. Rather, we seek Christ in the uncovering of our hurt, pain, anger, wounds, sin, guilt, loss, dark thoughts, motivations, assumptions, and the scripts we have been taught that bind us (and blind us). We find in this place forgiveness, repentance, reconciliation, the proclamation of the gospel, and the Spirit's authority to heal. Maybe this sounds too ideal, but anything less is not prodigal enough, not recklessly opening ourselves to the in-breaking kingdom of God.

We Learn to Become Friends

At the foundation of a welcoming and mutually transforming community must be the goal of renewing friendship: the practice of being "with" one another. In our society, there is a ubiquitous void of meaningful friendships, of relational intimacy, on any level. Much of this is caused by the oversexualization of all relationships (between men and women, between men, and between women) such that we are alienated from intimacy in any form. This has not only destroyed trust between the sexes but has created the loss of deep, caring, and intimate friendships within the sexes (men and women). The church's failure to speak to this loss of friendship has been deafening. Instead we have capitulated to our sexualized culture. Indeed we have often institutionalized these failures and have separated the sexes and called it "living above reproach."[11]

Within this unfortunate reality, the church has much to learn about friendship. Three years ago, when I (David) was blogging on some of these issues, I received a telling e-mail from a gay man that illustrates several of these issues. This man talked about his experience as a gay man spanning many years and across several relationships and friendships. "Coming out" for him was not just about sexuality but also about vulnerability and intimacy with other men. This man narrated how in the midst of the struggles and difficulties of life, he now had men who were there for him—to laugh and cry with him, to hold him in the darkest night. Even when the relationships were not sexual (and he said that often they were not), this man noted a level of love and care that straight men seemed incapable of. And for him, this was one of the most important aspects of being gay: the ability to share love and affection, true friendship, with the men in his life.

This man's story reveals the deep friendships that take place within the gay culture that are often missing in our culture at large and often in our churches. It reveals that much of gay life may have nothing to do with sex, indeed, that sometimes the level of intimacy and commitment shared in gay life puts the church to shame (although he did admit that there were the same problems of backbiting and jealousy we find in all human relationships and so was sure not to idealize the gay community). This man's journey illustrates how if we listen closely to our gay brothers and lesbian sisters, we might discover the truly good things going on there. It suggests that if we listen to them, we might see things missing in our own lives.

It becomes clear, then, that first and foremost, the prodigal church must create spaces for the restoration of friendship at the core of our life together. Such places of friendship must work to subvert the overly sexualized culture we live in. True friendship among men, among women, and between men and women, redeemed beyond the objectifying sexualization of our society, will begin a renewal of sexual redemption. We will start sorting out many issues that lie at the depths of our sexuality. Such friendship will give witness to the kingdom and be the foundation of a welcoming and mutually transforming community in mission.

We Are Called to Something Bigger

In May 2012, Intelligence Squared, a U.K. organization that stages high-profile debates around the world, held a debate in Sydney, Australia, on the statement, "Same-sex marriage should not be legalized."[12] One of the more interesting speakers that night, Annamarie Jagose, a feminist-queer theorist from the University of Sydney, surprisingly argued against the legalization of same-sex marriage. In her words, "The marriage we have been invited into is not a flourishing institution . . . it needs us more than we need it." She recited statistics on the large percentage of divorce and adultery in Australia. She asked why gay and lesbian people were aspiring to a failing institution and then asked, "Why should marriage be the category of social recognition that privileges certain sexual behavior above others?" For her, marriage was a troubled and obsolete institution.

Whether we agree or not with her, Jagose speaks to the position we find ourselves in as Christians in the new post-Christendom cultures of the West. Marriage in the West is failing. Meanwhile, the church insists on defending it without first defining it so as to make it meaningful again. We foist a view of marriage on society that we have not only failed to make compelling but have failed to live ourselves. We need communities that witness a kingdom view of marriage and celibacy that is bigger than what passes for sexual life in North America.

Sadly, Christians today are mostly driven by the same sexual assumptions that drive Hollywood. In other words, people marry based on the Hollywood fictions of attraction, compatibility, and the fantasy of "getting my needs met." We live the same account of marriage that Jagose and other large parts of society see as no longer compelling. We just throw a few restrictions on top of this ruse, such as no premarital sex and no divorce, to make it Christian, and then we break these rules anyway. Our witness as a result is duplicitous and false. Is it any wonder that the world, including LGBTQ peoples, looks at us and recognizes we ask something of them we are not willing to ask of ourselves.

But there is a sexual redemption in and through Jesus Christ made possible in his victory over sin and evil. It is large in vision, marvelous in purpose. This sexual redemption undercuts the idea that marriage is "for me." It pulls marriage into a participation in God's mission for the flourishing of the world.[13] It orders families and single people around the kingdom of God. And celibacy (shock of all shocks!) is not a fate worse than death in this kingdom. It is an adventurous choice that opens the way for us to live new possibilities in the kingdom. This sexual redemption calls us into the richness of community, friendship, and transformation. It calls us into something bigger than ourselves and our obsessive focus on sex. Our personal transformation sexually becomes an aftereffect of our entire selves entering into God's life and mission. A welcoming and transforming community then must be based in God's calling into a wider vision of life, the life in his coming kingdom. This call makes possible a profound and real personal sexual transformation. It is a redemption that concerns all people—straight, gay, lesbian, and everyone else who see themselves as "other."

We Are Missionaries Now

We are missionaries now in the new sexual worlds of North America. There is no longer a presumed social consensus concerning sexual behavior in most of our contexts. People do not necessarily know what we are talking about when we discuss premarital sex or heterosexual monogamy. We therefore find ourselves in a situation similar to those Western missionaries who engaged African polygamy years ago. Even if we do not believe same-sex sexual relations are normative for Christian life and practice (which we, Dave and Geoff, do not), we must still enter the missional far country recognizing that God is already at work in these places. Step by step, God is working to change the world, and we must incarnationally go into the far country.

This signpost, like all the others, does not present a clear and self-evident path. Yet the challenge is clear: we must follow the Son, humbly living among the sexual struggles of our day, listening, vulnerably walking alongside, and prodigally creating spaces for all who seek to enter God's welcoming and mutually transforming community.

PRODIGAL JUSTICE

AMONG OUR NEIGHBORHOODS: THE JOURNEY
TOWARD LOCAL JUSTICE

THE OCCUPY WALL STREET movement started in New York City in the fall of 2011 amid a lingering economic recession. The banks had been bailed out a few years before, and it seemed the U.S. government was taking care of the corporate elite while average citizens struggled to find a job. The wealth disparity between the top 1 percent and the rest of the country (the 99 percent) was at an all-time high since the Great Depression in the 1930s. The entire nation seemed discontented. Then a small group of people began demonstrating below the New York Stock Exchange and later at Zuccotti Park in Lower Manhattan. They declared, "We are the 99 percent." That protest gathered steam and spread across the country. Occupy became a national movement seeking to highlight the issue of economic injustice between the rich and the poor in the United States. In November 2011, it came close to our own little church in the northwest Chicago suburbs.

The pastors at Life on the Vine had already visited several demonstrations. We were asking whether the Vine should engage Occupy in some way? It was a controversial subject in our church. On occasions like these, "Viners" typically call for a Friday night town hall meeting. Any member of the church can call one whenever she or he believes the church is facing a key concern that requires discernment. So in this case, the pastors (the two of us and the other two pastors) called for a Friday night town hall meeting to discuss Occupy. We gathered to discern what God was doing in this movement. Should we join in? Should we start a protest ourselves? How could we witness to the kingdom of God with such a protest?

A few days later, we got an impassioned plea back from one of our most dedicated members. He urged caution, fearing that such a meeting would divide the church. He knew of many members who disagreed with the values of Occupy Wall Street and wondered if the pastors were letting their own political bias take over in their leading of the church. He advised the church to recuse itself from such political matters and let each individual to make up his or her own mind.

This episode illustrates that it is not always clear just what *justice* means. Some members of our community saw the economic inequality in our society as unjust. They believed it was our duty to get involved in God's work to bring justice to this situation in the United States. Others felt just as strongly that the job of government is to create a level playing field so that all individuals can participate equally. Who gets what percentage of wealth should be left to who works the hardest and smartest. To these folks, that was justice. And to still others, justice, especially "social justice," was not even the business of the church. The church should stick to ministering to individual souls. Amid this confusion, it was clear why communal discernment is so important.

Justice, especially social justice, means different things to different people. It is so controversial that many churches and many pastors prefer to leave it alone. And yet we know that the far country is full of injustice, exploitation, and oppression and that God is bringing justice and righteousness into the world. God in Christ has already begun making the world right. This is the kingdom. This is the gospel. This is our story. It is therefore not possible to proclaim God's salvation in our neighborhoods and ignore injustice as if it is unrelated.

But how should we respond to injustice? How do we discern what justice is in each situation? Does each individual Christian make up her or his own mind on something so important? We don't leave doctrine up to each individual Christian. Yet even for those who already agree on the definition of *justice*, these are hard questions to answer. How do we lead a church prodigally across boundaries amidst the world's injustice?

Individuals First, Society Later

New York city pastor Tim Keller is known for leading a church that joins mission with justice. In his book *Generous Justice*, he argues that God calls all Christians into justice because justice is at the very heart of God's desire for the world. Keller argues that "the image of God," created in each individual person by God, is the basis for a broader justice. As children of God, each one of us can see that image in the other person, especially in the least among us. This moves us toward compassion and justice. He describes how, in and through our relationship with the Father, we come to see that we own nothing but are stewards of God's gifts and must work for God's purposes. It only makes sense, then, that all who truly have a relationship with God will be motivated to work for God's justice in the world.[1]

How does this happen? For Keller, the individual's experience of being justified by faith naturally moves us to see victims of injustice differently. When you receive the unmerited gift of God's forgiveness in Christ, you see yourself as undeserving of God's grace. Grace changes you so much that when you "see a poor person, you realize *you* are looking into a mirror."[2] A life that has truly received the grace, love, forgiveness, and relationship with God cannot help but be generous with love and mercy toward others. A truly redeemed person, then, cannot *not* get involved in the justice of God in the world, the making right of all relationships.[3]

Keller champions the indelible link between individual conversion and reconciliation in the world. He helps us see the deep connection between personal forgiveness and the seeking of justice for others. He shows us that an individual's personal justification by faith leads that person into God's justice in the world. Out of a newly restored relationship with God, we are set into motion for God's reconciliation and work for the whole world. We applaud Keller's work. He corrects those who believe justice is either separate from or inconsequential to our salvation in Christ.

I'll Pray the Prayer If You Pay My Bills

And yet (there's always a "yet," right?) frontloading individual salvation like this—making one's personal justification by faith the prior entrance point for justice—can have some unintended consequences.

One time a woman named Brenda visited the Vine's worship gathering: she needed assistance for a place to stay and came seeking funds for the local hotel where she wished to stay for a couple of nights. She had asked us for help several times before, and we had helped. Our habit at the Vine is to give someone assistance the first few times with no questions asked. On the second or third time, we seek a deeper relationship. And so after a few visits, we sat and listened to Brenda. She revealed a broken relationship with her sister, which was why she was without a place to stay. Yet Brenda did not want to discuss her relationship with her sister. Instead she presented her material needs as desperate. And then, quite surprisingly and unprompted, she declared that she was a sinner and needed help from Jesus. "I know I need Jesus for salvation. I will pray the prayer if you'll just help me," she said, "and I'll come to your church too!"

Brenda seemed to think that if she just confessed her spiritual need, we would help her with her financial need. Later we found out she was a regular at many other local churches looking for help. She had, it seemed, been learning this protocol well. And perhaps we had fed into this problem. As a result, our relationship with Brenda had taken on a client mentality. She seemed to put reconciliation with her sister off limits, and in the process, the salvation of her soul had become separated from her call to reconciliation to her sister.

By getting to know Brenda better, we had the opportunity to offer her the good news that God had forgiven her for any wrongdoing toward her sister, and, indeed, God had forgiven her sister as well. God was at work reconciling the two of them. Could she receive that? "Yes. Now can I have money for a hotel?" Knowing Brenda a bit better now, we tried to help her find other ways to get shelter, but we also gently asked, "Do you think it's time to seek forgiveness from your sister?" Brenda resisted. She wanted nothing to do with her sister and left. We didn't see her again for over two years.

Some may want to warn that we didn't know the whole story. Perhaps Brenda's sister was an abusive and violent person. From what Brenda said, it didn't seem that this was the case, but even so, we would seek reconciliation (taking precautions, of course). What we learned with Brenda and many other people inside and outside our congregation is how easy it is to separate personal justification from justice in our relationships (in this case, reconciliation). When you separate the two, it is somehow possible to refuse the one while doing the other. And in the process, the contradiction thwarts what God wants to do in all the parts of our lives. The contradiction prevents the kingdom from breaking in among us and around us and invalidates our witness in the world.

Certainly God can work his justice in the world through getting individuals saved. We believe this. But Keller seems to make the Christian's justification the a priori to his or her work of justice in the world. This is dangerous because it makes justice an after-effect, an option for someone after being saved. Justice is the consequence of the kingdom of God instead of being intrinsic to the kingdom of God. It becomes something we do, not something God is doing.

But as we cross boundaries into messy, unjust, and abused places in the world, we will discover the two must be part of the one thing God is doing in the world: God's working to make all things right.

The Wrong Story

For Brian McLaren, biblical salvation is the social transformation that God is working in the world. It is almost as if social salvation is prior to personal salvation. So for McLaren, we participate in salvation by joining in with God's work for justice in the world. He would take issue with Keller's view by noting that individual salvation often does not lead one into social justice (e.g., note the lack of evangelicals within the civil rights movement). McLaren often observes how individual salvation gets absorbed into the wrong story, a story that has underwritten destructive economic or social forces in the world (our financial security has a surprising hold on our politics). We, for instance, "get saved" and end up pursuing wealth as our own personal blessing from God at the expense of others. McLaren challenges us to look at our stories.

According to McLaren, Jesus has been wrongly framed within a story that supports the world's global exploitive economic forces. This story frames salvation in terms of humanity's need of forgiveness because of its infractions against God. Humanity is condemned and deserving of eternal punishment, and Jesus is the solution. God offers us pardon from the guilt of that sin in Jesus's sacrifice on the cross. McLaren worries that this story "relegates Jesus to practical irrelevance in relation to human social problems" because "his message is about the soul, its guilt before God, and its afterlife."[4] This version of salvation allows us to abandon changing the world today for a grand march to heaven tomorrow.

Instead of an infraction against God, McLaren wants to frame the story of Jesus as the cure to the lethal infection of sin that is plaguing humanity and slowly killing us all.[5] According to McLaren, this is Jesus's story. Sin is a social disease that breaks down human relationships on every level: personal, social, and political. Jesus brings the kingdom of God as a revolution to all those relationships. Jesus comes proclaiming the kingdom of God as an alternative to the narratives of power and oppression we have been held captive to.[6] In McLaren's view, the story of the kingdom changes the way we relate to God and everyone around us. Living this story brings in a social justice that permeates our everyday lives and all our relationships. This is the salvation offered in Jesus Christ.

We applaud McLaren for renewing an emphasis on salvation as God's justice in the world. He has spurred a revival of sorts in social justice movements among Christians, and for this we are thankful. But again, as has been our habit in this book, we must probe a bit further. Is it enough to change our perspective with a new story about God's justice in the world? Is it enough to call individuals into the way of Jesus? What are the problems in this approach to justice and salvation in Christ?

From My Front Door to the World

In response to McLaren and others like him, Christians from everywhere have radically changed their lives in order to respond to the needs of the world. And so we have witnessed thousands of Christians, from baby boomers to millennials, from CEOs to suburban moms, who have joined celebrities like Bono to subvert unfair lending practices and work for the freedom of oppressed people, to end hunger, to participate in racial reconciliation efforts through Promise Keepers and other organizations, and to participate in the Campaign to Make Poverty History. We know many recent college graduates who reject high-paying jobs to serve others with their work, teaching in underfunded school districts, and working for nongovernmental organizations in developing countries. And we know countless people who have sponsored children through Compassion International and other agencies. Our church has participated in many of these efforts. We may now be witnessing the greatest invigoration of social activism since the 1960s.

Several years ago I (Dave) experienced a bit of this revival in a Vine leadership meeting. In the early days of Life on the Vine, we called this meeting the "worship committee," but it was more than that. It was a group of leaders who regularly met to discern what God was doing among us in all the areas of church life. This particular night, we heard from several members of our church in their twenties who proposed we join in with a famous Christian rock band and its campaign to eliminate AIDS in Africa. We listened to their impassioned pleas for almost an hour and then opened it up for questions. I asked if we knew where the money was going. "It is going to relieve AIDS!" someone responded. I probed further: "Will it buy drugs? Fund hospitals? Who will the money go through and to whom? How much money are they raising?" They could not answer most of these questions, and it became obvious we were rallying around a cause we had no relational connection to.

I tossed out for discernment what I called the $100,000 rule. I said that whenever the sums of money get big (say $100,000) and we funnel that money through nonrelational means, it is inevitable that these funds will reinforce the existing structure and authorities that are responsible for the injustice in the first place. Sure, the funds will likely provide some immediate relief, which is something we should consider. But large amounts of money, goods, and services by definition require distribution through the existing structures because no other means are available (apart from personally knowing people already well established on the ground). We strengthen these structures with our money. So these ostensibly good works can do the opposite of what is intended: support injustice, not justice. I argued that we should pursue justice through relational means whenever possible.

Surely the $100,000 rule is an oversimplification. But I reminded everyone that night that we already had a direct, ongoing relationship with a hospital in rural Africa ministering to one thousand AIDS patients a year. We even had a medical worker from that hospital talk to our church in person. Somehow that hospital had gotten lost in the euphoria over a seemingly more grandiose campaign.

It is getting harder and harder to discern God's justice in the world. We've had countless friends go to impoverished countries to work for a nongovernmental organization or other form of relief organization, only to discover that the very problems they came to relieve were being perpetuated or even made worse by foreign aid detached from relationships. Meanwhile, we also know firsthand many workers on the ground in impoverished places who, after many years of inhabiting a place, are being used to bring a new righteousness and justice to the land. Being with—living the gospel relationally with people as part of everyday life— seems to be the common practice from which God's justice breaks in. In this way, in submission to his reign, Jesus's presence is extended incarnationally through our lives (as we learned in signpost 7).

Jerry Falwell and Jim Wallis: Two Sides of the Same Coin

Most of us are constantly tempted to join larger, more magnanimous justice efforts in the world that promise big things. There is an allure around the promise of changing the world through "the world's ways": big government, big fundraising campaigns, and heroic relief efforts. Frankly, a lot of good has occurred through these efforts. But many times these big campaigns distract us from just being present with the poor in the simplest, most patient everyday ways that God can use to bring in the kingdom.

Whenever I (Dave) encounter people arguing over whether a good Christian should be a Republican or a Democrat in the United States, I usually insist they are arguing for the same thing. Whether it be over issues of abortion, school prayer, progressive tax structure, or national health care, they may differ on their version of what a Christian America should look like, but they are both using the same tactic to work for God's justice in the world. For them, God's justice is a matter of first figuring out what policies are most Christian and then advocating for a government that carries out these policies. Many leave it there, thinking their contribution for God's justice is complete.

Jerry Falwell, in the 1980s, once argued for "taking America back" for God and started what became the Moral Majority. In the same way, James Dobson argued for a Christian America on his radio show, *Focus on the Family*. America was a blessed nation, both said, founded on Christian principles, and we must work to "turn America around or prepare for her destruction."[7] The goal was electing Christian candidates who would legislate the right policies as agreed on by all good Christians. Ironically, in similar fashion, progressive evangelical activist Jim Wallis of Sojourners, in his 2005 book *God's Politics*, argued for much the same thing as Falwell and Dobson had. According to Wallis, we should pursue a government that is compassionate toward the poor. We should work for education, health care, and economic reform to help the poorer classes escape poverty. Wallis arguably worked on more theocratic and biblical terms than either Falwell or Dobson did. He called his policies "the Isaiah Platform," after the book of Isaiah.[8] In his next book, he called for a great awakening, invoking the vision of church revivals of hundreds of years ago.[9] And so Wallis was arguing for a Christian nation (although not in those words) just as Falwell and Dobson were, albeit with several different items on his political agenda. That's why we say Falwell and Wallis are two sides of the same coin.

Where has any of this gotten us over the years? We extract issues from their contexts—justice, capitalism, equitable taxation, prayer in public schools—and argue about them, making them into concepts that have little engagement with what's happening in our neighborhoods. We exhaust ourselves getting officials elected. Churches split between the right and the left and engage in unsightly antagonisms. We end up feeling good for a while in the election cycle when our side wins. Then the other side takes its turn in the next election cycle. Meanwhile, right in our own churches, hurting people go unnoticed. We are blind to racism taking place in our own neighborhoods or our own church communities. We remain distant from those in our cities, neighborhoods, and even our own churches who are in need and hurt from unreconciled lives, racism, injustice, oppression.

Please don't read us wrong. There is a time for discussion and discernment on the political issues of our day, but we must be careful when these political efforts lead us back to where we started this whole chapter. Whether it's Jerry Falwell (or his successor) or Jim Wallis, they turn the church into a recruitment center for individuals to go out and seek a justice in the world that is more conceptual than real. And the church itself, the social embodiment of the Lordship of Christ on earth, is never considered as an entity that lives God's justice and reconciliation before the world and in the world. This is where the prodigal justice of God must begin: in communities of people who share the new reality of reconciliation and renewal, love and transformation in their neighborhoods.

No Jesus, No Justice

I (Dave) was at a conference in Toronto when a friend asked me to interview theologian Stanley Hauerwas for a video program. I knew Hauerwas from my Ph.D. work and began the interview by asking him to explain the relationship of Jesus, the church, and justice in the world. After some brief comments, Hauerwas paused and said, "No Eucharist, no justice." This very odd statement prompted some puzzled looks around the room. So I attempted to try to translate it for a less-Catholic-oriented crowd. I asked if he might just be saying, "No Jesus, no justice." And, for that matter, "No justice, no Jesus." Acting perturbed as if I had just said the obvious and made things more confusing, he responded rather loudly, "Of course."

Despite the oddity of the phrase, Hauerwas is saying something worth clarifying. For Hauerwas, the church is a social manifestation of God's Lordship over the world in and through Jesus Christ. It is a foretaste of God's kingdom in the world, a sign of God's justice working in the whole world. This work of justice for Hauerwas is seen in the Eucharist (or Lord's Table): the eating and drinking together of Christ's body and blood. As we partake, each of us enters into a communal process that shapes us into the reconciliation, forgiveness, and renewal of all things God is working in Christ by the Spirit. In the process, we together become the lived-out, enfleshed reconciliation, and justice of God for the world to see.

This is why the apostle Paul is shocked at the economic divisions around the table at Corinth and tells everybody "to go home" (1 Corinthians 11:22). He was telling them that God's justice was not there, that the lack of justice was invalidating their practice of "Communion." Jesus proclaimed that his kingdom is birthed here at the Communion table in a way that defies how the world uses power against other people (Luke 22:25–29). For Hauerwas, no true justice is complete until it finds its true end in the reconciling work of Christ. And this work is wonderfully made real in the practice of Communion.

The implications of Hauerwas's statement are basic. If there is no justice in our lives, then Jesus is not present. If we are not with the least of these, we have no stake in the kingdom (Matthew 25:41–43). If we do not forgive others, we have not been forgiven (6:15). If we hoard our resources to secure only ourselves, we cannot inherit eternal life (Luke 18:18–29). And on and on it goes. Being "in Christ" personally is an act of participation in his work of justice in the world. There is no separating the two. This is what it means to say, "No justice, no Jesus."

Likewise, if there is no Jesus in our actions to make things right, then ultimately there is no justice. There may be glimmers of goodness, hints of grace, beginnings of mercy and restoration in the world. Such glimmers happen all the time. But ultimately every act of justice is completed only in its fullness in Jesus Christ, the reconciliation of all things.

When we see our lives in Christ this way, we relate differently to someone like Brenda. She had come to us for help with her housing, but as we got to know her, she revealed that she had left her sister's house over an argument and would rather hit the streets than give and receive forgiveness. We gave food and shelter to Brenda, but ultimate justice would not be complete until she had been reconciled to her sister in Christ.

This reconciliation in Brenda's relationships was already made possible in Christ's death and resurrection. It is not just some managed compromise between two individuals. Rather, the practice of reconciliation (Matthew 18:15–20) is a participation in God's worldwide reconciliation of all things in Christ (2 Corinthians 5:17–21). The work of God in Christ on the cross for the world makes possible a new level of reconciliation that goes beyond any human conflict management process.

This is the salvation God is bringing into the world in Jesus Christ. It is the new creation, the reconciliation, the righteousness (justice) of God. And it spreads from Brenda into Brenda's former place of employment, the places of social assistance that had abused her, the local police station where she was mistreated and discriminated against. Often, and we've seen examples of this, this justice goes all the way up to the levels of county, state, and even the federal government. Every local practice of justice plants the seeds for justice to flow wider and higher into the entire world.

Signpost Nine: The Journey into Local Justice

This leads us to the "rubber meets the road" questions. How can a people come together and spread this kind of justice throughout a neighborhood? How can we keep justice from becoming a T-shirt logo or bumper sticker that makes us feel better but keeps "the least of these" at a safe distance? How do we keep justice from becoming another program at our local church? God is calling Christians to be communities of justice everywhere we live, to cooperate with God's mission in bringing justice into the world. What might this look like? How do we do this?

We know from signpost 1 that we cannot take for granted what justice might mean in a post-Christian culture. We know from signpost 2 that God is always at work in the world—not in some vague manner but concretely in the world through the Son and Spirit. Signpost 3 directs us to see the incarnation as both God's way in the world (through a combination of power and humility) and God's presence in the world extended by the Spirit through us. Signpost 4 shows us that all of this must take shape in a communal way of life that gives visible witness to the kingdom before the world. Such a way of life will discern justice by living out our story, discerning the gospel in each situation, in living communities of the kingdom (signposts 5, 6, and 7). But we need some direction (a signpost). Here are three ways to follow the radical prodigal justice of the Son that moves into the neighborhood.

We Keep the Relational in Justice

First, let us reiterate that God's prodigal justice happens through being with people in the midst of their lives. It is intensely and simply relational. We do not mean to suggest that all Christians must immediately move into impoverished neighborhoods in order to remedy injustice. But God works for his righteousness through everyday relationships. The person who has slept in her car for three years learns how to work, think about a home, and think about relationships by being with people who do these things in everyday life. And when we who have jobs let hurting people into our lives, we see things about everyday life we never would have seen apart from these friends. It's a mutual relationship.

We are not saying that everyone should invite a homeless stranger into their homes. This would in fact be treating that person differently (almost like a project) because we invite only those we know as friends (or as friends of a friend) to stay at our house. Instead, we simply notice the hurting around us and begin to be available to them in relationship as our schedules allow. Soon after, as we know the hurting as friends, not as clients or people who need us, and commit to each other's growth as friends, something changes, and God works in that relationship. Kingdom breaks in. This is the pattern of being with that is talked about in so many ways in the New Testament (Matthew 25:31–46; 18:1–5, for example)

At Life on the Vine, we've learned that being with the poor is something that does not come naturally to most people. And so, instead of our church developing another program for meeting some need in the community that people can volunteer for, we've learned we must teach God's justice as a way of life. We have to teach people awareness of the hurting ("the least of these") in our surroundings. We must teach people how to see differently so we can take notice of the least of these and make space for being with them as part of everyday life. Without scheduling more time, just making space within what they already do every day, people learn how to be available to the hurting people God is bringing into their path. We find this learning starts best with the hurting in our own local church communities. Once we are practiced there, then we can more easily make space for the hurting in the neighborhood. And from there, as God allows us the time and skill, we can even develop relationships with the hurting overseas in ways that are not patronizing.

We must also learn, out of our everyday lives, how to stop and spend an hour a week at the shelter with those struggling with domestic abuse and just be with them. We must learn how to take an hour a week at the train station hanging out with the homeless or a night a week with the neighbor being foreclosed on in the neighborhood, or an evening a week volunteering at the local hospital with the sick. We must resist making a program out of it, another commitment at the church. Instead we do it relationally within our neighborhoods as part of our life routine. We engage the hurting as people who have something to offer, who have been created by God with great gifts. We come not with solutions but to connect people to people, friends to friends, and watch God work. In short, we teach and learn the skill of being with the least of these in our lives— not as a program but as a way of life that we carry on for a lifetime.

In a middle- to lower-class neighborhood northwest of Life on the Vine's building, we had some people band together to live in the neighborhood under the Lordship of Christ (you may remember we call these gatherings missional orders). This small group had been praying for the neighborhood, discerning what God was doing there and how they should respond. One couple chose to move to the low-income housing in the neighborhood. It was what they could afford. They noticed many immigrants being forced out as apartments got gentrified. Racism was rampant in these evictions. They chose to be "with" them, inviting them for a meal. Relationships were built in the hallways. Meanwhile, another couple in the missional order was spending time being with the principal at the local school. They learned she was a believer and had a heart for the local immigrants. She knew many of the immigrants were struggling with basic computer skills to get jobs, basic news from their homeland, and important papers.

The principal proposed opening up the school one night a week for both tutoring and access to computers. So they gathered: people from the missional order with computer skills and the local immigrants to learn from one another and provide help getting jobs and government papers. Soon one of the members began to work with a fair housing activist group to expose inequities/racism in the community's housing practices. His inside knowledge gave him credibility with the community. God was reordering the way this neighborhood worked politically and socially, yet it was not a program: it all happened relationally out of everyday life with God. God was working simply and quietly to bring an unmistakable righteousness and reconciliation into the neighborhood. The kingdom had broken in.

We must teach the practice of how to be with the hurting, how to be present in the midst of unjust structures and racist divisions no matter where we live or what income level we live at. God is at work everywhere. Wherever we are present, we bring the practices talked about in signpost 7. It may be reconciliation, proclaiming the gospel, hospitality, forgiveness, or kingdom prayer. Amazing things happen we could have never believed through our submission or faithfulness to Christ's reign. When we enter the world to be with people, the kingdom breaks in.

We Enter from a Posture of Humility

When we come to be with a community, we never presume we already know what is needed. The justice of the prodigal always comes in humility and vulnerability. We do not send millions of dollars to an urban ministry we have never spent time with. We do not come as "white people" to African American communities with our money, presuming to know what they might want or need. We do not go to our town councils and dictate what we think should be done based on our interpretation of the Bible. We must inhabit a place and listen. We must come to know people as friends. We must presume we have much to learn about God through them. And then God will use our joining in with the neighborhood to bring fresh eyes and fresh words and Christ's authority against oppression and evil. Again, this is not a matter of making a program to solve our community's social problems as if we are in charge. This is being present so as to become witnesses to what God is doing to reconcile the world to himself.

We must be careful not to assume that all city organizations (city government, public schools, the arts institutions) need is a few more Christians in leadership. God might have other plans. Some cultural institutions might be too far gone, given over to the powers of sin and destruction. The public schools, for instance, might simply not make sense anymore. Parochial schools or home schooling might make more sense. Or the public schools may be transformed with two or three teachers and tutors banding together to bring peace. The arts might better be renewed in the local coffee houses as opposed to gigantic institutions with money and power. We cannot presume that putting Christians in city hall is the way God will save the city. We are not arguing for one approach, just that we do not know how God might work until we are in the middle of discerning it.

We know of one place where the medical care situation was irreparable. The medical costs of giving birth in the hospital system were spiraling out of control. Basic health care for a mother giving birth cost three times what it should have and was out of reach of the poor. For normal births, the hospitals were charging the rates for high-risk births that did not require special medical procedures. These costs had become entrenched within the medical insurance system, and because people were making so much money off this system, it was impossible to change. Simply working as a Christian in the hospital system would not overturn the ways money and corruption had rigged the system.

But we know of a Christian doctor, at the top of his field, who had worked for years to change the system. He then discerned God was directing him elsewhere. He started a birthing center across the street from one of the hospitals and charged only 25 percent of the average medical costs to birth a healthy child. The hospital systems tried to buy him out. He refused. He single-handedly threatened the cost structures of the local system and in so doing bore witness to another order: the order of the kingdom that puts human needs above money. The birthing clinic itself poured forth the hospitality of the Lord's Table and offered hope. Since then, other physicians have begun taking notice, asking if they should do the same. Through this one doctor, a space was cleared for a simpler way. It is a way that does not take advantage of the "least of these" but instead brings local people together with skills under his reign. And the kingdom broke in.

We Bring Jesus

Signpost 7 shows us how communities are formed when people come together in a place and submit to Christ's rule. The presence of Christ is extended through the practices, and God's kingdom becomes visible in the changing relationships and structures penetrated by it. We must never forget that prodigal justice will always bring Jesus into the neighborhood. When we eat in the neighborhood, we bring the hospitality of Christ born out of his death and resurrection (localized in the Lord's Table). The Lord's Table brings people of all races together under the Lord's forgiveness and new life. When this happens in the neighborhood, the kingdom has broken in. When we see hopelessness, we bring the proclamation of the gospel: "Jesus is Lord and he is working." When gangs bring violence, we can pray "thy kingdom come" over that drug-infested corner. When faced with unreconciled relationships, hate and murder, division between economic, racial, and social classes, we can bring the practice of reconciliation made possible in the cross. In each case, we are not alone in our neighborhoods, for Jesus promised, "Lo, I am with you always" (Matthew 28:20 KJV). We witness the possibility for the completion of all justice in Christ's reign.

As we have said throughout this book, whenever we are being with a person or situation, we bring Jesus. By *bring*, we do not mean control Jesus or possess him. Rather we are witnesses to the unique reconciliation and renewal made possible in the life, death, and resurrection of Jesus Christ. As we saw with Brenda, her need for food and a room was inseparable from her broken relationship with her sister and her ultimate need to be in fellowship with God. So when we offer food or a room, we are already pointing (witnessing) to the true end of her body and soul in the reconciliation and renewal God is working in the world through the Son. And so as space opens in her life for the kingdom, we can only expect that it will eventually lead to its fulfillment in Christ being Lord over her life and her relationships. As with Brenda, so also with every other situation of injustice we are present to in our neighborhoods and world. In a sense, as witnesses, we bring Jesus and the kingdom breaks in.

Why Justice Must Be Local: "The Revolution Will Not Be Televised"

One day, a developer came to our church building asking for a meeting with the pastors. Our property was right behind a large tract of land that this man was hoping to develop into a shopping center, but it lacked the required traffic access. The developer was trying to buy adjacent residential properties in order to convert them into an entrance road, but no one was taking him up on his offer. So the developer proposed they use a narrow section of our church property as an entrance road in and out of the shopping center. They would then allow us to use all their parking for free (for when we became a big church!) and get free water from the new water system, and they offered various other enticements as well (like free snow removal for the church property). Dave got quite excited. He saw the financial benefits and the free upkeep on the property, and he liked the idea of the church building being next to the new center of the community.

Of course, Dave did not live on or near the property. He had his own missional territory south of the church's gathering place. But I (Geoff) did live nearby and knew the neighbors. I was hearing an earful from them. They were staunchly against the development because all of the benefits would be going to another part of the town while our neighborhood got all the downsides, including severe ecological impact and challenging traffic congestion. The neighborhood as we knew it would be wiped out. We were experiencing the NIMBY effect: Not In My Back Yard! I spent many hours with the neighbors. After a few weeks of prayer, discussion, and discerning, we decided not to sign the lease and instead work with our neighbors to protect the neighborhood.

It is one thing to talk economic progress, clean water management, or tax legislation on a national or federal level; it is another thing to work for justice on all those matters locally and relationally, bringing God's justice into the neighborhood. There no doubt will be times when we have to work for justice in Washington, D.C. (or Ottawa), but it will most likely start locally. One church rejecting health care restrictions and starting up its own insurance co-op or medical halfway house could perhaps cause a local medical system to change. Then maybe the whole city gets involved. One church taking in a young pregnant woman, offering an alternative to abortion, could reshape the possibilities for adoption in the entire country. One son being drafted into a war (if we had a draft again) can lead others in the church to apply for conscientious objector status, and then perhaps could lead thousands to refuse to go to war. The reconciliation meeting between rival gang leaders in the neighborhood could lead to gun law change and new neighborhood mediation practices. A white racist landowner seeking forgiveness from an African American he has refused housing to could lead to national awareness education in the real estate brokers' association. God's justice starts local, and we cannot predict where God will take it.

The incarnation teaches us more than a way to follow or a principle of missiology. It is the way God works to bring salvation, justice, and righteousness into the world. It starts in the smallest of ways, in relationships, and then spreads. Slowly, one relationship or structure at a time (God will not overwhelm our personal choices), God's victory overwhelms the powers and ends murder in the streets, brings reconciliation amid racial strife to a city, opens medical clinics to serve the poor when for-profit hospitals no longer see a reason to be there. It starts locally and builds. In the words of Gil Scot-Heron, "The revolution will not be televised." It will not overtake the world through the world's systems. Prodigal justice will not be just another program at your local church or of the Republican or Democratic party. It is a way of life under his Lordship through the Spirit that takes up residence in communities that spread across the nations.

PRODIGAL OPENNESS

FOR THE GOOD NEWS: THE JOURNEY
INTO DIVERSE WORLDS

I (DAVE) REMEMBER MEETING BOB "the Bolshevik" while we were all sitting around one morning jabbering at the local McDonald's. I was taking a break from my work over in the second "cubicle" on the right and Bob came over, sat down next to me, introduced himself, and promptly announced that he's an agnostic. He had evidently heard I was a Christian and thought this was important to get clear up front. But to me, it was not clear, so I asked what he meant. He explained that he believed God could be discovered in any number of ways. This of course disqualifies him as an agnostic since an agnostic by definition is unsure if God exists. Nonetheless, he talked on. "If there is a God," he said, "I am sure he is at work in any number of religions revealing good things about humanity and how we can all be better people." Bob then urged me to look for the good in all people.

Bob was unsure (which is what I think he meant by "agnostic") about how God works in other people's religions. He wasn't even sure that God was a force for good in the world. What Bob *was* sure of, however, was that any claim for Jesus being divine and the exclusive way to God was patently unbelievable. The guys at McDonald's called him Bob "the Bolshevik" because his wife's ethnic heritage was from a former Communist bloc country, so maybe he married into a culture of suspicion toward religion. But to me, he had actually articulated the dominant "religion" of North American post-Christendom: religious pluralism.

According to various reports, cities like Miami (60 percent immigrant), Toronto (over 50 percent), New York (over 40 percent), and Los Angeles (over 40 percent) have huge populations not born in the United States or Canada. Each immigrant brings a different religious and cultural heritage that is vastly different from what used to be the North American Protestant Christian consensus of the mid-twentieth century. And even those who have no religion still unequivocally agree that it is imperative that we accept all other religions and not judge them. This is the "religion" of the nonreligious. This is post-Christendom (signpost 1).

When I (Dave) was in my twenties and working as a representative in a downtown Chicago financial services firm, a coworker once asked me if I was a Christian. A bit sheepishly, I said, "Yes."

"What kind of Christian? Catholic, Lutheran, Baptist?"

"I'm a Protestant," I replied.

And then he asked, "Are you one of those evangelicals who believe unless you make a decision to accept Jesus into your heart you're going to hell?"

Sheepishly, I said, "Maybe."

"How can you possibly believe that one little moment of a decision can get people out of hell and into heaven?" he blurted out in disdain.

I remember sensing the huge disconnection between the salvation of my childhood, typified by the great Billy Graham's crusades, and the society I was now living in. It was stunning how all the people around me had no way of understanding what a "decision for Christ" might even mean. The backstory of how Jesus came to save us from sin, so common in the culture twenty years earlier, had been lost. Now, within the seas of pluralism, people resist seeing Jesus as anything more than one of many possible ways to God.

This is the far country of the new post-Christendom cultures of North America, a place our parents and grandparents never knew. How are we to cross into these places where the grand story of God sending the Son has been forgotten? Where the language of salvation has been lost? Where the prejudice is now against Christianity because of past and present abuses? How do we witness to what God has done in Christ when people hear the uniqueness of Christ as intolerant? How can we be present among the many religions and cultures without losing who we are: the people of God, followers of the Son, and witnesses in the far country?

Like the previous two signposts, journeying into the place of pluralism reveals the movement of prodigal Christianity. We move together into these places with God's mission already in motion. We participate in it by extending the incarnation and becoming an embodied witness. Indeed, the context of pluralism gathers together all the signposts of signposts 1 to 4 and shows concretely how prodigal Christians might live in the missional far country. And just as in all the previous signposts, the prodigal engagement of pluralism pushes us beyond the two given theological options we've encountered to an on-the-ground expression of the gospel in every context.

Overcoming Our Violent Ways

Brian McLaren responds to pluralism by calling us into a wider vision of what God is doing in the world. Instead of presenting people of other religions with a prepackaged truth message, Brian asks us to humbly join what God is doing already in the lives of all people.[1] He recounts the history of violence between religions in the West and notes that even now, many are "planning new ways to kill one another, and many believe that in doing so they are obeying and even pleasing and honoring God."[2] For McLaren, religions in the West have an inherent "exclusivist" attitude that breeds this violence. He asks us to "defect from destructive ways" of coercion and violence that we have inherited from Christendom in the West.

McLaren claims that Jesus gives us a different story—"a story that sends us into the world with Christ-like love for our neighbors of other religions." We go with love, "not suspicion; with humility and respect, not disdain, with a desire to understand, serve, and know, not a desire to conquer and colonize; with a passion to share—both receiving and giving—because we each have been given treasures for the common good."[3] McLaren calls us into the humble way of following Jesus by walking beside other religions in search of a common good. In these ways, McLaren helps us see something wonderful: God is at work in the world, outside the church, even (dare we say it?) in other religions. We cannot predetermine where God is working. It therefore behooves us to be present among all people, listening, allowing God to work, and responding appropriately.

Tony Jones, another Emergent leader, tells the story of how he and some Emergent friends put a meeting together with the local rabbis in his city to "talk about the future and God's kingdom." Some Christians objected because Jews, they said, could not possibly be involved in the work of God's kingdom because they did not believe in Jesus. Jones responded, "To Emergents, this kind of thinking binds God's work to the church and implies that outside the lives of professed Christians, God is handicapped." But Jones also stated that he did not want to participate in "a kind of lowest-common denominator spirituality" where it is predetermined what you can talk about so that "very little robust theological conversation" can take place that truly affects people's lives. He asserted that this flattening of all dialogue has crippled liberal churches across America. For Jones, the real issue is that "we've got to figure out a way to be robustly and distinctly who we are yet authentically open and respectful of the other . . . for me, that means being truly Christian, yet profoundly open to the rabbis."[4]

In a marvelous way, Jones and McLaren realize that dialogue with other religions is about more than just the bland tolerance so common to American political life. It requires us not to leave our history at the door. We enter dialogue as followers of Jesus Christ.

Nonetheless, is there not more to a Christian's engagement with other religions than a posture of listening and mutual respect? Is not the mission of God more than working together for "the common good" as McLaren describes it? What would it look like to envision the place where we engage in mutual dialogue with people of other religions and cultures as the very site of the in-breaking kingdom?

As much as McLaren and Jones move us in the right direction, we wonder what it would mean to give witness to the reign of Christ in both its humility and power in these dialogues. Isn't Jesus more than a "way" to follow in the hope that the world will become a better place? Doesn't God's mission (*missio Dei*) include the particular human being, Jesus, who in his life, death, and resurrection now reigns from the right hand of the Father? Sitting and talking is essential to this in-breaking reign. But such a dialogue fails to follow the prodigality of the Son if it does not also bear witness to the power and authority of Christ, the Son of God, at work overcoming the powers of sin and death among us.

If we believe (as we must) that God has invaded our broken and estranged world in the Son through the Spirit, bringing a particular work of forgiveness, reconciliation, resurrection, and renewal, then we must walk forward, even into relationships with other religions, in the prodigal particularity of Jesus and his cosmic (yet humble and benevolent) reign.

What We Need Is Absolute Truth!

In March 2011, Grand Rapids, Michigan, preacher Rob Bell published a book called *Love Wins*. Bell, often associated with the Emergent crowd, took on the questions of "heaven, hell, and the fate of every person who ever lived."[5] Though he is not a universalist and does believe in hell, he nonetheless argued for a more inclusive answer to the questions, "What is the destiny of the unevangelized? Will they all pass into an eternity in hell?" Before the release of the book, his publisher offered a video in which Bell asked whether Mohandas Gandhi, India's nonviolent leader, was in heaven. "Jesus was very clear," Bell said. "Heaven is full of surprises." Bell was pushing the envelope in exploring what he called "the mystery" of God's great intention to save the whole world.[6]

Yet for the average person growing up in conservative Christianity, Bell was opening up a huge can of worms. In the book, he seemed to blur the distinctions among religions. He seemed to make one's faith commitments in this life less consequential for the next. This made conservative evangelical leaders nervous. So even before the book was released, based solely on this promotional video, John Piper ignited an Internet firestorm when he tweeted, "Farewell Rob Bell." For Piper, Bell had crossed the line of heresy and so it was "farewell" to Rob as he left the orthodox faith. Bloggers such as Justin Taylor of the Gospel Coalition and Tim Challies of Canada followed suit. To these men (again, even before the book came out, so they likely had never had a chance to read it), Bell was misleading God's people by giving the impression that hell was not the eternal destiny of all those who pass from this life in their sin. For them, Bell was not taking seriously the justice of God and the very reality of hell.

There is something worth paying attention to in the Neo-Reformed reaction to Bell's book. Even if Bell was not guilty of an appeal to universalism, he seems to affirm that God is at work for salvation outside of Jesus Christ. Whether this is right or wrong, Bell seems to be nudging us closer to a flattening of the particular ways God's kingdom breaks in through Christ in power and authority. Is there a way to acknowledge God's work in the world outside Jesus Christ without losing the efficacy of God's incursion into the world in the Son?

At the time, others worried that Bell's book undercut God's work of justice in the world. New Testament scholar Scot McKnight, for instance, worried that "Rob has so distanced God from hell . . . and so distanced God from disestablishing injustice that the oppressed person may well find in Bell's God little more than justification for the oppressors."[7] If God's work lacks justice in eternity, how can we trust him to work for justice in the present? We need again to ask, Have we lost something here? Have we lost the God of justice and, in the process, the true sense of God's mission: that God is setting things right in the world?

These things really do matter.

Long before Rob Bell, the great missiologist Lesslie Newbigin recognized that pluralism is not just a sociological reality. It is an ideology celebrated and cherished as an accomplishment of Western society.[8] It is a religion unto itself. Don Carson, professor at Trinity Evangelical Divinity

School, agrees with Newbigin and argues that "philosophical pluralism is the most dangerous threat to the gospel since the rise of the Gnostic heresy in the second century."[9] Cultural pluralism makes anything said about God into an issue of personal preference and emotive sentimentality. It reduces Christianity to a form of personal therapy. In response to this kind of relativism, the Neo-Reformed camp champions truth. We need "objective truth" they say—truth that stands on its own, truth in propositions.[10] In the face of such ubiquitous pluralism, they believe we must assert the uniqueness, supremacy, and divinity of Christ as absolute truth. We must declare with all our might that "Jesus is Lord" and then vigorously defend him.

There is something to be listened to in the Neo-Reformed response to Bell. Pluralism, heaven, hell, and the uniqueness of Christ are all matters of life and death, justice, and eternity. God *is* a God of justice, and his coming disrupts the status quo, exposing lies, rendering justice, intruding into our lives, and reordering all things. Our witness in the world must take into account that God has come into the world in the Son and the Spirit to set the world right. This is the kingdom breaking in. This is justice. This is prodigal Christianity. We cannot give up on this.

Fighting Against or Standing With

And yet something is also amiss in the Neo-Reformed response to Rob Bell. I (Dave) remember reading Justin Taylor's blog response where he wrote (referring to 2 Corinthians 11:14–15) that "even Satan disguises himself as an angel of light. So it is no surprise if his servants, also, disguise themselves as servants of righteousness. Their end will correspond to their deeds."[11] I was taken aback as Taylor's words were imitated around the Internet as numerous bloggers responded in a similar way to what they believed was Bell's dangerous and "shoddy" theology (this even before they had read the book). The response was excessive and seemed defensive to an extreme. With some bloggers, the response took on an almost twisted pleasure in accusing Bell of heresy. There was a win-at-all-costs theo-blogical war. What are we to make of this?

Too often Christians behave in these ways, acting as if no one from the outside world is watching. But outsiders are watching, and they see the insecurity at the core of our theology. We look as if we are more interested in winning an argument than engaging those who are outside the faith who have legitimate questions. People distrust Christians because of this. Since we ourselves are not willing to patiently discern what God is saying in Scripture for this time and place in our lives, why should outsiders consider that we would help them answer their questions carefully without a winner-take-all mentality?

As we gaze across the post-Christianized postmodern landscape of North America, seeing the vast numbers of people who do not even have the insider language to understand these debates, we sense the time has passed for winning arguments. Surely we must ground ourselves in the historical beliefs given in Scripture, but when challenged, we must avoid excessive defensiveness.

On one Easter, some Muslim friends suddenly showed up at our family's door as a group of us were sitting around the table, enjoying good food and beverages and celebrating the day. Most of us had been awake since 5:30 a.m. when the celebration of resurrection begins at Life on the Vine around a bonfire before the sun rises. We were tired, relaxing, and telling stories of resurrection and new life. So we were surprised when Raja and Nusrah showed up (although it had happily happened before).

As we invited them into our fellowship and dispersed around the house into discussions, one of our fellow church members engaged Raja (the husband) in a vigorous discussion over whether Jesus was God and indeed whether he had risen from the dead. As she recited numerous historical and logical arguments, the conversation turned rather tense. Someone else rushed into the room and warned me that if I wanted to keep Raja as my friend, I better intervene. I walked in to hear Raja say, "I won't try to convert you, and you shouldn't try to convert me!"

Thankfully, that discussion ended with no one taking serious offense. But I also remembered that over the past two years, I had talked with Raja many times. On one occasion, we were sitting together in his back yard chatting over a very sweet Iraqi dessert. In this instance, we were discussing Raja's struggles to find a job and gain acceptance in the United States. Instead of the conversation turning toward an argument about his beliefs, I described to him how I had come to see the world as the place where God is working, where the resurrected Jesus is Lord. I gave witness to the times I had walked in faith and trusted in him to guide and protect me through these struggles. I asked whether I could pray for him. A little glimmer of the kingdom shone through.

My experience with Raja illustrates that the time for aggressive defensiveness has passed. The posture of wielding truth against an opposing religion is over. It separates us from those outside the Christian faith and prevents us from crossing boundaries. It does not allow for the listening to or the being with through which the kingdom breaks in. Instead God calls us to stand with while witnessing *to* the Lordship of Christ in our lives. And so as much as Don Carson, Justin Taylor, and others help us see the importance of the exclusive claims of Christ amid the worlds of pluralism, they are not radical enough. We need a signpost that will lead us into the far country of pluralism.

Signpost Ten: The Journey into Diversity

Several years ago, one of the largest churches in the Chicago area invited representatives of the three other major religions to share the stage with a Christian and talk about the differences between the various faiths. I (Dave) was intrigued, so I went. On stage were professional clerics from each faith: an Orthodox Jewish rabbi, a Buddhist *sangha*, a Muslim cleric, and a Protestant Christian pastor. Thousands flocked to the auditorium that night. The evening, entitled "Christianity Encounters the World Religions," was advertised as a learning experience. There was no attempt to suggest that one religion was going to be proved right over the others. It was only going to be informative, helping people understand the differences so as to help everyone "make up their own mind" in a more informed and sensitive manner.

What evolved during the hour and a half was fascinating. During the exchanges, the Christian would notice contradictions in the Buddhist account of God (or not God). He would say, "You cannot say both A and B if they contradict each other." The Buddhist would then look at him puzzled and say he had no idea what the Christian was talking about. To the Buddhist, the accusation of self-contradiction was an imposition of Western logic. But then the Muslim would chime in and ask the Christian how he could say that God is both one God and yet three persons. To the Muslim, this was a total contradiction that flirted with polytheism. Of course, the Christian could not easily explain to the Muslim or the Jew why he was a monotheist while believing in the Trinity.

After a while, it became clear that the expectations of the moderator were not being met. He was hoping it would be a dispassionate, objective look at these religions. But it was hardly objective: the Christian representative on the panel kept asking Christian-oriented questions before a Christian audience that the non-Christians could not understand. The Buddhist therefore could not answer the Christian's question, "How do you come into a personal relationship with God in your religion?" despite being prodded numerous times. The Buddhist could only respond, "I do not understand the question." When the Christian representative said, "Jesus Christ is the Son of God, the only way to heaven apart from whom all people go to hell," the Muslim responded that he was absolutely sure Jesus is the son of God, one of many such sons. In the end, the moderator of the whole evening thanked all the representatives for coming and said, "We need to learn how to live together and love one another."

There is a temptation to think that when we enter into dialogue with people of other religions, all we Christians need to do is to exchange information and then the superiority of our faith will be revealed. We seem to believe that if we know our facts, know our apologetics, and give reasonable evidence, then we will be able to prove our points over against the questions and claims of other religions.

But this misses the point of how God has come into the world in the Son. God has not come into the world to win an argument but to incarnationally engage a lost and fallen world by inviting all peoples to be reconciled and renewed in Christ. This is the mission of God, and God will accomplish it according to God's way (which is the way of the cross and kingdom).

Therefore, we need to go into the places of the new post-Christendom pluralism and be with people of all faiths. We need to create spaces where our lives can honestly intersect those of other faiths who live among us. As communities, we must inhabit places with people in everyday life so that out of these places, God's kingdom can break into the worlds of religious diversity. Such communities will participate in the *missio Dei* by walking in the ways of incarnation and witness. We have two suggestions we hope can direct churches into living prodigally amid pluralism: enter pluralism incarnationally and enter pluralism as witnesses.

Enter Pluralism Incarnationally

First, we must create space to be with people of other religions or spiritualities. The way these places take shape will differ from church to church, neighborhood to neighborhood, city to city. Whether we gather in coffee shops or in each other's backyard, we must extend the presence of Christ into those places. We must settle in, be comfortable, and spend time with people from all religions. This means we come humbly, vulnerably, and without coercion. As the Son came to us, so also we come to our neighbors of other religions. This is incarnation.

Each religion speaks its own language. Even the secularists of our day have a well-thought-out atheological culture. It is a way of life. So rather than seeking a point from above from which to translate our message to our friends, we must, just as Jesus did, enter into their language world (even if they speak English!) and be there long enough, deeply enough, and vulnerably enough to truly understand what their questions are, what their fears are, and who they are. Without a universal language to rely on (as we saw in signpost 1) we must enter each life and each religion locally and concretely as part of our everyday life. This is the humble way that abandons positions of power and coercive authority.

In such places, there is no a priori foundation that we can appeal to in order to win an argument. As Anabaptist theologian John Howard Yoder says, the appeal to some universal foundation is a me-versus-you "power play to avoid being dependent on your [the other's] voluntary assent, to bypass my becoming vulnerable to your world in your otherness."[12] But the way of Jesus takes all such posturing off the table. Instead we renounce all avenues of coercion. We do not enter a relationship ever thinking this person or group "must believe" what we believe. Instead we seek to live in these places alongside people of other religions and seek to be there long enough to witness with our lives what it means to say that Jesus is Lord. We do not communicate the gospel until we have learned how (or have the right opportunity) to say it in such a way that it can be received as good news.[13]

There is no need for us to make judgments about other religions in these places. We leave that to the Holy Spirit. The Spirit will be present in our dialogue to clarify and lead. As theologian Stanley Hauerwas has made clear:

> The command to be a witness does not entail *a priori* judgments about the beliefs and life of others—e.g. what is right or wrong with Hinduism or Islam—though such judgments after time may be appropriate, but rather witness derives from no other source than that which invites us to "look what manner of life has been made possible among us by the power of the cross and the resurrection of Christ." The invitation to join such a life is made not on the assumption that there is something wrong with the others' beliefs, but it is made because we are all sinners and through participation in this community we have the possibility of finding redemption.[14]

We therefore engage in dialogue knowing we have as much to learn in this relationship as anyone else. This dialogue becomes the arena of the kingdom to work in my life as well as the other's. Reconciliation, hospitality, ministry, and the proclamation of the gospel itself will happen in the course of everyday life. This kind of dialogue forms the place for the in-breaking presence of Christ as we come humbly and vulnerably submit to his work.

Such a place of dialogue teaches us that we do not possess Jesus Christ "like a proposition, which we hold to be authoritative and to be exempted from the relativity of hermeneutical debate." Instead, we enter into relationships with persons of other faiths in and through his presence. We learn that we cannot escape the "need to be corrected" as if we already possessed all the answers. Our relation to Jesus is located in the very engagement of becoming vulnerable to the other in this moment and time and place.[15]

Enter Pluralism as Witnesses

As spaces for conversation form in the neighborhoods, we must live daily knowing that Jesus is Lord. In terms of God's mission, God has made Jesus Christ Lord over the world. We can now come to our friends of other religions and share life with them already knowing the Triune God is at work making all things right in the world. This is all encapsulated in the affirmation that Jesus is Lord. Prodigal Christianity lives this one affirmation as the basis for our engagement with all other religions.

The affirmation that Jesus is Lord may seem off-putting, even undercutting the very space of dialogue and openness we seek. Surely such a claim for the supremacy of Christ pits us against other religions and other ways to God. But the conviction that Jesus is Lord actually does the opposite: it frees us from coercion and control. It is Jesus that is Lord, not us. We do not need to land a knockout punch to win an argument against another religion. We are witnesses! We do not need to be prosecuting attorneys on behalf of Jesus. We are witnesses!

African theologian Kwame Bediako, in his book *Jesus and the Gospel in Africa*, explores the question, "How is Jesus Lord?" within the context of African religious pluralism. In line with our previous signposts, he sees three dynamics going on in the affirmation that "Jesus is Lord." The first, related to the incarnation, affirms "that in Christ, God humbled himself and identified with humankind" such that "the Incarnation is supremely the unique sign and demonstration of divine vulnerability in history." The second, related to the cross of Christ, affirms the way divine love works through a "suffering forgiveness" in the face of evil. The third aspect, related to the Lord's Table, affirms that all are invited into a reconciliation of "broken relationships across racial, ethnic, national, cultural, social and economic barriers."[16] In these three concrete ways, we see the dynamics of vulnerability, the forgiveness amid evil, and reconciliation amid division that are at work at the core of Christ's Lordship in the world. Together, the incarnation, cross, and table reveal how exclusivity and domination are overthrown when we say, "Jesus is Lord." It is to this reality that we are witnesses.

"Jesus is Lord" therefore must govern our entry into the places of religious pluralism. Knowing Jesus is Lord helps us enter each relationship with humility (for what we do not know) and trust (that God is working in ways we cannot expect). In the words of John Howard Yoder, "to confess Jesus Christ is Lord makes it inconceivable that there should be any realm" in which Jesus does not rule. Yet his authority is never coercive, never violent. "It cannot be imposed, only offered."[17] To say that Jesus is Lord confesses we don't need to be in control for God to convince people of the truth.

When our convictions are challenged by other religions, this too is an opportunity for God to deepen our understanding not just of the other's religion, but also of our own understanding of what it means to walk in the reality of he who was crucified, raised from the dead, and now sits at the right hand of God. We can patiently listen, consider, and respond in confidence because we are submitted to him as Lord. We can rely on the Holy Spirit, when prompted, to give us the right words to say (Luke 12:11–12). We need not fear apostasy because if there is anything evil and corrupted in a religion we are dialoguing with, the Lord who reigns by his Spirit shall reveal it (and, of course, this goes for our own sinful manifestations of Christianity). If God's love (or the gospel) is rejected, we can deal with that too knowing that Jesus is Lord. Instead of being obsessed over heresy, we are freed in prayer and submission to discern the kingdom of God in our midst and proclaim the gospel when an opening is offered.

In light of all this, the Christian conviction that Jesus is Lord makes possible the open, gentle, discerning dialogue that we describe as prodigal. As opposed to those who uphold the rules of "tolerance" for interreligious dialogue, we enter incarnationally, under the reign of Christ, believing that God works in these places to clarify and purify our knowledge of God through others and bring others to himself. This is our witness within pluralism.

Welcome Pluralism

Perhaps this sounds too good to be true. Perhaps we need a new imagination for the ways we can cross the boundaries that divide us without aggressive defensiveness or loss of identity. Could it even be possible to see pluralism as God's ordained way to accomplish his purposes in the world?

In Genesis 11, the people started building the famed tower of Babel. They were not "filling the earth" as God told them to do (Genesis 9:1). Instead they were consolidating themselves as an empire and building a giant city with a tower reaching to heaven. They were speaking only one language. It was common in that day for a conquering people to suppress the native languages of the conquered. It was the means of control. And so John Howard Yoder suggests that Babel was an idolatrous attempt to overthrow God's plan to "fill the earth." As a result, God scattered all the peoples into multiple languages at Babel, preventing them from consolidating and becoming sufficient in themselves. Instead they now had to be dependent on God as he works through and among other people. The scattering was not a curse. It was God redirecting the sin of the people toward God's purposes. And the pluralism that resulted was actually a divinely intended "gracious act" of God.[18] And so we learn from Babel that God works to clarify, not obscure, the gospel through pluralism, through our vulnerable interactions with and being challenged by other people in other religions. This dependence, made necessary after Babel, is God's design for human flourishing.[19]

Pluralism then is not a bad thing for the church. In fact, it is something we cannot do without. Through the loss of one singular language at Babel, God has enabled us to see the gospel (God at work) in many and various ways through encounters with other religions. It forces us as God's people to be an open community, vulnerable and dependent on other communities for discerning God in the world. Pluralism is the nonviolent condition for God to work out the truth of the gospel in each of us, slowly over time and in relation to others (even other religions).

We can now say that in a way, pluralism is how God has chosen to work in the world, and we should cooperate with God in that. God has called us to follow the Son into this pluralist world, as exemplified in the incarnation itself. Because we now live under the Lordship of Christ and are confident in God's mission, because we know pluralism has been given to us as the way we must engage the world through incarnation, we can enter pluralist situations with the anticipation that God is working there. Yet it requires participation in Christ's work as opposed to being in control of it ourselves. There should be no defensiveness. There should be little reason to hide behind bland tolerance. We are called to a prodigal Christianity that recklessly risks itself deep into the places of pluralism.

Open Communities of Witness

One night I (Dave) was relaxing at home after a long day's work, and my wife told me Raja and Nusrah were in the hospital with their newborn. Their baby girl had severe jaundice, and my wife said I should get over there. So I grabbed a cigar and my Bible and walked over to the hospital, praying along the way.

I sat quietly asking Raja and Nusrah how they were doing. I was there with no agenda but to minister Christ's presence. I carried with me in body and soul the specific witness that Jesus Christ is Lord, the hope and healing of the world. I asked if I could read a psalm. They said that would be fine. I asked if I could pray for their baby. They said of course. After this I said, "Well, it might be time for me to go."

As I got up to leave, they said, "Now that you have done all the stuff you're supposed to do, could we ask you some questions?" And the night went on for another two hours about who Jesus was. Was he the One True God? Or was he one of ten thousand gods? I said I believed he was the Lord, and in the midst of their fears, I remember saying something like, "This is what this means to say 'Jesus is Lord' over little Aakifah. No harm can touch her apart from his plan. God in Christ has his hand over her right now." It was a simple act of proclaiming the gospel out of everyday life lived with and among them. It did not seem coercive, defensive, or blandly tolerant.

I admit I have not spent enough time with Raja and Nusrah and their family. I admit they have not embraced Jesus as Lord of their lives (yet). Nonetheless, I am confident that they have experienced an open community of witness and have witnessed Jesus's presence. In nonviolent ways, defying any colonializing of one culture or religion by another, God has allowed me to inhabit their world and they mine. My family and I have simply cooperated with God in making a space available for Raja and Nusrah to come into a fuller knowledge of God in Christ Jesus. In the process, I have grown and learned much in extending the presence of Christ into another religious world. This is incarnation, the kingdom. This is the way the gospel goes forth.

The prodigal God crosses all boundaries between heaven and earth, between culture and culture, and religion and religion. Christ's vision for his people in the new post-Christendom world of North America is for communities that live lives of peace and reconciliation among those of other religions or no religion. These open communities of witness are incubators for dialogue and transformation. They make possible the proclamation of the gospel. Wherever they happen, the kingdom of God breaks in. God draws people to himself in Christ Jesus.

As we gather in these new post-Christendom cultures, God is calling for us to be present among the world's religions (and no religions). We need not fear, for Jesus is Lord. And we need not demur from affirming, "Jesus is Lord." We take his presence with us, ever ready to proclaim the gospel as the Spirit prompts, preparing the way before us. May his kingdom break in!

THE PRODIGAL RETURNS

REMEMBER THE CLIMAX OF THE parable of the prodigal son? The son comes into view down the road, and the father sees him in the distance and rushes to meet him. With arms wide open, he embraces his son, celebrates his return with a party, and restores him to full relationship as both his son and a member of the family. This is the prodigal love of the father for the prodigal son.

Karl Barth (whom we mentioned in the Introduction to this book) says this return of the prodigal son prefigures another return, the Son of God returning to the Father. The Son, after the resurrection, returns to the Father and is exalted to his right hand, crowned as ruler over the whole world. This return of the Son, Barth says, is the way of all humanity's return to the family of God.[1] Jesus takes up his reign over all things, and the Spirit is sent into the world to extend this reign until he comes again. This is the way the world will be drawn back to God. In the words of 2 Corinthians 5:17–18 (REB):

> For anyone united to Christ, there is new creation: the old order has gone; a new order has begun. All this has been the work of God. He has reconciled us to himself through Christ, and has enlisted us in this ministry of reconciliation.

This is the purpose for the sending of the Son. In the sending and return of the Son, the pouring out of the Spirit, and then the sending of the church (as ambassadors), God is reconciling the whole world to himself. God is drawing all people into the kingdom and then "the end will come" (1 Corinthians 15:24 RSV). Prodigal Christianity is an invitation to be caught up in this work of the Triune God to restore the world to relationship with God and the flourishing of God's purposes in all creation. Our incredible invitation is to participate in that.

The Invitation to Participate: The Promise of Missional Incarnational Communities of Witness

No one book can change the world, and no one person can change the church (except Jesus by the Spirit). But maybe a few of us, maybe ten or twelve of us at a time, can respond to the invitation of the Son and begin to live together in the radical excessive prodigal Christianity of his journey into the far country.

We disavow any illusion that this book can provide solutions to the problems that pastors, leaders, and all other Christians face in their churches today. Indeed it might be fair to say that even looking for solutions in a book like this locates part of the problem we face as Christians in North America. Amid the multitudinous cultures within the United States and Canada, we search for one solution that will work for everyone across all contexts. But there is no single universal way, no solitary new product that can change our churches and make them into what we think they should be. We must instead be provoked to think anew about what it means to be the people of the Triune God caught up in his mission in these strange and exciting times and then begin to do the patient work of cultivating it anew for each individual context.

We hope this book provokes us all to be faithful to the prodigal mission of God through the Son by the Spirit. Let us delve into the places where we live and begin to discern the prodigal way of the Son among us. Let us discern what the Triune God is doing so that we can join in the mission that has begun anew in Christ, who has sent us into these very places by the Spirit.

We believe this will inevitably result in local, place-driven communities that practice submission to the Lordship of Christ out of everyday life. Whether it is organized by three or four singles or couples in their neighborhoods, or megachurches organizing their masses by neighborhoods, *Prodigal Christianity* invites us to intentionally practice God's kingdom by joining together in every city block, neighborhood, and subdivision and practice bringing in God's kingdom. In these communities (of baptism) we recover Table fellowship, gospel, reconciliation, being "with," the fivefold ministry, and kingdom prayer. When this happens, the new life of the kingdom takes shape and bleeds into the world.

We believe there is unlimited promise to this simple life of faithfulness. Because this ultimately will be nothing we do, it will not be a set of programs or another list of to-dos for Christians. It will simply be discipling people into the marvelous reign God is birthing in and through Jesus Christ. By learning to invite people into the practices of the kingdom, it takes the pressure off us as individuals. The kingdom now depends more on our obedience than our skills, more on our integrity than our technique, more on what the Holy Spirit will do than anything we have figured out. It is ultimately dependent on one gospel reality: Jesus is both Savior and Lord. Jesus is King. We pray for many laborers for this great harvest, for a grand joining in with God's great prodigal act of mission in the Son. May it be so to God's Glory.

NOTES

INTRODUCTION

1. This is the famous title of Brian McLaren's book of the same title published in 2001 by Jossey-Bass: San Francisco.

2. For our Reformed friends, we recognize that the Neo-Reformed movement in the United States is not prototype reformed theology in keeping with its historic European lineage. Some have likened the Neo-Reformed to a rebirth of American Puritanism. They have therefore advocated we call this group "Neo-Puritan" to clear up the confusion. Nonetheless, this group of pastors/thinkers and the media have continued to use *Neo-Reformed* (or *new Calvinism*, or both) as their primary label. We shall follow suit. See, for instance, David Van Biema, "The New Calvinism," *Time*, March 12, 2009, where the authors refer to the group as "New-Calvinism." http://www.time .com/time/specials/packages/article/0,28804,1884779_1884782_1884760,00 .html. Collin Hansen, at that time an editor at large for *Christianity Today*, wrote the book that defined the movement: *Young Restless Reformed* (Wheaton, IL: Crossway Books, 2008).

3. Tim Keller, *The Prodigal God* (New York: Dutton, 2008), xviii.

4. Barth exposits this Christological interpretation in *Church Dogmatics*, ed. G. W. Bromiley and T. F. Torrance, trans. G. W. Bromiley (Edinburgh: T&T Clark, 1967), 4:2, 21–25.

5. Barth realizes the danger here of "strained interpretation." Nonetheless, he shows how the parable's Christological interpretation completes the other interpretations. Indeed, it is a corrective to those who "hastily conclude" that "not the Son and the atonement accomplished in Him, but only the Father and His goodness belong to the Gospel as preached by Jesus Himself." Barth, *Church Dogmatics*, 4:2, 22.

6. Today, much to my chagrin, much of the Red Hill Valley is now a highway called the Red Hill Valley Parkway.

SIGNPOST ONE: POST-CHRISTENDOM

1. Peter Rollins has made this argument. See *How (Not) to Speak of God* (Brewster, MA: Paraclete Press, 2006).

2. Authors like Rollins, *How (Not) to Speak of God*, and Brian McLaren, *A New Kind of Christianity: Ten Questions That Are Transforming Faith* (San Francisco: HarperOne, 2010), repeat what has been called the "Hellenization thesis" (that early Christianity was corrupted by Greek philosophy) put forth in the scholarship of Adolf Harnack (1851–1930) and others. This claim seems to be exhausting itself, along with its semiracist basis. For the idea that perhaps instead of "Hellenizing Christianity," the early church was in a process of missionally "Christianizing Hellenism," see Robert Wilken, *The Spirit of Early Christian Thought* (New Haven, CT: Yale University Press, 2005). For the claim that that the very categories of Hellenism and Hebraism reflected Enlightenment racism, see Dale B. Martin, "Paul and the Judaism/Hellenism Dichotomy: Toward a Social History of the Question," in *Paul Beyond the Judaism/Hellenism Divide*, ed. Troels Engberg-Pedersen (Louisville, KY: Westminster John Knox Press, 2001), 29–61.

3. Our use of *Christendom* overlaps with a related term: *Constantinianism.* Both refer to the church's official recognition by the Roman Emperor Constantine, who issued the Edict of Milan (313 A.D.), making Christianity a legal religion. Many Anabaptist thinkers see this Roman sponsorship as the beginning of the church's alliance with culture and power and the fall of the church. For us, however, the issue is not a historical one. Christendom is about the church's fundamental alliance with the broader culture as a cultural strategy. We draw from the writings of John Howard Yoder and Stanley Hauerwas on the themes of Christendom and Constantinianism and the impact on today's faithful Christian witness. We agree with Yoder when he says that "'mission' by definition should mean a forsaking of the Constantinian relationship for a pilgrim status in the world." *The Priestly Kingdom* (Notre Dame, IN: University of Notre Dame Press, 1984), 145.

4. For a helpful introduction to these ideas, see James K. A. Smith's excellent book, *Who's Afraid of Postmodernism? Taking Derrida, Lyotard, and Foucault to Church* (Grand Rapids, MI: Baker Academic, 2006).

5. Jacques Derrida, *Of Grammatology*, trans. G. Spivak (Baltimore, MD: Johns Hopkins University Press, 1976), 158.

6. Jean-François Lyotard famously argues for the incredulity of all metanarratives in *The Postmodern Condition: A Report on Knowledge*, trans. G. Bennington and B. Massumi (Minneapolis: University of Minnesota Press, 1993), xxiv.

7. Mark Driscoll, *Vintage Jesus: Timeless Answers to Timely Questions* (Wheaton, IL: Crossway Books, 2008).

8. For the contrasts with the Roman Imperial Cult, see Sylvia C. Keesmaat, "Crucified Lord or Conquering Savior: Whose Story of Salvation?" *Horizons in Biblical Theology* 26:2 (2004): 69–90.

SIGNPOST TWO: *MISSIO DEI*

1. Sam Harris, *Letter to a Christian Nation* (New York: Knopf, 2006), 87. Christopher Hitchens, *God Is Not Great: How Religion Poisons Everything* (New York: Hachette Book Group, 2007).

2. Kenda Creasy Dean, *Almost Christian: What the Faith of Our Teenagers Is Telling the American Church* (New York: Oxford University Press, 2010).

3. David Lamb, *God Behaving Badly* (Downers Grove, IL: IVP Press, 2011). I recommend this highly readable book on the common misperceptions about God from the Old Testament.

4. Quoted by Audrey Barrick, "'God Is Sovereign,' Says John Piper After Japan Disaster," *Christianity Today*, March 14, 2011, http://www.christiantoday .com/article/god.is.sovereign.says.john.piper.after.japan.disaster/27664.htm. The hymn is, "God Moves in a Mysterious Way."

5. For an examination of the source of guilt as a pivotal theological category, see Krister Stendahl's influential essay, "Paul and the Introspective Conscience of the West," in his book *Paul Among Jews and Gentile* (Philadelphia: Fortress Press, 1976).

6. Lesslie Newbigin, *Open Secret*, rev. ed. (Grand Rapids, MI: Eerdmans, 1995), 37.

7. Doug Pagitt uses this image wonderfully in *A Christianity Worth Believing: Hope-Filled, Open-Armed, Alive-and-Well Faith for the Left Out, Left Behind, and Let Down in Us All* (San Francisco: Jossey-Bass, 2008).

8. Up-rooted, "Summary of December Up/rooted.City Gathering," January 10, 2008, http://up-rooted.blogspot.com/2008/01/summary-of-december-uproot edcity.html.

9. Newbigin, *Open Secret*, 37.

10. Brian McLaren, *Everything Must Change* (Nashville, TN: Thomas Nelson, 2007).

11. Newbigin, *Open Secret*, 19–29.

12. Despite the feminist critique of father-son language, which we recognize as valid, we still prefer the biblical language of fatherhood in part because we acknowledge that to pray "our Father" through the Son subverts all previous

understandings of abusive fatherhood we may have learned through our earthly families. Praying "our Father," in other words, can be the means to both destroy the false male patriarchies of our day and to open the doors to new righteous relationships between the sexes, genders, and parental roles. To remove *father* from our language for "God" could in fact remove the possibility for this healing. All this happens, however, while acknowledging that God is not masculine because we know God does not have a gendered physical body. So to learn to call God our father is to learn deeply the experience of God's loving sovereign care over us as children, which changes everything. See Stanley Hauerwas, *Matthew* (Grand Rapids, MI: Brazos Press, 2006), 76–77.

13. Joel Marcus, *Mark 1–8*, Anchor Yale Bible (New Haven, CT: Yale University Press, 2000), 165. This section is shaped greatly by Marcus's insights in this commentary.

14. Space does not allow a full articulation of the Trinity here. For recent accounts of trinitarian theology and their relation to mission, see also our "Mission amid Empire: Relating Trinity, Mission and Political Formation," *Missiology: An International Review* (forthcoming).

15. In this sentence, we are subtly assenting to the controversial yet classic *filioque* clause in the Western creedal statements. By so doing, we affirm that the Holy Spirit is indeed active in the world. Yet we also recognize implicitly that the Spirit ultimately cannot be fully known separate from the Son and the Father.

SIGNPOST THREE: INCARNATION

1. Nikos Kazantzakis, *The Last Temptation of Christ* (New York: Scribner, 1998); Norman Mailer, *The Gospel According to the Son: A Novel* (New York: Ballantine Books, 1997).

2. Representative of such a position is John Starke, "The Incarnation Is About a Person, Not a Mission," *Gospel Coalition Blog*, May 16, 2011, http://thegospelcoalition.org/blogs/tgc/2011/05/16/the-incarnation-is-about-a-person-not-a-mission/.

3. Of course, those from the Neo-Reformed perspective would answer that we live our present lives in gratitude and thanksgiving for our deliverance from sin (on the cross in the past) and in view of our hope in heaven (in the future). But this still leaves our current lives disconnected from Christ and his work.

4. Brian McLaren, *A New Kind of Christianity* (San Francisco: HarperOne, 2010), 128.

5. Marcus Borg, *Jesus: A New Vision* (San Francisco: Harper & Row, 1987), 191.

6. Brian McLaren, *The Secret Message of Jesus* (Nashville, TN: Thomas Nelson, 2006), 75.

7. Borg, *Jesus*, 17.

8. We recommend McLaren, *The Secret Message*; Borg, *Jesus*; and Mark Scandrette, *Practicing the Way of Jesus: Life Together in the Kingdom of Love* (Downers Grove, IL: IVP Books, 2011).

9. To be fair, Marcus Borg tells us that this Jesus invites us into the supernatural, that God truly is at work in the world. Borg decries the Enlightenment for stripping our world of the Spirit and God's work in the world. Borg invites us into the fullness of God's kingdom and what God is doing to transform the world. He draws us into the experience of a relationship with God through the Holy Spirit that draws us into his work in the world. Yet in the end, Borg wants to deny the divinity of the Son. Because of this, his portrayal of Jesus doesn't match the prodigal nature of the radical incursion that is God in Christ by the Spirit. His version of Christianity is not a prodigal Christianity.

10. It is interesting and yet typical of Neo-Reformed theologians to separate what is joined in Mark: the proclamation and presence of the kingdom. Kevin DeYoung and Greg Gilbert look to Mark 1:15 and claim from this text that what drove Jesus's ministry was primarily the proclamation of the kingdom. This comes from a narrow view of the gospel and the kingdom of God such that Jesus's ministry was less about making present the kingdom and mostly just proof of his divinity en route to the cross. See their *What Is the Mission of the Church? Making Sense of Social Justice, Shalom, and the Great Commission* (Wheaton, IL: Crossway, 2011).

11. This notion of how Mark uses *tear* in chapter 15 is a common observation most recently described in detail by M. Eugene Boring, *Mark: A Commentary* (Louisville, KY: Westminster John Knox Press, 2006).

12. Some biblical scholars will note that the announcement of Jesus as the "Son of God" is more a royal title indicating kingship than divinity such that at baptism, Jesus is anointed as the expected coming king and at the cross is confirmed as king (ironically by the centurion). On one level, we agree that the gospels depict Jesus as King just as much as (if not more than) being God. But we also see that the drift of the gospels is to identify Jesus not only as God's agent, the King, but also as himself God.

13. Lesslie Newbigin, *The Open Secret*, rev. ed. (Grand Rapids, MI: Eerdmans, 1995).

14. For more on the history and meaning of this pivotal hymn, see Ralph Martin and Brian J. Dodd, eds., *Where Christology Began: Essays on Philippians 2* (Louisville, KY: Westminster John Knox Press, 1998).

15. The same understanding of the church as Jesus's presence holds true for the temple of God. Remember how the curtain was torn in the temple, signifying that God was loose in the world, that God's presence is no longer contained in the temple. If the literal, physical temple is no longer the place of God's presence, the writers of the New Testament quickly discerned that God's presence was now located in the lives and communities of Christ followers.

The first letter to the Corinthians asks, "Do you not know that you are God's temple and that God's Spirit dwells in you?" (3:16 ESV), and the letter to Ephesians adds that we are being grown "into a holy temple in the Lord," built into a "dwelling place for God by the Spirit" (2:21–22). Peter tells us that we "like living stones are being built up as a spiritual house, to be a holy priesthood, to offer spiritual sacrifices acceptable to God through Jesus Christ" (2:5). This new, living temple does not begin with all those who follow Jesus; it actually starts with Jesus. John says this most powerfully in his gospel when he says that in Jesus, "The Word became flesh and dwelt among us" (John 1:14 ESV). We often think about this in the sense that Jesus walked around, or lived with us, or "moved into the neighborhood," as the *Message* has it. But the word for *dwelt* literally means to set up a tent, or a tabernacle, as the Old Testament would say. And the tabernacle was the first temple of God, a portable version used from the time of Moses until Solomon built God a stationary temple. John is telling us that with the coming of Jesus, God is again moving around the landscape in a portable, living temple. Everything the temple stood for (the intersection of God and humanity) is now centered on the body of Jesus, the tabernacle among us. And from here, from Jesus, all of this is now extended to the followers of Christ, who are also the body of Christ. The Sent One, Jesus, is still living and moving in the world through his followers. The Sent One is still in the far country as the true prodigal. For more on this, see N. T. Wright, *Simply Jesus: A New Vision of Who He Was, What He Did, and Why He Matters* (New York: HarperOne, 2011), 132–135, and for an in-depth study, see Nicholas Perrin, *Jesus the Temple* (Grand Rapids, MI: Baker Academic, 2010).

16. Alan Hirsch and Michael Frost, *Shaping of Things to Come* (Grand Rapids, MI: Baker Books, 2004), 35.

17. Taken from Alan Hirsch, "What I Mean by Incarnational," posted on his Facebook page, May 9, 2011, http://www.facebook.com/notes/alan-hirsch/what-do-i-mean-by-incarnational/10150189514096009.

18. In the same piece, Hirsch writes, "I think people misunderstand me when they think that incarnational mission does not mean that we evangelize people but just have to identify with, and love, them. That we simply go to them and be with them. This is clearly not the case as proclamation is a vital part of incarnational mission."

19. Alan Hirsch, *The Forgotten Ways: Reactivating the Missional Church* (Grand Rapids, MI: Brazos Press, 2009), 113. The word in parentheses is ours. Hirsch subtitles this section "A Conspiracy of 'Little Jesus.'"

20. Michael Frost and Alan Hirsch, *The Faith of Leap* (Grand Rapids, MI: Baker Books, 2011), 63.

21. See *The Forgotten Ways: Reactivating the Missional Church,* 142–144.

SIGNPOST FOUR: WITNESS

1. Douglass Grootius, *Truth Decay: Defending Christianity Against the Challenges of Postmodernism* (Downers Grove, IL: IVP, 2000).

2. Kevin DeYoung, "Glory of God: Preventing Truth Decay," *Gospel Coalition*, June 24, 2011, http://thegospelcoalition.org/blogs/kevindeyoung/2011/06/24/glory-of-god-preventing-truth-decay/.

3. In *Deep Church: A Third Way Beyond Emerging and Tradition* (Downers Grove, IL: IVP, 2009), 71–90, Jim Belcher tries to navigate between two approaches to truth: the "foundationalist" approach of the traditional church and the "relational" approach of the emerging church. While Belcher's postfoundational approach is a step in the right direction, it is telling that his very first constructive piece relates to questions of truth. This seems to belie a certain fundamental orientation shared with modernity. Rather than focus on the nature of truth from which witness will follow, we must focus on the nature of witness out of which our understanding of truth emerges.

4. Lesslie Newbigin, *Proper Confidence: Faith, Doubt, and Certainty in Christian Discipleship* (Grand Rapids, MI: Eerdmans, 1995).

5. See Tony Jones, *The New Christians: Dispatches from the Emergent Frontier* (San Francisco: Jossey-Bass, 2009).

6. Michael W. Goheen, *A Light to the Nations: The Missional Church and the Biblical Story* (Grand Rapids, MI: Baker Academic, 2011), 125–126. For the Old Testament roots of witness, see Christopher J. H. Wright, *The Mission of God's People: A Biblical Theology of the Church's Mission* (Grand Rapids, MI: Zondervan, 2010).

7. Neo-Reformed scholars unfortunately separate the question concerning the kingdom from the commission to be witnesses. Those like DeYoung and Gilbert, *What Is the Mission of the Church? Making Sense of Social Justice, Shalom, and the Great Commission* (Wheaton, IL: Crossway, 2011), assume that the question of the kingdom has nothing to do with the commission (128–136), giving *witness* the typical meaning of preaching (48–52) instead of the embodied witness we argue for below.

8. Darrell Guder, *The Continuing Conversion of the Church* (Grand Rapids, MI: Eerdmans, 2000), 53.

9. Quoted in ibid.

10. Ibid.

11. Richard Bauckham, *Bible and Mission: Christian Witness in a Postmodern World* (Grand Rapids, MI: Baker Academic, 2003), 99.

12. See Roberto S. Goizuetz, *Christ Our Companion: Towards a Theological Aesthetics of Liberation* (Maryknoll, NY: Orbis, 2009), where the author elaborates on how defending the truth is done from within a society's position of power. It is in essence defending the privileged.

13. In using this quote from John and the previous one from 1 John, I am following Darrell Guder's explication of *witness* in *Continuing Conversion of the Church* (Grand Rapids, MI: Eerdmans, 2000).

SIGNPOST FIVE: SCRIPTURE

1. Christopher Hitchens, *God Is Not Great: How Religion Poisons Everything* (New York: Hachette, 2007), chap. 7.

2. Bart Ehrmann, *Misquoting Jesus* (San Francisco: HarperOne, 2007).

3. Albert Mohler, "The Devil Is in the Details: Biblical Inerrancy and the Licona Controversy," *AlbertMohler.com*, September 14, 2011, http://www.albertmohler.com/2011/09/14/the-devil-is-in-the-details-biblical-inerrancy-and-the-licona-controversy/.

4. Albert Mohler, "Yahoo, Yoga, and Yours Truly," *AlbertMohler.com*, October 7, 2010, http://www.albertmohler.com/2005/03/16/modernitys-assault-on-truth/.

5. John Piper, *Contending for Our All* (Wheaton, IL: Crossway, 2011), 63.

6. The systematic theology of Wayne Grudem, *Systematic Theology* (Grand Rapids, MI: Zondervan, 1994), is an example of this tendency to argue that all we have to do is comb through the Bible and collect all the different statements related to each doctrine to understand what we need to know and how we are to live. In his view, the Bible is a really large compendium of propositions that needs to be sorted and organized for referral. See, for example, chapter 8.

7. Brian McLaren, *A New Kind of Christianity: Ten Questions That Are Transforming Faith* (San Francisco: HarperOne, 2010), 80.

8. Ibid., 81, 92, 96.

9. Christopher J. H. Wright, *The Mission of God: Unlocking the Bible's Grand Narrative* (Downers Grove, IL: IVP, 2006), 208.

10. Ibid., 211.

11. Much of the remainder of this section is indebted to Richard Bauckham's *Bible and Mission: Christian Witness in a Postmodern World* (Grand Rapids, MI: Baker Academic, 2003), chap. 2, and Michael W. Goheen's excellent *A Light to the Nations: The Missional Church and the Biblical Story* (Grand Rapids, MI: Baker Academic, 2011).

12. Goheen, *A Light to the Nations*, 31.

13. Wright makes this distinction between creation and mission in *The Mission of God*, 211.

14. Bauckham, *Bible and Mission*, 36.

15. Ibid., 37. Bauckham cites Exodus 9:16, 2 Samuel 7:23, Nehemiah 9:10, Psalm 106:8, Isaiah 63:10, Jeremiah 32:20, Ezekiel 36:22–23, and Daniel 9:15 to support this claim.

16. Goheen, *A Light to the Nations*, 56.

17. For an outstanding recounting of the entire Old Testament history in terms of God's peaceful rule over against the violence of the world in sin, see John Nugent, *The Politics of Yahweh* (Eugene, OR: Cascade Books, 2011). This rehearsal of Old Testament history relies on Nugent's take on John Howard Yoder's Old Testament theology.

18. The above is indebted to Bauckham, *Bible and Mission*, 49–54.

19. N. T. Wright, *Scripture and the Authority of God* (San Francisco: HarperOne, 2011), 117.

20. Wright, *The Mission of God*, 52–58.

21. The interpretation of scripture always happens within a tradition—a history as God's people in the past. This authority is manifest through creeds, confessions, denominations, and other means. Stephen E. Fowl lays out the necessary reading practices in his *Engaging Scripture: A Model for Theological Interpretation* (Eugene, OR: Wipf & Stock, 2008).

22. For a fuller account of this understanding of scripture, read David Fitch, *The End of Evangelicalism?* (Eugene, OR: Cascade Books, 2011).

SIGNPOST SIX: GOSPEL

1. This is N. T. Wright's shorthand for the gospel proclaimed by Paul. See *What Saint Paul Really Said: Was Paul of Tarsus the Real Founder of Christianity?* (Grand Rapids, MI: Eerdmans, 1997), 46.

2. We must be careful not to blame Martin Luther for the reduction of the gospel that occurred after the Reformation in revivalist movements in North America. He may have provided the seed for such developments, but

Luther's actual doctrines of sin, salvation, and sanctification were much deeper and more profound. Luther provided the needed corrective to medieval Catholicism and made great sense within the matrix of medieval Christianity.

3. Scot McKnight makes this helpful distinction in his *The King Jesus Gospel: The Original Good News Revisited* (Grand Rapids, MI: Zondervan, 2011).

4. This is basically how Neo-Reformed pastor-teacher Greg Gilbert has defined the gospel in *What Is the Gospel?* (Wheaton, IL: Crossway, 2010). McKnight offers a critique of Gilbert in *The King Jesus Gospel*, 58–60. Along with McKnight, we do not think Gilbert is wrong in what he says. We just do not think this "plan of salvation" is the same thing as the gospel.

5. See Stanley J. Grenz, *Theology for the Community of God* (Nashville, TN: Broadman & Holman).

6. See Brian McLaren, *The Secret Message of Jesus* (Nashville, TN: Thomas Nelson, 2006). Thankfully McLaren denies the need to bifurcate Paul from the Jesus of the gospels.

7. See N. T. Wright, *How God Became King* (San Francisco: HarperOne, 2012).

8. For an extended discussion on 1 Corinthians 15, see McKnight, *The King Jesus Gospel*. We are summarizing from his discussion there.

9. N. T. Wright, *How God Became King* (San Francisco: HarperOne, 2012).

10. We must remember that saying the gospel is the "power of God for salvation" in Romans 1:16–17 speaks of its effects, not its content. This verse is in essence a Pauline challenge to Roman power. It is therefore problematic when those explaining the gospel from a Neo-Reformed perspective jump to Romans 1:16–17 without properly dealing with Romans 1:3–4, for this only reinforces the separation between kingdom and cross, reading "the righteousness *of* God" as being a "righteousness *from* God." See DeYoung and Gilbert, *What Is the Mission of the Church? Making Sense of Social Justice, Shalom, and the Great Commission* (Wheaton, IL: Crossway, 2011), 102–104.

11. N. T. Wright, *Justification: God's Plan and Paul's Vision* (Downers Grove, IL: IVP Academic, 2009), 203. We have changed the ESV translation of *pistis Iēsou Christou*, which is rendered "faith in Christ" to "faithfulness of Christ." Many commentators follow this translation even though most Bible translations do not. Wright, as well as others, points out the shift that takes place when we translate Paul's justified "by *faith in* Christ" in Romans 3:23 and Galatians 2:16 with the subjective genitive translation: the "*faithfulness of* Jesus Christ." In simple terms, it changes the nature of how we are justified, for we are now justified not (only) by personal faith in Christ but by

joining the faithfulness of Christ in the covenantal work of God in the world. We immediately move from a faith that is our own to a focus on Christ's faithfulness to complete the covenant in obedience to the Father and our participation in that work (see also *Justification*, 117). Jesus becomes the fountainhead of a new corporate covenantal people who have been saved—put right with God and each other—as part of the first fruits of the covenantal promise of God to make the world right.

12. Wright, *What Saint Paul Really Said.*

13. Wright, *Justification*, 209.

14. The use of the word *gospel* as a verb or adjective is a linguistic habit of Scot McKnight's we are borrowing from him in this sentence.

SIGNPOST SEVEN: CHURCH

1. John Piper, *Let the Nations Be Glad! The Supremacy of God in Missions* (Grand Rapids, MI: Baker, 2003).

2. Kevin DeYoung and Greg Gilbert, *What Is the* Mission *of the Church? Making Sense of Social Justice, Shalom, and the Great Commission* (Wheaton, IL: Crossway, 2011), 62 (emphasis added).

3. Ibid.

4. Ibid., 129.

5. Ibid., 69 (emphasis in original).

6. Ibid.

7. Ibid.

8. Brian McLaren, *A New Kind of Christianity* (San Francisco: HarperOne, 2010), 165.

9. Tony Jones, *The Church Is Flat: The Relational Ecclesiology of the Emerging Church Movement* (Minneapolis: Jopa Group, 2011), 166.

10. David Bosch, *Transforming Mission* (Maryknoll, NY: Orbis Books, 2000), 384.

11. McLaren, *A New Kind of Christianity*, 135.

12. Jones, *The Church Is Flat*, 165, 166.

13. See Alan Hirsch, *The Forgotten Ways: Reactivating the Missional Church* (Grand Rapids, MI: Brazos Press, 2006).

14. This is explained at length in ibid., 142–144.

15. "However difficult it is to remain open to God, it is vital that this relationship must take the form of a direct and unmediated relationship with Jesus. It must involve a constantly renewed, up to date experience with our Lord."

Alan Hirsch and Michael Frost, *ReJesus* (Peabody, MA: Hendrickson Publishers, 2009), 50. Hirsch and Frost are affirming here Kierkegaard's understanding of contemporaneousness. They write that "contemporaneousness is a conscious effort by the believer to reach beyond the church's entire two-thousand year tradition and free of inherited presuppositions, encounter Jesus, seeing him with eyes not of the first Christians but of the first eyewitnesses" (55).

16. Ibid., 105, 111. "Wild Messiah" comes from the subtitle of their book.

17. "The more one replaces a fresh daily encounter with Jesus with religious forms, over time he is removed from his central place in the life of the church. The result of this removal (by whatever means) is the onset of dead religion in the place of living faith." Ibid., 71.

18. David Fitch, "Stop Funding Church Plants and Start Funding Missionaries!" *Reclaiming the Mission*, June 28, 2011, http://www.reclaimingthemission .com/stop-funding-church-plants-and-start-funding-missionaries-a-plea-to -denominations/.

19. Jason B. Hood, "The End of Church Planting?" *Christianity Today*, July 15, 2011, http://www.christianitytoday.com/ct/2011/julyweb-only/theend ofchurchplanting.html.

20. Alan Hirsch and Michael Frost highlighted the fivefold ministry out of Ephesians 4 in their groundbreaking book, *The Shaping of Things to Come* (Peabody, MA: Hendrickson Publishers, 2003), chap. 10. Later they developed it in terms of the APEST (apostle, prophet, evangelist, pastor, teacher) model. See Alan Hirsch and Tim Catchim, *The Permanent Revolution* (San Francisco: Jossey-Bass, 2012). Mike Breen, in his book written with Steve Cockram, *Building a Discipleship Culture* (Pawley's Island, SC: 3DM Ministries, 2012), as well as J. R. Woodward in his book, *Creating a Missional Culture* (Downers Grove, IL: IVP Press, 2012), have also written extensively on the fivefold ministry. Though we may differ some on exegesis and functioning, these authors have contributed much to our thinking on the fivefold ministry.

21. In a way, this entire chapter is playing off John Howard Yoder's *Body Politics: Five Practices of the Christian Community Before the Watching World* (Elgin, IL: Herald Press, 2001). On the practices as "sacraments," see 72–73.

SIGNPOST EIGHT: PRODIGAL RELATIONSHIPS

1. This letter can be found on the website of *The Drew Marshall Show* under the heading "June 25, 2011": http://www.drewmarshall.ca/listen2011.html.

2. Polygamy has long been an issue for discernment in Africa among the churches. As far back as 1862, controversial Anglican missionary John William Colenso arranged for the baptism of polygamist families as long as

the husband committed to taking no more wives. He did this in order to avoid breaking up families. See John Draper, ed., *The Eye of the Storm* (London: T&T Clark International, 2003). Many conservative evangelical mission churches, including my own denomination, the Christian and Missionary Alliance, had to make similar discernments in the twentieth century. As recently as 2009, *Christianity Today* published an article linking the issue of polygamy with gay and lesbian marriage, asking how the church can engage same-sex marriages when they enter Christian conversion already married. See Susan Wunderlink, "What to Do About Unbiblical Unions?" *Christianity Today*, June 25, 2009, http://www.christianitytoday.com /ct/2009/july/12.17.html?start=1.

3. "Brian McLaren on the Homosexual Question: Finding a Pastoral Response," *Out of Ur*, January 23, 2006, http://www.outofur.com /archives/2006/01/brian_mclaren_o.html.

4. "Brian McLaren on the Homosexual Question 3: A Prologue and Rant by Mark Driscoll," *Out of Ur*, January 27, 2006 http://www.outofur.com /archives/2006/01/brian_mclaren_o_2.html.

5. The article is Denny Burk, "Why Evangelicals Should Ignore Brian McLaren: How the New Testament Requires Evangelicals to Render a Judgment on the Moral Status of Homosexuality," *Themelios* 35:2 (2010): 213–237. Brian McLaren, *A New Kind of Christianity* (San Francsico: HarperOne, 2010).

6. Interestingly, McLaren does not propose that all changes in the church's position be put on hold until a consensus can be reached. This has been one prominent way of understanding the process of historical discernment in church councils.

7. I (David) owe some credit to Brad Sargent (from futuristguy.wordpress.com) for the suggestion to include "mutually" into the "welcoming and transforming" framework I was developing on my blog in 2010 to discuss these issues. His suggestion in a comment helped me better express what I was getting at in terms of a community's ability to come together and submit to one another in Christ for his work of transformation. His work on community and culture dynamics remains some of the best I've ever read.

8. Famously, through Stanley Grenz's book, *Welcoming But Not Affirming: An Evangelical Response to Homosexuality* (Louisville, KY: Westminster John Knox Press, 1998), conservative evangelical congregations began labeling their position on the issue in these terms. And those who wished to reject Grenz's position labeled themselves "welcoming and affirming."

9. The entire post is at "Club Unicorn: In Which I Come out of the Closet on Our Ten Year Anniversary," *Weed*, June 7, 2012, http://www.joshweed .com/2012/06/club-unicorn-in-which-i-come-out-of.html.

10. By saying "delicate" here, we are recognizing that many issues require swift judgment for the protection of the innocent.

11. Dan Brennan has written a book entitled *Sacred Unions, Sacred Passions: Engaging the Mystery of Friendship Between Men and Women* (N.p.: Faith Dance Publishing, 2010), in which he argues against the oversexualization of friendship and the harm it has done in the church. I (Dave) have learned much from Dan on this subject. Although I am not in agreement with some of his analysis (including some of his analysis of Freud and subjectivity), I have learned much from his attention to the sexualization of friendship. He has provoked me to hone my thinking on this subject.

12. The entire IQ2 debate, "Same-Sex Marriage Should Not Be Legalised," can be downloaded: http://www.abc.net.au/tv/bigideas/stories/2012/06 /25/3530504.htm.

13. David Matzco McCarthy describes this as "open households" in *Sex and Love in the Home* (London: SCM Press, 2010), chap. 5.

SIGNPOST NINE: PRODIGAL JUSTICE

1. Timothy Keller, *Generous Justice* (London: Hodder & Stoughton, 2010).

2. Ibid., 103.

3. John Piper makes similar points concerning racism and justice in his *Bloodlines: Race, Cross, and the Christian* (Wheaton, IL: Crossway, 2011).

4. Brian McLaren, *Everything Must Change: Jesus, Global, Crises, and a Revolution of Hope* (Nashville, TN: Thomas Nelson, 2007), 81.

5. McLaren credits Frederica Matthewes-Green for the contrast between *infraction* and *infection*.

6. Ibid.

7. Jerry Falwell, *Listen America* (New York: Doubleday, 1980), 17–23.

8. Jim Wallis, *God's Politics: Why the Right Gets It Wrong and the Left Doesn't Get It* (San Francisco: HarperOne, 2005), chap. 15.

9. Jim Wallis, *The Great Awakening: Reviving Faith and Politics in a Post Religious Right America* (San Francisco: HarperOne, 2008).

SIGNPOST TEN: PRODIGAL OPENNESS

1. Brian McLaren, *A New Kind of Christianity* (San Francisco: HarperOne, 2010).

2. Ibid., 207. McLaren is playing into the standard account that religious belief has been the cause of the history of violence in the West. We question the assumption that religious belief always leads to religious violence and that

only the secular state can peacefully arbitrate such conflicts. See William T. Cavanagh, *The Myth of Religious Violence: Secular Ideology and the Roots of Modern Conflict* (New York: Oxford University Press, 2009).

3. McLaren, *A New Kind of Christianity*, 223–224.

4. Tony Jones, *The New Christians: Dispatches from the Emergent Frontier* (San Francisco: Jossey-Bass, 2009), 136.

5. Rob Bell, *Love Wins: A Book About Heaven, Hell and the Fate of Every Person Who Ever Lived* (San Francisco: HarperOne, 2011).

6. "Love Wins Promo Video," http://vimeo.com/20272585.

7. Scot McKnight, "Exploring Love Wins 9," April 21, 2011, http://www.patheos.com/blogs/jesuscreed/2011/04/21/exploring-love-wins-9/.

8. Lesslie Newbigin, *The Gospel Is a Pluralist Society* (Grand Rapids, MI: Eerdmans, 1989).

9. Donald Carson, *The Gagging of God* (Grand Rapids, MI: Zondervan, 1996), 10.

10. Prominent examples are Douglas Groothius, *Truth Decay: Defending Christianity Against the Challenges of Postmodernism* (Downers Grove, IL: Inter-Varsity Press, 2000), and Donald Carson, *Becoming Conversant with the Emerging Church* (Grand Rapids, MI: Zondervan, 2005).

11. Taylor later deleted those words and replaced them as reported by *Christianity Today*. See Sarah Pulliam Bailey, "Rob Bell's Upcoming Book on Heaven and Hell Stirs Blog, Twitter Backlash on Universalism," *Gleanings*, February 28, 2011, http://blog.christianitytoday.com/ctliveblog/archives/2011/02/rob_bells_book.html.

12. John Howard Yoder, "Meaning After Babel," *Journal of Religious Ethics* 24 (1996): 134. This section is indebted to Yoder's essay.

13. "That Jesus Christ is Lord is a statement not about my inner piety or my intellect or ideas but about the cosmos. Thus the fact that the rest of the world does not yet see or know or acknowledge that destiny to which it is called is not a reason for us to posit or to broker some wider or thinner vision, some lower common denominator or halfway meeting point, in order to make the world's divine destination accessible. The challenge to the faith community should not be to dilute or filter or translate its witness, so that the 'public' community can handle it without believing, but so to purify and clarify and exemplify it so that the world can perceive it be good news." John Howard Yoder, *For the Nations* (Grand Rapids, MI: Eerdmans, 1997), 24.

14. Stanley Hauerwas, *Community of Character* (Notre Dame, IN: University of Notre Dame Press, 1982), 105.

15. John Howard Yoder, *Priestly Kingdom* (Notre Dame, IN: Notre Dame University Press, 1985), 70.

16. Kwame Bediako, *Jesus and the Gospel in Africa: History and Experience* (Maryknoll, NY: Orbis, 2004), 41–42.

17. John Howard Yoder, *For the Nations* (Grand Rapids, MI: Eerdmanns, 1997), 25.

18. Yoder, "Meaning After Babel," 132.

19. According to Yoder, "Meaning After Babel," the Enlightenment sought to replicate this universalized knowledge and thereby overcome diversity within one dominant philosophical and cultural program. For a fuller exposition of Yoder on Babel, see also John Nugent, *Politics of Yahweh: John Howard Yoder, the Old Testament, and the People of God* (Eugene, OR: Cascade Books, 2011).

EPILOGUE

1. Karl Barth, *Church Dogmatics*, ed. G. W. Bromiley and T. F. Torrance, trans. G. W. Bromiley (Edinburgh: T&T Clark, 1967), 4:2, 24.

ABOUT THE AUTHORS

David E. Fitch is founding pastor of Life on the Vine Christian Community of the Christian and Missionary Alliance in Long Grove, Illinois. He now pastors and coaches all three churches that Life on the Vine is part of, as well as other churches and church planters. He received his Ph.D. from Northwestern University and holds the B. R. Lindner Chair of Evangelical Theology at Northern Seminary in Lombard, Illinois, where he teaches and speaks regularly on the topics of congregational formation and mission. He is the author of *The Great Giveaway: Reclaiming the Mission of the Church* and *The End of Evangelicalism? Discerning a New Future for Mission* and blogs at www.reclaimingthe-mission.com.

Geoff Holsclaw is a copastor at Life on the Vine and an adjunct professor of theology at Northern Seminary. He helped form the first Emergent Village Cohort with David Fitch (in Chicago) and later coordinated the cohorts nationally. He is a doctoral candidate at Marquette University.

INDEX